HINDUISM
Clarified
and
Simplified

HINDUISM
Clarified
and
Simplified

*An Authentic Intellectual Analysis of the most
Emotional, Spiritual and Religious Topic*

Prof. Shrikant Prasoon

V&S PUBLISHERS

Published by:

V&S PUBLISHERS

F-2/16, Ansari road, Daryaganj, New Delhi-110002
☎ 23240026, 23240027 • *Fax:* 011-23240028
Email: info@vspublishers.com • *Website:* www.vspublishers.com

Regional Office : Hyderabad
5-1-707/1, Brij Bhawan (Beside Central Bank of India Lane)
Bank Street, Koti, Hyderabad - 500 095
☎ 040-24737290
E-mail: vspublishershyd@gmail.com

Branch Office : Mumbai
Flat No. Ground Floor, Sonmegh Building
No. 51, Karel Wadi, Thakurdwar, Mumbai - 400 002
☎ 022-22098268
E-mail: vspublishersmum@gmail.com

Follow us on:

For any assistance sms **VSPUB** to **56161**
All books available at **www.vspublishers.com**

© **Copyright: Author**
ISBN 978-93-813847-2-5
Edition 2014

Printed at : Param Offseters, Okhla, New Delhi-110020

DEDICATION

Dedicated to all
Human Beings,
Particularly, to those that
Wish to absorb cosmic energy and
Imbibe humane, sublime and divine qualities
And
To my elder brothers
Late Āchārya Vishnukant Pandey
And

Sri Ramākant Pandey 'Vijay.'

Prof. Shrikant Prasoon

Preface

While writing the book my own raw concept of Hinduism hammered at my mind. People call it Hinduism, so I'm also calling it 'Hinduism' but throughout my childhood I heard only *Sanātana Dharma*. For brief intermissions I used to get confused; 'Are Hinduism and *Sanātana Dharma* two different religions?' It was a foolish question to ask to the elders. Hence, during my youth, I got it confirmed in different ways, from different persons and books.

Now, I'm the last man to accept it as Hinduism. I accept it to be *Manava Dharma* and *Sanātana Dharma*: Eternal Religion for Human Beings. I thought that it was the first thing to be clarified and simplified. I have done it. These three words are the same; the three religions are different names of the same religion. Fortunately and happily enough, this very clarification simplifies Hinduism. Now, it's easier to understand it.

I'm a follower of that 'Eternal Religion for Human Beings' and am proud of it, proud of my tradition, culture, civilisation, the forefathers and the Scriptures. I'm proud of this land and the people, and everything that is Natural and Indian.

Then, I bowed again to Lord Shiva, Goddess Saraswati and Shri Ganesh and started writing the book. It took another six months to write the book and get it typed and corrected. When the book was ready I read and re-read it and then finished it after two months.

While writing a book it's not important to write all that we know on the selected topic but to hold the important points on different aspects and save them. Writing is easier but holding back is difficult. By checking the speed, flow and material of writing one can write a good and balanced book but if such a check or control is not applied, if all the matters are hurriedly written, then, the book will become an assembly of repeated ideas.

'Don't write all the ideas as they flow. Keep them by making notes: mostly points and a few elucidations and explanations too; and write them at their proper places to avoid repetitions'. Of course, it's tough, to control important and worth writing matter. But it has to be done for writing a great or a good book. The temptation was always there to write similar matters at one place but the danger of repetitions was looming large, so, I resisted the temptation.

There was another difficulty. Indian life is a mixed life, its culture a mixed culture and its religion is a mixed religion. It's so integrated and amalgamated that the separation of each part is not possible. It was neither needed nor attempted.

I have used short tales and incidence to elucidate this universal religion. The Indians take inspiration from such short directly didactic tales; from the symbolic meaning and significance attached to them and from the short, compact, condensed meaningful and suggestive *shlokas* and *dohas* (couplets). It would have been better to quote the couplets but it did not allow space for them. I must add here that whatever truth has been revealed in and through the *shlokas*, was also expressed through couplets but at a later age. These are the greatest possessions of the Hindus. They try to keep them on the tip of their tongue.

'**Hinduism: Clarified and Simplified**' presents each and every aspect of the greatest, most complex and complicated religion. The book is complete and comprehensive despite its thinness. At least, there has been an honest and conscious effort to see and present the illusive 'Whole.'

I used many techniques while writing, '**Hinduism: Clarified and Simplified**'; and I feel it's the strength of this book; but I had to repeat the Brahman; He pervades the complete book. It may or may not be treated as repetition. The inner brightness increased and guided me all through these months.

The outcome, '**Hinduism: Clarified and Simplified**' is in your hands now. While reading it you will feel the grace and blessings of gods, goddesses, Rishis and saints, throughout the book. Read it, follow it and get bliss, beatitude, peace and salvation.

Only ā has been taken from scriptural transliteration for long 'a' sound, which is otherwise impossible to write in the Roman script. Rest everything is as written in government papers, magazines, newspapers and general books. It will help the readers to read the few Mantras and Shlokas quoted in it and also the names of many persons and books.

Hari Aum Tatsat!

Prof. Shrikant Prasoon
www.shrikantprasoon.com
shrikantprasoon@yahoo.co.in
M. 09868082133

Foreword

In this book there is an honest attempt to clarify and simplify Hinduism and hence, it bears the title: **'Hinduism: Clarified and Simplified'**. But one should never think that it has been done in one chapter or one paragraph. For getting a clarified and simplified view of Hinduism one will have to consciously and slowly read the whole book. Only after finishing the book one can get a glimpse of complete Hinduism; can understand it and can take its help for benediction, bliss, beatitude, prosperity and salvation: mukti; and much more than what is claimed separately by different Rishis and different books. Hinduism gives more but claims less.

All the obvious things, prevalent misconceptions, often-raised doubts, common prejudices against and known aspects of Hinduism have been discussed, analyzed and answered in a subtle way. **Hinduism Simplified and Clarified** is the central theme and the only aim behind the book. Hinduism is a complex and the most primitive religion. It's not easy to clarify and simplify it.

The author, Prof Shrikant Prasoon has done justice to the theme and has concentrated his knowledge, mind and resources to that declared theme and has succeeded in clarifying and simplifying Hinduism.

Living and illuminating Hinduism is present throughout the book; the clarifications are apt, appropriate and straightforward. The common and lucid language has adequately simplified the intricacies and complexity of the *Original, Eternal, Human, Hindu Dharma*.

Because of the spirituality, subtlety and divinity of *Dharma* I'm sure the book will be appreciated and accepted by all.

Prof. (Dr.) Birendra Nath Pandey
Vice-chancellor,
Magadh University,
Bodhagaya, Bihar.
M. 09431233398

Contents

Prayers

Prayers

Abhayam mitrādabhayamamitradabhayam
gā̃tādabhayam puro yeh,
abhayam naktamabhayam diwā nah
sarvā āshā mama mitram bhawantu.

Atharva Veda 19:15:6

अभयं मित्रादभयममित्रदभयं ज्ञातादभयं पुरो यः ।
अभयं नक्तमभयं दिवा नः सर्वा आशा मम मित्रं भवन्तु ।

O God! We should not be afraid of friends or enemies; make us free from fear of known persons and all other things; we should be fearless during day and night; there should not be any cause of any fear in a country; and everywhere we get friends, and only friends.

Bhadram no api wātaya mano dakshamuta kratum.

(Rigveda 10:25:1)

भद्रं नो ऽपि वातय मनो दक्षमुत क्रतुम् ।

O God! Give us liberal heart, generous work and bountiful strength.

Vaishwānarjyotirbhuyāsam.

Yajurveda 20:23

वैश्वानरज्योतिर्भूयासम् ।

O God! Make me absorb your bountiful light.

Aum purnamadah purnamidam
purnāt purnamuchayate;
purnasya purnamadāya purnamewavashishyate .
Aum shāntih shāntih shāntih.

Aum, the Sachidānandghan, Divine Brahman, the Perfect is always perfect from all the points of view. The universe is also complete and perfect because of Him as this perfect has come out of that perfect. Therefore, the universe is perfect because of His perfection; that is why He too is perfect. Even when we take out perfect from that perfect Divinity yet the Brahman remains perfect.

Vedas, the eternal source of knowledge, are perfect. Perfect knowledge of 'one' 'some' or 'many' can be taken out of it, yet it'll remain perfect. Thus both will remain perfect.

It's really wonderful that one perfect tree comes out of one perfect seed and again that tree yields many such perfect seeds for many more perfect trees; and thus the continuity is maintained. That is perfect and this is also perfect; and after getting one perfect from another perfect; both remain perfect. It's the system behind the creation and on this system the creation has sustained so far. And if man refrains from interfering into that eternal system it may continue and grow for billions of more years to come.

Aum viswānideva savitarduritāni parāsuva
yed bhadram tanna āsuva.

O God, keep everything bad and impure away from me; and send everything good and pure to me.

Hinduism in Spiritual Quadruplets

One ॐ

Hinduism contains all the known Religious Trends;
It absorbs freely whatever novelties Future sends;
It grows from inside and sustains under duress as:
On right tracks it turns and righteously itself mends.

Two ॐ

Hinduism is not only a Religion but also a culture;
Human, Divine and Sublime that chisels as sculpture;
Keeps as idol, loves as self, fosters with tender care:
It's Cosmic, Personal and Social and follows Scripture.

Three ॐ

Religion in Hinduism has a wider connotation;
It includes 'All' and the 'Whole' with ovation;
Individuals see others as projection of the 'self':
It aims at and prays for the general redemption.

Four ॐ

It's not possessed; instead it possesses 'All':
Human, living, non-living beings big or small;
Diversities and changes are easily accepted:
Obeys dictates of Gods and Rishis to evade fall.

Five ॐ

In four divisions it divides the society as active parts;
In four stages it divides life as clear, balanced charts;
It gives four pursuits to be attained in the long life:
Every sort of knowledge practical, eternal it imparts.

Six ॐ

Hinduism protects Religion that in turn protects life;
Gives energy, hope, tolerance, and sustenance in strife;
Religiosity releases from painful cycle of birth-rebirth:
For salvation it encourages the devotees to strive.

Seven ॐ

It is devotion, surrender, Oneness, spiritual wealth;
It's willpower, confidence, humility and lasting faith;
It's inner growth, peace and belief in non-violence:
And finally it's freedom from cyclical birth and death.

Eight ॐ

Only they feel ceaseless pain, live in constant strain;
That deviate from righteous path to turn to material gain;
Only they're suffering that fail to follow 'words of God':
By performing deeds with attachments, waste life in vain.

Nine ॐ

They are the blessed ones that possess purged self;
He is the enlightened one that knows his inner self;
Union or Oneness with the self is our cherished aim:
As self is godly, self is god and god lives in the self.

Section-II

Introduction
to
Hinduism

The Origin of 'Hindu' and 'Hinduism' Words

Khaiber Pass was the thoroughfare and the bank of Indus River, known as Sindhu Nadi was the first major stoppage, for the persons coming to India (mostly invaders and traders). Either they were unable to pronounce Sindh or they got the wrong pronunciation and started calling it (either by mistake or deliberately) Hind. From Hind Aryāvarta became Hindustān, its people became Hindu and its religion Hinduism or Hindu Dharma, and from Indus it became India. They may be said to be of Indian origin but these are the words created by foreigners and imposed upon India. It happened in such a remote past that (a) nothing could be said with assurance; (b) it is known only to the elite mass and (c) it has been accepted and become a part and parcel of our thinking and expression.

We, the Indians, follow Mānava Dharma (Human Religion) that is also called Sanātana Dharma (Eternal Religion). Emperor Manu, one of our original forefathers, declared and established it through his *Manusmriti,* although, it was thought over and created by the Brahman and on His instance by the first Rishis and expanded, explained and enriched by other Rishis, Munies, Saints, Seers and Āchāryas. It's the only Religion that has been growing incessantly and enriched by the wise, sublime and saintly souls. It has never remained dormant. It has been flowing and refreshing itself over the myriads of centuries. *Manu or our other seers and saints never preached Hinduism. Hinduism is in fact and in essence, that Eternal Human Religion.* The Manusmriti 2:20 mentions that the rules so framed are for all the men on the earth: *prithivyām sarvamānawāh.*

Hinduism is originally the religion for all human beings so it's Human Religion (Mānava Dharma) and it is eternal so it's

Sanātana Dharma. **Some of the other Religions, were there in remote past, they are not now. Some of the other Religions were not in the remote past but they are at present. Hinduism is the only religion that was in the remote past and it still exists. That is why Hinduism is Eternal.**

The invaders and the traders had their own religion and weaknesses of different kinds. Had they called us 'Humanists' then it would have looked 'black and sinful' to attack on humans and humanists. So, they carefully thought over and planned, and deliberately rather by force called us Hindus to be morally and ethically free from falling down because their attacks would have been on 'humans' and 'Humanists'. Just by calling us Hindus they saved themselves from falling down in their own eyes. Now, they were morally and ethically right in attacking Hindus, abusing Hindus, robbing Hindus, killing Hindus and destroying Hindus.

All Are Related

There was yet another reason. Had they accepted Humanism as our religion, then, they would have become a part of us: as our forefathers claimed *vasundhawai kutumbakam,* universal brotherhood, or the world is a family or all the human beings are related. It would have been an acceptance that their religion had too come out of 'Humanism' or 'Eternal Religion'; that they too belonged to our family. They were not and are not ready for that. The whole world is a divided lot: in sects, castes, religions, sub-religions, colour and creed, etc. Even in the wake of internationalism and globalization, amalgamation and humanism are distant dreams. Like the moderns they too wanted to distinguish themselves and maintain the distinguishing features. They had to justify the killings in the eyes of their own people; otherwise, there was a chance of revolt from the soldiers. It was easier to keep the soldiers as butchers in the name of religion and nationality. As usual, the soldiers were made brutally prejudiced. They had no way out but to make and keep the Hindus different that we are not. *Scientists may sing different tunes and the philosophers may come with stunning logic but the eternal fact is that all human beings are evidently, obviously, genetically, scientifically, socially and psychologically related.*

This fact was known to and accepted by only the most ancient Indian 'civilized, cultured, humane, sublime, divine and wise men' that all of us belong to one family, that we have been created by the Almighty, by one Absolute Power, by the Brahman. Even today, all the religions of the world, somehow and someway, believe in One Absolute God. Whether they call Him Brahman or not is a different matter. Only an ancient wise man was in a better position to know who had migrated to which place and when. For them most of the things must have happened in recent past that is for us very remote past. If all the continents were one continent then it was easily possible for men of the same root to have drifted to distant continents along with the continental plates. It is hypothetical for us but it would have been an incident of 'recent past' during that 'remote past'.

At their heart they all accept India as the most ancient civilisation; the birthplace of human beings, knowledge, culture and religion but on their lips and in their writing they are bent upon proving that Indian civilisation developed and flourished at a later stage. The writings of Indus Valley Civilisation, the most developed among the ancient civilisations, have not as yet been deciphered yet it's not accepted as the oldest one. It's sad that even Indian historians are following them and quote them as authentic proof. They are not giving enough time and mind to search out the missing links and prove beyond doubt "why only ancient Indians claimed the world to be a family; why they wished health and happiness for 'All'; and why only Indians say the earth to be mother. The acceptance that the earth is the mother and the sky is the father, carries some obvious and some hidden meaning. The truth that India was and to a certain extent still is the Viswa Guru has some essence in it. The truth will not alter even if one denies at the peak of one's voice or writes in books or advertise in different media. There is yet another truth that when there was no language in the world Samskrit was the most developed and sublime language. There is still no language in the world closer to its perfection. Vedic Samskrit is still the best though the latter epics were composed in worldly (laukika) Samskrit.

In different parts of the world this or that force of Nature was worshipped. Only in India all the forces of Nature were and are worshipped. It is obvious that the other countries knew the creative and destructive powers of few forces, while Indian knew a lot about all the forces that give energy and help life to sustain.

We are the Aryans. We had visited distant lands. Some might have returned back to their original motherland. That does not prove that they belonged to or had origin in another country. Only in India Aryans had and have settled life. Geographically speaking only India was most suitable for life and arrival of man. It was the 'Garden of Eden' and life first appeared here. That is also a reason that India has everything "really very ancient".

Creation, Arrival or Birth or Evolution of Man

Creation, Arrival or Birth or Evolution of Man is a different topic for discussion or debate, as it needs balanced scientific views and deep religious faith. But if man evolved from Apes, as the modern scientists are claiming, then man was evolved only in India because apes are found only in Asia. Geographically and scientifically speaking the place for the evolution of man is India. It could not have been China for it's in leeward side of the great Himalayas and sunrays and rain are not evenly distributed. It's only India that gets correct and balanced light and rain throughout the year in this or that part. It could not have been Japan because Japan is a cluster of islands full of volcanoes and the earthquakes are very common there. India is least affected by such dangerous and deadly natural phenomenon. It could not have been Arabian nations because of the deserts and hot climate. Till a few decades back it was difficult to live there for lack of water resources. Oases are not enough for life to evolve.

Only India had and has balanced climate, all the known six seasons, rivers with clean and healthy water and slow current, water plants (particularly, lotus leaves) and great fertile plains. It has the most soothing and convenient latitude and longitude (in the north and south of the Tropic of Cancer) with protective triangular shape. Other places with similar latitude and longitude are not lands and have no rivers. It includes the continents of America. At this point North and South America join together. It could not have been Africa for the whole Africa is a table shape stair-like plateau, equator passes through its middle and it has a very hot and wet climate with too much sunrays and too much rain that results in huge and dense forests. One can hardly pass through the middle of Australia or Africa. It must have been India for only India has different soil rich in minerals and humus and is balanced.

Life must have evolved between 16^0 N to 26^0 N in Tropical Zone. Life could never have evolved in the sea because of the devastating currents. And, if it was a single celled creature then it could never have sustained the fast-flowing currents of oceans or seas. Life must have evolved in a river because rhythmic flow and some plants to stick to were essential. Lotus leaves are like placenta and the ancient literature accepts the presence of lotus flowers in Indian rivers. It could not have been Southern Hemisphere because it is completely surrounded by water and the few islands have least protection.

Life came in India first then it spread out to other places. That explains the fact that only our forefathers treated the earth as mother, river Ganges as mother, the sky as father (for heat, light, space and energy), the five gross elements to be at the root of creation, the Sun as God; and only they claimed universal brotherhood and sang for the health and prosperity of all. India is the only country that has not attacked on other countries for it knew that all human beings belong to one family.

Now, it makes hardly any difference whether man was created, man arrived, or took birth or evolved on itself or from monkeys or apes, it must have happened only in India. That is the reason that it's the most ancient country. Civilisation grew here first. Settled human life began here. Kingship developed from the heads of the tribes and villages and took the form of Chakravarti Rājā (Emperor of the Circle).

Those that went to and settled in Southern Hemisphere or African or American continent or South India got different colour, ate different things and lived a different life. It happened also in the context of the people that settled in extreme north. The men from the central India became more balanced because of agriculture and helpful water bodies and fertile plains. In a nutshell, the same things happened to the persons that went to and settled in Egypt, Arabian Desert, Europe or even China. The local climate and seasons and also the available natural food and habitat changed their life and created greater difference. The "Three Wise Men" that predicted the birth and birth place of Christ and took a great journey to meet him and tell the world who he was; are definite proofs that Indians used to travel to distant lands during ancient times. They went there and presented gifts to Christ that started the tradition of Gift. In Christianity that journey is known as the Journey of Magi and the gift as the Gift of Magi.

The men of 'Champā Dynasty' that once ruled in Vietnam must have been from Champakāranya (the forest of Champā) in the valley of Himalayas bordering (actually extending into) present day Nepal. The men that captured Rome were also Indians that had settled at different places myriads of years before that incident; and the persons that bought Rome from them and freed it were also Indians, Indian traders. Red Indians or Africans are not dreams; they are true and truly Indians. The West is trying hard to prove that Homo sapiens, i.e. Man, fall in four different categories on the basis of physical construction. It's nothing but an effort to counter the Indian theory *"vasundhavai kutumbakam'*; that all human beings are related.

It's not clearly known or there may be many reasons that during the time of Harshavardhan (according to modern and European Historians) smaller kings revolted, declared free and India was divided into smaller kingdoms. This may be true but it was the general practice and way of 'administration' in India. India was always divided in hundred of segments and there were different kings but they were undr one Chakravarti Rājā. In the Mahābhārat hundreds of kings participated. But it's a fact that something went wrong and the invaders got sporadic success during Harshvardhan but they established their rule by the time of Prithvirāja Chauhān. From there onwards India lost everything very fast and steadily; and unfortunately it's still losing.

It is a known and accepted fact that the conqueror tries his level best or worst to destroy the language, culture, religion and civilisation of the conquered. It was done vehemently and successfully in the case of Hindus. As a result most of the Indians are far away from their real culture, civilisation, language, religion and philosophy. They are taught and they think that the borrowed ideas are correct and good for their health, happiness and prosperity. It is definitely thrice removed from reality. India is and Indians are still the richest people in terms of mineral wealth, skilled human power, character, wisdom, knowledge, philosophy, religion and spirituality. Those that have retained Indian-ness are healthier, happier and far away from the modern rat race.

☙

The Elephant and Seven Blind Men

In a famous story seven blind Indians were/are proved to be wrong and foolish. They wanted to know what an elephant was. How did it appear? They were blind so they had only the touch for knowing the fact. They touched different parts of an elephant and declared an elephant to be like the part that they had touched Their findings were based on the single part that each touched.

The story is a satire on Indians and on their way of living; their beliefs and Religion. It has been termed as blindness. It's clearly established through the fable-like tale that Indians are blind and incapable of knowing the truth. At least, it is the way, the narrative poem is taught in the class-rooms. It's a must. It has to be taught to every student as early as possible and definitely before the final Secondary School Exam with a clear intention that the immature mind will never forget the psychological impact of the poem.

But is it 'True'? Are the Indians really blind and foolish? The narrative has a moral in it or a couple of morals like such other stories. It has decidedly deeper meanings than the established foolishness of the Indians.

The story declares that 'all men are blind.' Each man looks at or feels one part; and that way learns about a part of the whole; and definitely like the blind Indians claim 'the part to be the whole'. Only seven parts of the whole were touched, there is a chance that the whole contains 70 or 700 or 7000 parts or may have infinite number of parts like the Cosmos or the Hinduism.

All men are correct in parts at their respective place and in a particular context. But in the light of the whole, the whole truth, they are all wrong.

Are we not all wrong? Are we not living in and with illusion or illusions? Are we not taking the part to be the whole? Are we not going all out for one or two pursuits? Are we not living an incomplete life? Are we not dividing society; family? As persons are we not fragmented?

Some myriads of years back our Rishis declared that whatever we see, feel, learn and know are illusions (Māyā). The creation is Māyā. Life is Māyā and the climax is that death is also Māyā. We have yet to realise it. They proved this and numerous other things at a time when there was no other culture and civilisation elsewhere in the world. Culture and civilisation flourished there wherever Indian knowledge reached.

The height and depth of that culture, civilisation and knowledge is incomparable. No civilisation and culture has come closer to that. To surpass it is still a dream. The refinement and sublimity of their language is living proof. They had such a great command over language that they wrote the books of Physics, Chemistry, Botany, Medicine, Mathematics, Astrology, Astronomy, etc in poetry; and gave their theories in *Sutras* (comparable to a maxim or an aphorism).

Hinduism is that elephant which is being seen from 7 or 70 or ---- different angles, and 7 or 70 or ---- different parts are being seen, touched, felt; and declared to be either this or that. No one is interested in knowing 'the whole'; all about Hinduism. Their immediate aim is being completely fulfilled. They don't want to know more or at least to assimilate all that has been declared by others. They are touching only the outer reality of Hinduism. Through that or those parts the whole is beyond conception or perception or both. The parts, that they are able to touch because of prejudiced blindness brings them to grotesque conclusions. This way neither the blind men will know the elephant nor the prejudiced persons know Hinduism. Its real and inner truth will always evade them.

The story "The Elephant and Seven Blind Men (from India")" was originally created by the Indians. During the Middles Ages 'from India' was added to it. The story is easily applicable to Hinduism. Most of the men, including philosophers, scholars and spiritualists have felt only a part of the great and most ancient religion and announced their verdict. The verdict is far from the reality and is definitely not complete. Hinduism is so vast and varied that it's almost impossible to see, understand and explain it from one point or an angle.

In the story, the blind men touched and felt only the outer part of the elephant. The elephant remained elusive for neither they felt the whole of the outer reality nor they had inkling into the inner reality. The moderns are restless and in a hurry. They give a passing glance and announce their final findings and results. At least it's expected that the findings should be given only after a comprehensive study, analysis, synthesis and assimilation of inner and outer parts. The hurry is the reason, that numerous scientific theories were replaced by new theories during the last fifty years.

The 'Elephant' is just a symbol. The 'Elephant' is the Brahman or the Vedas, or Eternal Religion, or Humanism, or Hinduism; the Scriptures; anyone of them or all of them. The 'Elephant' in itself is a symbol of 'bigness', 'heaviness', 'difficult' or such things. In Hinduism it symbolises 'problems'. In dreams or in reality, a man chased by an elephant symbolises a person facing problems. In dreams if the elephant returns or changes direction is explained as relief from the problems.

Existentialism in Mahābhārata

In the Mahābhārata, complete 'Existentialism' is expressed through this symbol. In that symbolic presentation, an elephant is chasing a man. He is running away from it and the elephant is coming closer. He sees a dead and dry well. He jumps into it. The moment he jumps, he sees snakes at the bottom of the well. A big branch of a banyan tree has come down inside the well. In order to keep himself away from the snakes he caught the branch. The elephant came up to the well and tried to catch the man with its heavy trunk. When the man looks up towards the elephant he sees that a white and a black rat are nibbling (cutting) the branch. He looks up and finds a beehive. Honey as drops was falling on the leaves. It falls on a leaf nearby. He licks the honey happily.

The symbols are very clear. We are all the time facing problems. We run away from it to get relief. We take shelter inside a protective wall but death is also there. It is represented by the snakes. We take the help of others. But they too are mortal like the big branch of the banyan tree that is being cut by a white rat and a black rat.

They are the symbols of Time. The white rat symbolises day while the black rat symbolises night. The Time is swiftly passing by. Death is all around; up and below, in different forms. There is no respite from it. The protective wall is unable to save. The help that one seeks from the branch is also ephemeral, not safe. Under such deadly circumstances the Nectar-like honey drops down from the beehive above. The honey is the life and the beehive is the perennial source of life. The man licks the drop of honey. It is the life: a drop of sweetness and delight. Our existence is limited to that or such sweet and delightful moments. We can spend our life solving or running away from the problems or make healthier and happier like the honey. It's the whole of 'Existentialism.'

The 'Seven Men' are the men from the seven continents, including the Indians. It is the blindness of man towards religion, self, the duties, etc, that is depicted in symbolic manner in the story. Because of the prejudices against India the word 'from India' was added, and the story became popular. Its popularity sprouted and blossomed only because of 'the Seven Indians', meaning thereby that only the Indians are blind. Of course, Indians have not been excluded. They too were and are blind to the realities. They may have failed to unveil the 'whole truth' or they don't believe in the unveiled truth. Most of them or often all of them have been declared 'ignorant' by the Rishis, seers and saints.

We are able to touch, feel and know only a part of the Elephant and take it as the whole of it. We know only the parts and claim it to be the whole truth, the complete truth or the only truth.

When the story was first invented or created and narrated some literate, learned and wise men were blind, but at present, the whole world is blind. (We are touching the parts of the problem of extinction looming large in the form of either pollution, water pollution, air pollution or as acid rain, dilapidated ozone layer, thinning of atmosphere, growing diseases, arm-race, terrorism separately while it is growing at supersonic speed. What the scientist predicted to happen after hundred years is happening only after three years. We are blind to the greatest problem of existence of the earth and the life on it but are following the devastating principle of destroying everything one by one separately, adding to the danger and asking others to 'save the earth'.)

On the other hand, the more the world is trying to be 'global' the more selfishness is growing in individuals. The more the scientists are trying to know the cosmos, the more it's growing; and in exasperation the scientists are now telling that there are millions of 'galaxies'. Once upon a time there were millions of stars. Now, one galaxy comprises of millions or billions of stars, then how many stars are there in millions of galaxy? The cosmos has become the 'elephant' and the scientists are the blind men, touching and feeling only its parts and coming out with dubious projection and decisions. One is claiming the other to be ignorant. One is proving the already proved and accepted theories to be wrong. 'Millions' is an indefinite number but has become an integral part of the scientists' statements.

The truth is that even the parts in themselves are so complicated and mysterious that thousands of scientists have been trying to know the whole truth of a part (say: blood, skin or heart, a system or a star, a tree or an animal) but have not as yet completed and closed the chapter. They are often repeating, 'There is the need of more scientific research in the field.' The scientists have a habit to study and analyse one system, either respiratory system, skeletal system or circulatory system; nervous system or digestive system; and every time they fail to realise that all these are a part of a different and larger system, a greater and more intricate, complicated and complete system.

Those that think speak and write about religion, particularly Hinduism, talk either of Vedas or Vedānta; Upanishads or Smritis. Saguna or Nirguna, Vaishanavites or Shaivites, of idol worship or sacrificial rituals, meditation and penance. They rarely try to see the 'whole of Hinduism', its inner integral self and the outer worldly form at a glance. Naturally, they fail to realise that 'all these' and 'many more' constitute Hinduism. It's not dependent on one book, was not created by one person, it does not follow one system or only one ritual. It's the creation of many learned and divine figures and it inculcates 'everything', that a complete religion needs or can give. *Hinduism is the only religion that absorbs all, possesses all. It cannot be possessed by any.*

Only after a determined, consistent and concentrated effort of a few years that one can prepare an authentic and dependable list of the branches of Hinduism yet there is every doubt that it would be incomplete. It will take another couple of years to prepare the names of Hindu gods or the chart of rituals. It was the usual practice (it still continues) that many wise men worked on different aspect of one thing and exchanged their knowledge in congregations. It was co-related by a greater Rishi and then a theory was propounded. That way knowledge grew, culture flourished and religion developed.

Enormity of Hinduism

Hinduism is bigger than the Hindus, greater than the country, more compact than the earth, deeper than the seas and wider like the cosmos for it absorbs and possesses the cosmos; for it was created by the Almighty Brahman, and was fostered, saved and propagated by His wise sons, the Rishis and Maharshis. Hinduism is endless, infinite and happily enough, it's still growing like the universe. The cosmic law of non-stop change is the law that has been at the root of Hinduism and it's behind its incessant growth. It has kept on changing and growing; and the system indicates that it will keep on growing. That is the reason behind its rejuvenation and immense vitality. The only fixed law in Hinduism is the cosmic law; the law of change.

Any conclusion, enlarged with details or synthesized with precise statements, about Hindus will remain inconclusive for Hinduism includes and inculcates 'All'. The life force and the living element in Hinduism are so forceful that the continuity of life is regarded as the supreme duty: unsaid, undeclared but meticulously followed. Hinduism is natural, unprofaned and simple, and convincing so much that it keeps on inspiring each sane man of each religion and of each generation. It makes no difference whether they agree with it or not.

Hinduism has not and will not come to a saturation point for it keeps on flowing: neither it turns into solid nor changes into gaseous and light. Hence, it was neither broken nor blown out. It will remain inconclusive for it will keep on growing and flowing like cosmic energy in every direction to cover greater space.

Hinduism covers each and every aspect of life and the universe, and the life in relation with the universe. It does not treat them to be separate entities. These are inseparable and hence, Hinduism explains, aims at and achieves Oneness. It sees the individual and the cosmos and shows both their independence and dependence.

Thus, Hinduism is both the tree and the seed. It believes in the seed growing into a tree, yielding fruits and changing into the seed again. It's a continuous process, a part of the greater system. That is the reason that despite all the modernity, materialism, industrialisation and globalisation India is still an agricultural country; and 70% of its population still lives in the villages and is dependent on agriculture. **It is because Hinduism is basically the religion of living with, on and for Nature**. Nature teaches us to wait, endure and tolerate. Adjustment is its basic philosophy, so control and balance are the characteristics of the Hindus. Rishis taught and modern science accepts that those that acclimatise with Nature and natural elements and forces have greater durability, tolerance and can survive in heterogeneous climate and adverse situations. *The greatest thing about them is that they have retained all the best things propagated by the seers and saints and needed for a healthy and happy life.*

On the other hand, the other religions have stopped growing. Each aspect of those religions is fixed. The rites and rituals, functions and festivals are fixed and counted. Neither changes are possible nor the changes will be accepted.

Ignorant about the 'Whole'

We don't know the whole of our body that we possess, the whole of our spirit that we are, the whole of our mind that we work with. How can we claim to know the whole truth of our family, society, country, the earth, the moon, the sun or the 'religion', human, eternal or local or personal or of a community.

We must accept that we are ignorant about the whole. We know neither the whole of 'problems' nor the whole of 'solutions'; neither of needs nor of demands, neither the duties nor the responsibilities; yet we praise ourselves as the most responsible and dutiful person and give rewards and certificates to that effect. Even the living persons are getting lifetime achievement awards. Man has a habit of praising his own self and deeds; and of late, has started to belittle the very Creator, the Almighty and has dared to claim that there is no god. We know only some parts of a part of the cosmos and yet are denying the Creator of the 'whole'. Is it not funny and ironical?

The funniest claim is that 'the universe has come into the drawing room, at the click of a mouse; or it's in the hand at the push of a button of a mobile. The Ancient Rishis were more refined and truthful when they claimed that the 'Cosmos is contained in the self.' They meant, the self is a replica of the cosmos when they said: *yat brahmānde tat pinde.*

Religion, Eternal Religion, Human Religion or Hinduism is like the elephant, vast and heavy; and as varied as the life on the earth and as idiosyncratic as the persons. We are like the blind men, touching, feeling and knowing only the parts and claiming to know all, telling with all confidence (that we can show) that we know 'all'. On the contrary, we say that the Omniscient knows not what He has created.

Man must ask some questions silently to the self and answer it silently. Is it the truth? Is it the whole truth? Is it the only truth? Is it religion? Is it human? Is it human religion? Is he a human being, a being as well as human? Has he got happiness? Has he given pleasure? Is he honest and sincere? Has he performed wholesome deeds? Does it guarantee the continuation of life on the earth? Are we safe? Does modern man contribute something to the ecology? Will we only destroy atmosphere, elements and life? What should we do? One must feel the responsibility and answer these questions to 'oneself'.

❧

What is Hinduism?

What is Hinduism? Is it a religion or is it a culture? Is it a way of life or a way to God? Is it more or less than what we conceive? Do we know Hinduism? Have we felt Hinduism? Is it conceivable? Can we perceive Hinduism? Can we possess it? Does it have an origin? Each question must be answered collectively and also separately.

Hinduism is a religion, a complete and dynamic religion. As a religion it paves the way, so, it's a way of life too to help and serve all. As a religion it shows the self and the Pure Energy, the Brahman and makes the union of the self and the Brahman possible. Thus it's a way to God.

The birth of Humanism or the Eternal Religion or Hinduism took thousands or myriads of years (it's so ancient that the time factor loses its significance), may be a few *Manus* or a few *Manwantars* (a cycle of five Manus). It was not created in a day. It has grown up among the selected wise men as well as the whole mass. It moved and it grew, it was followed and it grew, it helped and rescued others and grew. It made life easier and better and kept on growing. It defended from outer attacks and invasions and the growth remained unchecked. It was possible because **Hinduism is as much the religion of body as the religion of soul**. It took from the society what was worth to be possessed and accepted them; on the other hand it rejected all impure ideas and unwholesome deeds. It gave and took energy from the society with clear declaration:

dharmo rakshati rakshitah; religion protects when protected.

Hinduism is a philosophy, the oldest and most profound philosophy. But it's the half-truth. The complete truth is that Hinduism is the total effect of many philosophies and many branches of those philosophies. The philosophy has multiplied and each part has remained an integral part of the Religion. It is neither static nor limited to one sphere. It has opened the doors and new vistas; grown towards different directions; experimented, applied, accepted and practised different ways for final salvation; fixed the duties, rituals and festivals according to the changing seasons and climate; and finally, has kept all the doors and windows opened for fresh air as new ideas to fill the inner space and rejuvenate.

Brahman is the main root of the Tree (Gamut) of Hinduism, the *Rishis*, gods, *Munies*, seers, saints and other wise men are the roots or the hair roots as well as at the roots and hair roots. The stem has grown on its own like the branches, leaves, flowers and fruits. It has taken the sap, juice, minerals and vitamins from the earth, the hard and tough reality, and stored energy in different forms extracting from the elements and atmosphere, the Sun and the Cosmos; and has been preserved well by the Almighty Brahman and the self created sound 'Aum'. It has survived on subtle spirituality, meditation and penance, and worshipping the solid idols in or without temples, by recitations and chanting of divine and abstract Mantras and singing prayers and teachings: praising the Creator, His incarnations, the gods, the great souls and moral deeds.

The *Rishis* explored the truth behind our creation and existence, the cause and effect and our duties and rights. They propounded the theories: tested, explained and followed them, then asked others to follow. Those theories defined and established the truth, the best ways for pure and happy living. They knew and made the Hindus believe that purity and balance are the ladders of success, happiness, health and bliss.

Hindus completely surrender to their God. They do not possess the religion, they are possessed by it. The Scriptures say: *dhārnāda dharmah*, a religion is that which can possess all. Hindus lose their identity and identify themselves with the Supreme Lord, the Brahman,

aham brahmāsmi; I'm the Brahman;
yo ayam so aham, I'm the same as He is.

Thus, Hinduism is so vast that it covers all.

They created a set of rules for good living, for living in unison and in community, as a united family. That also is an integral part of Hindu religion while it comes in the domain of social set up and governance. These rules too are not temporary or a thing of a passing phase. They too are immortal for they are for ages, for all time. The changes and growth will be natural but the amendments are not possible. The latitudes are inscribed in them. But in themselves they don't constitute the Religion. Hence and thus, Hinduism assimilates, absorbs, contains and amalgamates all and yet gives and accepts the idiosyncrasy of each individual, region, sect and divisions and sub-divisions. Of course, it's difficult to sustain under such heterogeneity but Hindus have never thought life or growth to be easy. Purity and truthfulness are not easy qualities to maintain.

If one takes the long and varied history, life, civilisation, culture and over all 'living' of Hindus, the Hindu Scriptures and rituals then it will be obvious that it's very difficult to define Hinduism and to include in one definition all its strong limbs and colourful wings, and everything that Hinduism stands for, inculcates and gives forth. The picture will be clear when one by one each or most of the parts are closely seen, understood, and a final mental sketch of the whole is prepared. It will be that person's personal possession. One person's 'whole Hinduism' will not be the other person's Hinduism. It will be a bit different. In all probabilities, that difference will be the outcome of his personal character, nature and aspirations.

The diversity, the colour, heterogeneity and regional and local divisions in Hinduism are the outcome of the diverse soil, climate, seasons (It must be mentioned here that western four seasons are being taught in the schools of India while there are six distinct seasons here.) produce, food, relief, etc. That is the reason that in every ritual the Hindus have opted for *rituphalam* seasonal fruits. The locality is given the needed importance. Hindu Religion in itself does not stand apart and separate. The invaders and persons or communities with vested interest have cashed on it. On that natural divisions and sections they have tried to divide India and Indians and have partially succeeded in weakening India. It's entirely up to the Indians to know the rich and varied country, its rich and varied culture, civilisation and religion; its existing and growing needs and completely Indian and natural ways to fulfill them for sustaining under threats from many corners.

If the geography of India is read well then all the internal major problems can be solved easily. Unfortunately, the persons with the least knowledge of Indian geography have been trying to change India, always with adverse results.

A very clear conception of Hinduism can emerge only from its geography. Its geography alone can simplify 'Basic Hinduism'.

☙

Dharma in Hinduism

In Hinduism the word *Dharma* has the widest possible range and scope and is extremely elastic, so, the synonyms of *Dharma* from other languages don't project its 'depth, height and width.' It is related both with inner purgation and outer purification; with the growth of soul and physical deeds, with the society and spirituality; it contains both '*parā* and *aparā*'. It includes the personal and social behaviour and ethical and moral conduct; as well as the emancipation and salvation of soul. It's gaining in worldly prosperity and heavenly bliss. In its entirety, it includes all living beings and man's pious and human approach towards them.

In Hinduism *Dharma* (Religion) is a way to grow. It is the extent to which one develops: *dhriyate abhyudayanih shreasādanena.*

Religion is the power that saves living beings from irrational and thoughtless destructive deeds. The difference lies in the extent, degree and quality of growth. It is measured from the point one takes a start. Standing on a similar pedestal may mean growth for one and degradation for another. Hinduism states and has proven track that the growth is carried forward in another life. In Kundali Yoga it's very clear that one that reached up to *āgyā chakra* in the previous life, will start moving onward from there in the present life. He will not start again from *Mulādhār chakra*. It's the reason behind the beauty, handsomeness, brilliance and spiritual power in some people that come to fore at an early age.

The complete Hindu Dharma is based on āchār (conduct) or Sadāchār (good conduct). It is the highest Dharma and the fundamental root of all *Tapas*, Austerities and Penance. The inner disposition that gives the desire and will to keep good conduct constitute the character which is the aggregate of different general and peculiar qualities. They add value to life and character; and the values help in the realisation of self and God. He that leads a virtuous and moral life based on values and good conduct attains *Moksha*, i.e. Freedom, Perfection or Salvation.

In all the religious observances and conduct the Scriptures are the guides. It is declared in the Gītā: "Let the Scriptures be the authority in determining what ought to be done or what ought not to be done. One should work in this world after knowing what has been declared as the right path and conduct by the ordinances of the Scriptures." It must be mentioned here that in Hinduism *Ahimsā, Satya and Brahmacharya symbolise the three processes of avoiding sin, sticking to values and self-purification. Our misery is caused by our ego that manifests as ambition, desire and lust. We indulge in hatred, love, flattery, pride, unscrupulousness, hypocrisy and delusion under their influence; and drift far away from* Dharma, *God and* Parmānand.

According to Hindu thought: that power, other than the natural physical need, is religion that is not a cause of destruction but a stable means, in the eyes of Vedas, of development, enlightenment, attainment and pure pleasure (*parmānand*). Religion is very stable for it does not stand on one or two or three legs but is quadrupled; and the legs are very strong pillars of *Tapa, Gyāna, Yagya* and *Dāna*. There is yet another important fact that the Indian seers and saints have taken religion, virtues, and restraint of passion, just actions as synonyms: *dharmah punye yame nyāye swabhāwāchārayoh kratau.*

According to Gautam, the pioneer of *Nyāyadarshana*, "**Religion is a specialty of soul**". It originates from good intentions and good deeds. Maharishi Kanāda, the pioneer of *Vaisheshika Sutra* and the person that discovered atom concludes that **the action, that gives prosperity in the world and salvation after death, is religion**. Maharishi Kapila, the pioneer of *Sānkhyadarshana* takes religion to be a trait of inner self. **Religion is something like conscious deeds of conscience**. According to *Bharadwāja* Rishi those deeds are religion that destroy *Tamoguna* and increase *Satoguna*. *Yāgyavalkya* holds the opinion that to know the 'self' through Yoga is the best religion. In the opinion of the historians of the yore days, **moral and ethical behaviour is the best characteristics of Religion:**

Achāraprabhawo dharmaḥ; or more directly: *āchārah prathamo dharmah.* According to *Devarishi Nārada:* To follow the dictates and footprints of enlightened souls is religion. Maharishi Angirā claimed that **Religion is the deeds offered to God**.

Sutajee has taught Shaunaka and others, "The behaviour that helps in growing unattached devotion (without desire) to God; and makes and keeps the soul pleased and happy is the best religion for human beings":

Sa wai punsāmam parodharmo yato bhaktirdhokshaje,
Ahaitukya pratihatā yathā ātmā samprasidati.

Shrimad Bhvgawat 1:2:6

स वै पुसांपरो धार्मों यतो भक्तिरधोक्षजे ।
अहैतुक्य प्रतिहता यथाऽऽत्मा सम्प्रसिदति ॥

The Hindus accept that except the *Brahman* nothing is perfect in the Universe. Perfection is not possible. One can try to come closer to perfection but can't achieve it. Some impurity will remain there in every action, every deed and every person. So, the Gītā says (18:48) that one must do all the usual deeds because though, *yagya* is a pious deed but many innocent insects are killed:

Sahajam karma kaunteya sadoshamapi na tyajet,
Sarvārambhā hi doshena dhumenāgniriwāvritāh.

सहजं कर्म कौन्तेय सदोशमपि न त्यजेत् ।
सर्वारम्भा हि दोषेण धूमेनाग्निरिवावृता: ॥

Man and animals are the same in food, fear, sleep and sex but the good thoughts, ideal deeds and religiosity distinguish them. A man without a religion is just like an animal: *dharmena heenāh pashubhih samānā.*

Even among the humans there are categories. From among the eight accepted religious deeds: *Yajna* (Oblation); *Adhyayana* (Study), *Dāna* (Charity), and *Tapa* (Penance) can be performed with ego but the rest four can be achieved only by selected few that have won over their ego; in other words that have no ego. The rest four are: *Kshamā* (Foregiveness); *Dhairya* (Patience); *Alobha* (the state of no lust) and *Satyavrat* (Truthfulness):

Edyādhaina dānāni tapah satyamdhrite kshamā,
Alobhah iti mārgortham dharmasyāt vidhasmitah.

इद्याधौनदानानि तप: सत्यं धृते क्षमा ।
अलोभ: इति मार्गोंथं धर्मस्यात् विधस्मित: ॥

But in essence, Hinduism takes religion to be the deeds and duties described and prescribed by the Vedas and other Scriptures. Hinduism advocates that each one should follow religion and perform religious deeds. None should go against religion. Religion is the honour and life of the Universe: *dharmo viswasya jagatah pratisthā*; he is destroyed that tries to destroy it: *dharmam yewa hato hanti*: if killed religion kills.

Five Facets of Dharma

Medhātithi is accepted as the foremost commentator on *Manusmriti*. He has declared *Dharma* to be fivefold:

(i)   **Varna Dharma:** Varna Dharma is related to the duties of the people of each Varna in the fourfold division of society based on the division of labour; popularly known as *Brāhmin, Kshatriya, Vaishya* and *Shudra*.

(ii) **Āshram Dharma:** Āshrama Dharma contains the duties related to four stages of life namely *Brahmacharya, Grihasta, Vānaprashtha* and Samyāsa.

(iii) **Varnāshrama Dharma:** *Varnāshram Dharma* is related to the duties of the persons of each division to which he belongs to as well as the stage of life one has attained.

(iv) **Naimittika Dharma:** *Naimittika Dharma* is unconditionally obligatory duties given for special occasions.

(v)   **Guna Dharma:** *Guna Dharma* includes all the particular duties and responsibilities that are related to particular job; e.g. the duty of the head of the family to feed and protect other members of the family.

Sixteen Pillars of Hinduism

Hinduism accepts sixteen basic principles that are the pillars of religion.

(i)   **Moral Behaviour:** It includes all physical activities that must have proximity with religious teachings and in the best interest of others.

(ii) **Purity in thought:** It aims solely on the improvement in the inner-self and emancipation.

(iii) **Obey the division in social set up:** It includes living within and fulfilling the duties associated with the *Varna* one belongs to.

(iv) **Chastity and faithfulness of women:** The happiness and development of a family depends on the chastity and faithfulness of women; if otherwise, the family will be ruined.

(v) **To follow the four stages in life:** By following it the life remains organised.

(vi) **Belief in a world of spirits:** The concrete world is protected by the abstract world.

(vii) **Unshakable faith in the Divine Power of the Absolute God:** The Hindus believe in God and the incarnations of the Gods and Demons or *rākshas*.

(viii) **Prayer and worship:** Prayers and worship of Hinduism are based on devotion and yoga. It has the widest possible range of prayers and ways of worshipping.

(ix) **Idol worship:** By establishing temples and putting idols in it the Hindus declare the existence of God and worship His existence.

(x) **Purities-impurities and touchables and untouchables:** Hindus have definite scientific reasons for touching or not touching a particular thing or whether something is pure or impure but these things became a part of religion. So, people seldom think of the scientific reasons.

(xi) **Belief in *yagyas* (*yajna*) and *mahāyagyas*:** There are numerous *yagyas* and five *mahāyagyas* that Hindus perform.

(xii) **Belief in Vedas and other Scriptures:** Hindus have unmatched faith in the Vedas, Upanishadas, Purānas and other numerous Scriptures. They use this or that part of this or that Scripture in each *pooja, yagya* or *mahayagya*. Incidentally, there is no occasion when they can use the complete Scriptures because the Scriptures cover a vast area.

(xiii) **Faith in *Karma*, the seed of *karma*, *Samskārs*:** Hindus believe in the actions and deeds and the rewards and punishments (*kriyā* and *pratikriyā*).

(xiv) **Belief in Rebirth:** Hindus believe in the immortality of soul that does not perish with death and after a certain time takes rebirth.

(xv) **Belief in *Saguna* and *Nirguna*:** Hindus have different ways of worshipping, and believe in God without Qualities (*Nirguna Brahman*) and God with Qualities (*Saguna Brahman*).

(xvi) ***Kaivalya Prāpti (Moksha)*:** Hindus believe in eternal emancipation or liberation from the ties of the world, unity with the Almighty, or salvation through perfect purity.

Without getting at the root of these beliefs one can hardly understand Hinduism and Hindu culture.

☞

Hinduism:
A Panoramic
View

Basic Hinduism

Positive outlook, hope, faith, devotion, worshipping, surrender, festivals, spiritual and inner pleasure, music, dance and other colurful activities along with purity, pious deeds, helping others, kindness to all, no jealousy, no lust, no enmity, no revenge and forgiveness constitute **Basic Hinduism**. No stealing, expiation, atonement, oneness, salvation, control over sense organs, study, teaching, sermons are other integral traits of Hinduism.

Basic Hinduism is the main root and the main stem. The hair roots, numerous branches, countless leaves, different flowers, various fruits and the ever-changing local and temporal effects are all integral parts of the great religion, and are accepted unanimously on their face value. The changes are marked, talked about for sometime then are forgotten.

Basic Hinduism is neither the seed nor the seedling, it's neither the sprout nor the roots, neither the branches nor the boughs, neither the rind nor the leaves, neither the flowers nor the fruits. It's all, the complete tree; for some a big banyan tree, for others a sweet-sour mango tree. Like it, everything that Hinduism possesses is highly useful in healthy and happy living and beneficial in achieving personal goals, bliss and salvation.

Pure and **sacred** are the two words that define Hinduism the most.

Hindus have a positive outlook towards life. Despair is not for them. They keep on searching ways and means to be out of the woods and to be free from shackles: worldly or spiritual. They have faith and keep hope.

For the Hindus the glass is always half-filled up, it's never half-empty. They take life as something sacred and rare and wish to do the most. It's different about the criminals and persons with demonic nature but the rest always see life in a very positive manner. They never lose hope. The condition may keep on growing worse but the hope will be there. Such immense hope comes from symbolic teaching in the form of moral stories, true incidents and numerous fables. They take inspiration from such short directly didactic tales; symbolic meaning and significance attached to them and from the short, compact, condensed meaningful and suggestive shlokas and dohas (couplets). They are taught and moulded in that manner. They get both wisdom and confidence from them.

Undying Faith and Hope

The most astonishing fact about such stories and fables are that they never appear to be artificially created. The strength of this great Human Religion lies in its vast and sublime literature. A tale of hope will illustrate it:

A fish-couple was leading a simple and happy life in a pond. One year the rain was delayed. The water of the pond evaporated. The pond was drying fast. The female fish was worried. She tried hard to keep her worries to herself but she could not. She asked her husband, "The pond is drying fast. What will happen to us?" "It depends on the wish of God. Wait and see what happens." The male replied.

Some days passed. The pond almost dried up. The back of the fish-couple was out of water. The female was worried. She relayed her anxiety to the male, "Now, our back is visible. The fisherman can come any day and catch us. What will happen to us?" "Have patience and keep faith in the Almighty. He has plans for everything. He helps His devotees. Wait and see what happens."

Some more days passed and the fisherman caught them, put them in his fishing basket. The female fish was worried a lot, "What will happen to us? Now, the fisherman is taking us to the market. We will be sold." The male fish was as usual confident. "Wait and see, what happens. God will always do well to his devotees. Have faith in Him." The male fish tried to console her.

Of course, they were brought to the market and sold. A rich man bought them. His servant put them in a bag and carried them. The worried female shared her anxieties. "What will happen to us? We will be cut into pieces and cooked." The male fish knew that the ultimate end was near. But he had ample faith in his God. He said, "Wait and see, what happens. God helps His devotees."

Evening had come. Darkness was growing when the maidservant took them out of the bag. She had her sharp knife ready. She was ready to pick one of them up for cutting when she remembered that she had no ashes to have good grip over the slippery fish. She went inside to bring some ash. The female was anxious, "What will happen to us? The maid servant is ready to cut us into pieces." The male had not lost his inner confidence, "Wait and see what happens. The God is just and kind. The delay is only for testing the devotees. We are clueless, when out of water. God knows better and does good."

Yes, the God knew all and was just and kind. It started raining. The drops increased. The rains started in torrents. It rained cats and dogs. The rain continued. The ditches were filled up. The courtyard had ankle-deep water. Without any physical effort the fish-couple were drowned to the drain, then to a big drain. They were ecstatic. They enjoyed rain and swimming. They played and swam and reached a river. The female-fish happily informed her male partner, "We are safe." The male fish prayed, "O God! You are kind and caring."

The tale has all: devotion, faith, hope and bhagwatkripā (the grace of God). Along with the karma, these are enough for a satisfactory living and the shaping up of the soul for better days ahead.

If such trends are not there then it's not Hinduism. As for example: excess/extreme/top/bottom/edge are non-Hindu-regions. Hinduism has lived and survived in balance. The Hindus have attained the peaks but have returned to the valleys to live in peace and in concurrence with Nature. They have dived deep but have come to the surface to live on the plains for overall gain and growth, health and happiness. They meditate for long hours, often for days and return back to the normal self for fulfilling normal everyday activities. They fall in trance and are carried far away but they return to reality to face the music of the world. They don't vie or try for *shreshthatam* they are satisfied with *shreshthatam*; and that steady pace towards goodness gives them greater and higher qualities. They have been taught those qualities. They know the qualities that they need to absorb. They try to be like that. In such matters Rāma, Krishna and Shiva are their best guides. All other teachers, the saints and ācharyas guide them but mostly through Rāma, Krishna, Shiva. Krishna, with his Gitā, is more abstract and more direct. He has given the words, Rāma leads with example. As a conclusion to Gitā, Krishna has given a list of all those qualities in the 1st, 2nd and the 3rd Shlokas of the 16th Chapter:

Abhayam   satwasamsuddhi   gyānayogavyawasthitih,
Dānam damahcha yagyashcha swadhyāyastapa ārjawam,

अभयं सत्त्वसंशुद्धिः ज्ञानयोगव्यवस्थितिः ।
दानं दमश्च यज्ञश्च स्वाध्यायस्तप आर्जवम् ॥   (१६/१)

(Gentle, humble and refined persons are fearless; they possess a pure heart within; and regularly meditate to know the divine truth. They are sincerely engaged in charity and gaining control over the senses. They worship God and perform wholesome deeds. They keep themselves busy in self-study (of Scriptures and Classics); chant the name of the Lord and sing for Him. They take trouble and endure physical pain while carrying their religious duties. They have developed sense organs and are gentle.)

Ahimsāsatyamakrodhastyāgah   shāntirpaishunam
Dayā bhuteshwaloluptam mārdawam hanirchāpalam.

अहिंसासत्यमक्रोधस्त्याग: शान्तिरपैशुनम् ।
दया भूतेष्वलोलुप्त्वं मार्दवं ह्रीरचापलम् ॥   (१६/२)

(Gentle, humble and refined persons never give pain and trouble to others. They speak truthfully and sweetly. They are not angry even on those that do wrong to them and bring harm. They do things successfully but without ego. They have unshakable minds. They neither censure others nor speak ill of them. They are not attracted by the attractions even when they get easy opportunities. Smoothness is their characteristic. They are shy of going against the Scriptures and society. They avoid making useless efforts.)

Tejah kshamā dhritih shauchamadroho nātimānitā,
Bhawanti sampadam daivimabhijātasya bhārat.

तेज: क्षमा धृति: शौचमद्रोहो नातिमानिता ।
भवन्ति संपदं दैवीमभिजातस्य भारत ॥   (१६/३)

(Gentle, humble and refined persons have brightness, forgiveness and patience. Piety of outer body and inner self are their specialty. They have no enmity and no pride. Those that possess these qualities possess divine wealth.)

One shloka 16:8 of the Gitā is a proof that western scientists were not first to say that there is no God and man is a creation of the union of a man and woman. Such persons were there that doubted the existence of the Creator:

Asatyamapratishtham te jagadāhuran iswaram,
Aparaspar sambhutam kim anyat kāmahaitukam.

असत्यमप्रतिष्ठं ते जगदाहुरानीश्वरम् ।
अपरस्परसंभूतं   किमन्यत्कामहैतुकम् ॥   (१६/८)

(The men with demonic attitude say that the world has no Protector, it's illusory and has come out of the union of man and woman with the aid of God. So, one should enjoy everything. There is nothing other than physical pleasure. It's the summary of the western scientific view and material attitude. It was stated myriads of years before Christ.) It shows that even materialism is a part of Hindu religion, life and outlook. But they have shown *Sanyama* (control).

The modern and metropolitan Indians are either not learning about their religion or they are learning it by reading the books by wise men, philosophers and writers of western countries whose material inclination prevents them from understanding its depth, width, height, sublimity and divinity. In place of presenting the complete religion, the whole truth and reality, they are presenting misshaped, de-formed, discoloured and disfigured Hinduism. It is so because they are not acquainted with varied and fertile Indian soil, society, systems, seasons, climate, water, languages, rituals, customs, faiths, aspirations and many things more. They have their prejudices against India. They have read some books and articles; and base all their findings and conclusions on those fistful books; without witnessing the festivals and rituals. By reading their books the modern Indians are drifting far away from their root and soil, their religion and scriptures, and their culture and custom. Those prejudiced writers are getting immense success in creating confusion and chaos among the Indians.

The tragedy is that what Krishna has said in Gitā to be the characteristics of the demons, are seen in the modern man. Then there is a simple question, have men changed or are men changing into demons? Those that are interested in knowing the inner character of the demons can see it in the 16th Chapter of the Gitā: shlokas 4 - 20.

On the contrary, to the character of the demons, that are all out for violence; **non-violence is a major trend in Basic Hinduism.** In Hinduism *Ahimsā*, i.e. non-violence is absolute religion; absolute control, absolute charity, and absolute penance. *Ahimsā* is the greatest *yagya*; greatest fruit, greatest friend and greatest pleasure:

> *Ahimsā paramo dharmastathāhimsā paro damah,*
> *Ahimsā paramam dānamahimsā paramam tapah.*
> *Ahimsā paramo yagyastathāhimsā param phalam,*
> *Ahimsā paramam mitramahimsā paramam sukham.*

> अहिंसा परमो धर्मस्तथाहिंसा परो दम: ।
> अहिंसा परमं दानमहिंसा परमं तप: ॥
> अहिंसा परमो यज्ञस्तथाहिंसा परं फलम् ।
> अहिंसा परमं मित्रमहिंसा परमं सुखम् ॥

> महाभारत, अनुशासन पर्व, ११६:२८:२९

The first condition of non-violence is egolessness. An egoist can't practise non-violence. The 2nd condition is *ātmavat sarvabhuteshu*; one is like all else. It's that process that symbolises and absorbs the whole ocean in one drop of water. Hindus feel that Oneness.

When all are like the 'self', then there is no question of 'ghananti' (pushing or pulling down); 'dhananti' (beating) or 'hananti' (killing) another body or soul.

The concept of non-violence is closest to soul and far away from body; and only the soul survives, body is ephemeral.

Thus, the projected form of the soul is *Ahimsā*. The concept of *Ahimsā* was born in Indian mind, and is there only in India. Others don't possess it. Hence, they miss real human feelings and oneness with others.

🖎

Hinduism is Human Religion

It is very easy to say that Hinduism is the Human religion. It's not easy to make others believe that it's really so. Each one will raise doubts: both solid and imaginary. It has to be proved rationally and spiritually.

Apparently, Humarism has two meanings: the qualities of and in human beings; and the religion for all human beings. Only that Religion can be Human Religion which is human and for human beings with prejudice to none. Hinduism is the only religion that has been devised by a combined force of 'pure and wise seers.'

Hinduism has no preceptor or prophet as such to start it. It's a combined effort of many human beings of many epochs, ages and periods when there was no other religion. It was for all human beings and is for all human beings. There is no prejudice and partisan in it, and hence, it's called Human Religion.

The saints and seers that shaped Hinduism merely explained and reiterated the teachings of Vedas, of both the *Shrutis* and the *Smritis*.

Hindu word has not been used in any of the Ancient Indian Scriptures, or it has never been said that the Scriptures are for the people of *Aryāvarta,* the then India. It is for all human beings, for the whole mankind. It's not limited to a sect or the followers of one particular religion.

The time of Manu is not known, and it can't be accurately calculated but it's the fact that his book Manusmriti is the oldest known Scripture. Majority of people have not read it and most of the people don't know that during that primitive period Manu said:

Yetad   desh   prasutasya   sakāshadagra   janmanah,
Swam swam charitram shiksharen prithivyām sarvamānawāh.

एतद्देशप्रसूतस्य   सकाशदग्रजन्मन: ।
स्वं स्वं चरित्रं शिक्षेरन् पृथिव्यां सर्वमानवा: ॥

मनुस्मृति २:२०

"All the men of the world sit near the *Brāhmins* born in this country (India) and take the lessons about their individual character."

It's simply wonderful. It's adequate proof in itself that the Religion born and propagated in India is true Human Religion. If otherwise, then during those very early stages of human civilisation they would not have suggested all the human beings of all the continents to study and learn Religion from an Indian *āchārya* or *Brāhmin*. It's a general conception that India is **Viswaguru**, the teacher of the world, for all the knowledge spread over the world came from India. People hardly realise that India is *Viswaguru* because it gave the world Human Religion.

It's really sad that the people of the world for selfish gain, for physical pleasure and satisfaction to ego changed the human path. It's immaterial whether it was on self-volition or satanic influence but it was a misconception that most of the people of the world have opted out and are committed to "a life of high living and simple (rather ordinary) thinking confined to money and physical pleasure". Spirituality and Religion has vanished from their life. Spirituality has become a pastime and show and religion has become a matter of exhibition and advertisement.

On the contrary, the religion that India taught and follows basically aims at "simple (almost ordinary) living and high thinking"; universal brotherhood and blood relationship (black or wheatish or white colours are the outcome of the geographical features of different places; India is the best example with all the colours of human beings: *Shyāmavarna* from Kanyākumari to *Gauravarna* in Kashmir) with the slogan of *Vasundhavai kutumbkam*. With its prayers it's as generous as Humanism can and should be *sarve vawantu sukhinah* (everyone should be happy); *satyameva jayate* (Truth must prevail); *ātmawat sarva bhuteshu* (all others like oneself) *yoga* (union) and *mukti* (liberation of soul).

A very disappointing description of Kaliyuga proves that the Rishis knew about the degradation of mankind. So, they prayed 'Jantārana tāraya tāpitakam' (save this servant from this unhappy world).

Their Brahman is not for them only. It's the Absolute God of the Cosmos. It's thousand times more fruitful than the time and energy spent on the adjectives used for Brahman in the very first stanza of the quoted prayer, "Parameswarastrotram"; Hymn to the Absolute God.

Jagadish sudhish bhawesh bibho paramesha parātpar puta pitah,
Pranatam patitam hatbuddhibalam jantārana tāraya tāpitakam.

जगदीश सुधीश भवेश विभो परमेश परात्पर पूत पित: ।
प्रणतं पतितं हतबुद्धिबलं जनतारण तारय तापितकम् ॥

Jagadish (the God and creator of the Universe); *Sudhish* (the God of all Benevolence and Benedictions); *Bhawesha* (the God of the World); *Bibho* (Omnipresent, Pervading All); *Paramesha* (the Absolute God); *Parātapar* (God of Nature from the Beginning); *Puta* (Absolutely Pure) and *Pitah* (Father) are the words that have been used for the Brahman. It is prayed to that Lord to free a fallen, weak servant from the unhappy world.

Can such a Power be kept confined to one continent, subcontinent, country, region, religion or person?

Other religions are the creations of one person, so, they talk of one or two such greater aspects but because Hinduism was created as *Sanātana Mānava Dharma* (Eternal Human Religion) by many sublime and divine figures like Gods and Rishis so it incorporates all the best that mankind can ever think of. The ancient wise men have already thought over each aspect of inner and outer life; experimented with, discussed and refined and then asked the people to follow.

None other religions needed to be tested before teaching and asking the people to follow because the central figures had ample faith in the tests carried out by the ancient Rishis. Whatever is spread over all the continents is there in this Religion. The analysis and words differ a bit but the concepts and philosophy are the same.

All the irreligious talks and deeds are attaining their respective climax everyday because modern man has forgotten the real meaning of religion. Religion means that which holds and balances the world. The Scriptures are very clear on this point: *dharati viswam iti dharmah*: that which holds the world is religion. The more the religion is denied the more the hold is weakening. No police of any country, including the Interpol is able to control the rampant crime. Now the papers and electronic media are comparing the graphs of crime on the monthly basis: "The crime in the month of ---- was more in the year ----. It's on decline (or rise)." They say and change as they wish. There is no central power that can hold. Even the magnetic and gravitational power of the earth is weakening. It's unable to hold the atmosphere and ozone layers. **Malevolent deeds can't bring benevolence.**

The Scriptures say: *dharmo rakshati rakshitah*: Religion protects when protected. Most of the people don't know the Human Religion; their rights, responsibilities and duties as human beings. How can they protect religion? It seems that each one has the right to describe, explain, analyse religion in his personal way and follow a different path. They are all playing with words unforgetful of the fact that extinction is at hand. They must know this Eternal Human Religion that claims:

"Religion is the honour and prestige of the whole world. People prefer to visit religious persons. Religious deeds make us free from the sins. Everything depends on religion. So religion is the most sublime possession."

Dharmo viswasya jagatah pratishthā,
loke dharmistam prajā upasarpanti,
dharmena   pāpamapanudati,
dharma   sarvam   pratishthitam,
tasmāda dharmam paramam vadanti.

Taitiriya Āranyakka 10:63:7

धर्मो विश्वस्य जगत: प्रतिष्ठा लोके धामिष्ठं प्रजा उपसर्पन्ति ।
धर्मेण पापमपनुदति धर्मे सर्वं प्रतिष्ठितं तस्माद् धर्मं परमं वदन्ति ॥

तैतिरीय आरण्यक १०:६३:७

One thing must be marked: In the complete shloka, only the

word 'Religion' is mentioned every time. That is the greatest proof that this religion is for all human beings.

That is why Indian Scriptures say that 'judicious deeds is religion, immoral acts are anti-religion; it has been said by sublime and virtuous men':

Ārambho nyāyayukto yeh sa hi dharma iti smritah,
Anāchārastwadkarmeti atachichhasthānushāsanam.

आरम्भो न्यायुक्तो य: स हि धर्म इति स्मृत: ।
अनाचारस्त्वधर्मेति   एतच्छिश्ठानुशासनम्   ॥

S.N.	The Powers of Successful Men.	Virtues According to the Gita
1.	Amānitvam	Humility
2.	Adabhitvam	Modesty
3.	Ahimsā	Non-violence
4.	Kshamā	Forgiveness
5.	Arjawam	Forthrightness
6.	Gururshraddhāh	Respect to the Teacher
7.	Bhāvakaramashuddhih	Purity of Thought and Action
8.	Lakshyaratih	Consistency of Purpose
9.	Ātma Sanyam	Self-restraint
10.	Vairāgya	Detachment
11.	Ahamvisarjanam	To Shun Egotism
12.	Sambhāva	Balanced Thinking
13.	Anāsakta	Avoid Excess Affection
14.	Viswāsam	Reliance
15.	Daivoāsthā	Faith in Divinity
16.	Yekānt	Staying away from Crowded Places
17.	Ātmajnāna	Knowledge of the Self
18.	Ātmasangharsha	To Face Duality in Life
19.	Bhautiktopari	Aloofness from Materialism
20.	Muktiprayana	Effort to Get Free from the Cycle

It was but natural for the Rishis and Seers to declare: *Vedo akhilo dharmamulam*: Vedas are the roots of all Religions. All religions can be interpreted in many ways but the best way seems to be "everything that is for every human being." In a nutshell, Hinduism is Human Religion in its full bloom and laden with fruits.

Twenty Virtuous Qualities

Hindus cultivate or try their best to cultivate the 20 Virtuos Qualities preached by Sri Krishna in the Gita given above. It makes no difference whether they have read them or not. They know, they are taught and they imbibe. These virtues are not only for the Hindus but all the refined and cultured human beings. Human beings can claim to be human only when they possess such human qualities. This is one important reason that Hinduism is the Religion for all Human Beings.

Hinduism is Eternal Religion

It is very easy to say that Hinduism is the Eternal religion. It's not easy to make others believe that it's really so. Each one will raise doubts: both solid and imaginary. It has to be proved rationally and spiritually.

Hinduism has no starting point in human history. It was thought, analysed, explained, modulated, enlarged and accepted in a 'period' of time. It's timeless and hence, it's called Eternal.

In the context of the origin of Hinduism 'the period of time' plays an important role. Not only its birth has a period of time but the later explanations too came after long intervals of centuries apart and always in a period of time. In the whole of the history of Hinduism, and in the creation of its numerous Scriptures there is not a single 'point of time'; there is always a period of time, It's the reason of its immortality. It's the reason that it's Eternal. It is the reason that no point of time is mentioned.

Vedas, including the *Shrutis* and *Smritis*, that are the basis of Hinduism came into existence in a long period of thousands of years and contain the knowledge that is true for all time: the time in the past and the time in future or for Past, Present and Future. That is the reason that Hinduism is Eternal Religion.

The *Vedas* have no fixed place of origin and no point of time. The Mantras were envisioned by different *Rishis* at different places and in different periods of time. It is said that the *Vedas* existed from before the creation of human beings, as they are deemed to be, originally created by the Brahman. They were deluded and lost, and were envisioned by great Maharshis that had immense divine and spiritual power; that were able to connect to the cosmic power and energy; and were capable of doing unbelievable and miraculous things. Their stories and deeds are wonderful, captivating and revealing. They envisioned and collected the great Mantras. First it was compiled in one volume called 'Rigveda' but later on, when the number of Mantras increased considerably, Veda Vyāsa compiled, edited and divided them in four Samhitas called: Rigveda, Samaveda, Yajurveda and Atharvaveda.

The *Vedas* and the *Rishis* were the centers of educational system in ancient India up to the middle ages. Broadly speaking that educational system comprised of all the different spheres and phases of life: physical, mental, spiritual, scientific, medical, economic, philosophical, machinery, arms, sculptor, painting, artistic aesthetic, yoga and meditation.

Though labelled as Hinduism yet it did not change. It kept and retained the 'immortality and humanness' intact. Whatever the name is given to it, in essence and totality it will remain the same. That is also a proof that it's both Human and Eternal.

Sanātana or Eternal has many meanings and connotations. Hinduism is eternal because it contains and purifies us not only in this life but we are purged from the sins and misdeeds of the past life; and it also stores the fruits of our virtues and good deeds for future lives. In this way this religion gives and ensures continuity to its followers, so, it's Eternal religion. It makes possible the union of a devotee with the Infinite, Indefinable God, hence it's Infinite and Eternal. As the soul in this religion never dies, so it is Eternal Religion.

The Scriptures say: *sanātanasya dharma iti sanātanadharmah;* because it has been propounded by the Eternal Brahman so it is Eternal religion Moreover, this religion existed before the creation and sustains till delude and is again created. Hence, it's Eternal Religion: *sanātanashchāsau dharmashcha,* the religion that always exists.

The theist Hindu doesn't ignore religion as he believes in the words of Lord Krishna and follows the dictates of the Gitā:

> *Yeh   shāstavidhimutsrijya   vartate   kāmkāratah*
> *Na sa siddhimawāpnoti na sukham na parām gatim.*

Tasmāchchhāstram pramānam te kārākāryavyawasthitau
Gyātwā shāstravidhānoktam karma kartumihārhasi.

The Gitā: 16: 23-24

य: शास्त्रविधिमुत्यसृज्य वर्तते कामकारत: ।
न स सिद्धिमवाप्नोति न सुखं न परां गतिम् ॥
तस्माच्छास्त्रं प्रमाणं तं कार्याकार्यव्यवस्थितौ ।
ज्ञात्वा शास्त्रविधानोक्तं कर्म कर्तुमिहार्हसि ॥

–गीता (१६/२३-२४)

They, that cast aside the orders of the Scriptures and act in arbitrary fashion, attain neither perfection nor purity, neither happiness nor salvation. So, one should follow the Scriptures in deciding wholesome and unwholesome deeds. One should know the Scriptures first and then decide what should be done and what is not to be done.

Most of the Hindus don't know or don't read the scriptures. Some of them are illiterate too. They depend mostly on the Pandits (Priests) that guide them and make them perform the rituals. The greatest wonder in India is that without reading the Gitā people know the teachings of the great philosophical book and follow the dictates.

❧

Hindus

Pillars of Religion

There are four pillars of religion: *Tapa* (penance); *Gyāna* (knowledge); *Yagya* (worshipping and sacrifice) and *Dāna* (charity, donation). Thus *Dharma* (religion) is called quadrupled. *Satyuga,* the age of Truth had all the four pillars. Penance was lost in *Tretā,* so it's called three legged. *Dwāpar* (two) lost another pillar called *Gyāna* and remained biped. *Kaliyuga* has lost another pillar, *Yagya*. It's standing on one pillar. It's moving on its single leg called *Dāna,* i.e. charity, donation. In reality, in place of charity and donation, the modern age has survived on loans, debt, interest and fresh loans for the repayment of the previous one.

Just on the other it's clearly stated that they are like animals that don't possess these qualities:

> *Yeshām na vidyā na tapo na dānam na*
> *chāpi sheelam na guno na dharmah,*
> *Te martyaloke bhuvi bhārabhutā*
> *mansyarupena mrigāscharanti.*
> येशां न विद्या न तपो न दानं न चापि शीलं न गुणो न धर्म: ।
> ते मर्त्यलोके भुवि भारभूता मनुष्यरूपेण मृगाश्चरन्ति ॥

चाणक्य नीति १०:७

(Those, that have neither education nor penance; neither charity nor morality; neither quality nor devotion; are a burden on this mortal world and the earth. They are like deer grazing grass in the body of a human being.)

The aim of Hinduism is abnegation, abdication, renouncement, release etc. and not the physical pleasure or luxury or accumulation of wealth. Those, that keep themselves away from lust and accumulation of wealth, are more respectable in Hindu society than the seekers of wealth and physical pleasure. Great kings have bowed down to poor saints. Greatness here is measured not in terms of wealth but in terms of sacrifices for the society, human and non-human beings. Under the unhealthy influence of the west India is fast turning into a materialist country. Naturally, crime is growing faster; and all sorts of criminals are freely engaged in immoral acts, economic, ethical and sexual crimes. Scams, stealing, skin-trade, sale of women and children and organs are growing everyday. Murders and kidnapping have literally become a child's play. Normalcy will not return to society if stress is not on moral character and detachment from wealth is not made the aim of life.

Closeness to Nature

There is hope only in Hinduism. The destructive science that has created more fear than arms, and more arms than the number of human beings on the earth, has brought it to the brink of total disaster. Annihilation is just at hand. Only Hinduism can save the earth and the life on it because it's the only religion that is closer to Nature, and it gives preference to natural life than to anything else. Yet Hindus have hope, and most of the people are disillusioned. Dissatisfaction is growing. The demands and revolts are on for a life in the lap of Nature. People are getting tired of being shut down inside brick-built and glass houses; and of being searched extensively and intensively while visiting a temple. They know they are deliberately being kept away from the temples and their gods. The others have lost their god and faith; the same thing is being forced upon the rest in all possible ways. Economic, physical, cultural and psychological ways are the most prominent among them. They feel that modernity is taking great toll and giving only meaningless luxury and lust. They are turning away from it. It may prove to be a turning point in saving the atmosphere, the earth and the life on it.

Cooperation among Hindus

Hindus have a large canvas and they dominate it effortlessly for they have different Scriptures to teach them, guide them, and to prove and make them correct, if and when there is even a shred of doubt. Their inner character, contact with Nature and religion and intelligent ideas lead them to spirituality and God through the self and service to others. They see the top and know the bottom, but live on the plains and valleys. So, they are safe and secure. Their religion and Scriptures have given them shelter and protection.

Hindus are religious both at heart and in deeds. They build their nature soft and personality as elastic as possible, so, they are able to live in community despite apparent differences. They know the profit of mutual give and take, so, they cooperate and get cooperation without paying in money. It's reciprocal. Their household, yagya, agriculture and festivals depend on others. It's a rare and grand mixture of individual set-up and growth and community living. In every village (and villages in India still show 70% of the total population) each one know the other, his needs and the ways the needs can be fulfilled. That is the only reason that despite the negligence and obstacles they have been able to feed one hundred and seven crores of Indians. They are selfish and selfless and human in every sense of the term.

Hindus have a sense of unspecified mission, and get a specific and special satisfaction in the physical service that they do to others. They have their inner faith that by doing so they constantly get God's blessings that will help them in getting salvation. Some do it as a part of atonement. In this way they realise their hopes and dreams that they cherish. Their enthusiasm gives energy and satisfaction. As they feel contented so, their strain, fatigue and weariness are gone. They feel fresh early in the morning to start again the chores. They prefer and do a lot of physical labour, so they get tired by evening and go to bed early. When the metropolis and the rest of the world remained awakened till late in night Indians abide by 'early to bed and early to rise'. They need no weekends for freshness because they get energized by singing a few devotional songs in the evenings or just by sharing their problems with others or even by a wordy dual. For them all are the ways of getting refreshed. Only a few carry the load and anger of words they collected the previous day. Others forgive and forget but if the act is repeated they remember the incidents and retaliate. Actually, they do not forget, they suppress the words and incidence that cause pain and anxiety. That is the specialty. So, whenever they get an opportunity, they retort back but in the presence of people.

Psychologically speaking, it seems to be abnormal but again the psychological theories have been borrowed from western countries that are not tropical but cold. Tropics are different from colder regions, as equatorial regions are different from the tropics.

Climate Determines Food and Living

It's the place to lay stress on the land and climate of India. India stretches from 8^0 North to 37^0 North. Of course, it's hot in south India but less hot than the hottest equatorial zone; simply because it's triangular there and is surrounded by seas and at least 8^0 away from the equator. In the same way, it's not in the coldest polar area. It stretches only up to 37^0 North. The Tropic of Cancer passes through its middle and blesses it with the best possible climate and the most balanced one from very hot in Kerala (Kanyākumāri) to very cold in Kashmir. That is the reason that it enjoys all the six seasons. People never need a tie here (barring the winter during December and January); otherwise, they keep a few of their buttons open for the air to touch the chest and neck. They prefer half shirts. They don't need protection from cold air during the rest of the year. They relish air. Indians need fresh food. So, every household is a hotel here. They cook their food. So, they prefer a combined family. Stale food, fruit, vegetables are curse and poison to us (all). It is such a great difference that the western living (particularly thick, heavy cloth and tight fitting or refrigerated food) is causing diseases and obesity. The secretion of hormones, flow of blood, functioning of heart and hence alertness of mind are affected. The number of physically and mentally handicapped has grown many fold during the last 40 years. Indians must beware of this growing curse. It's better to study the good and healthy living habits than to fall ill and visit clinics. They must realise that only the climate and local produce determine food and living.

Life Span of Hindus

Because of the guidance from the Rishis the Hindus lived a longer healthy life. The death age has not gone high after independence, a bit of the record has been maintained which has shown the rise. In fact, Indians have not kept the records of the dates of birth and death. Even after a lot of pressure from the government most of them neither keep track of the dates nor try to get registered. So, it's impossible to know the average age of death in India. It's calculated on three terms: *alpyāyu* (death before attaining youth); *deerghayāyu* (death after living the life of a householder) and *purnayāyu* (death at around hundred years of age). It's the general conception not the actual age. They depend on religion, gods, healthy living, physical works and pious deeds for longer life.

There is a story to illustrate it. The young son of a religious brāhmin of Kāshi, named Dharmapāla was studying at Taksheelā. Once the young son of the āchārya died. The boy wondered and said, "Well! The young die here." It pinched all. Some asked, 'Does death come to your family after taking permission?' He said with wonder still in his voice, "That I don't know but I know that during the last seven generations only the old have died in my family. Young men have not died."

It traveled up to the āchārya. He felt aggrieved. He thought to test the statement. He went to Kāshi with some bones collected from the burning ghāta. He showed Dharmapāla the bones and sadly informed him that his son has died. Dharmapāla laughed and said, "O noble āchārya! You're mistaken. The dead young must have been someone else. No one has died young in my family since the last seventh generation."

The āchārya tried to convince him, "If someone has not died young that does not mean that no one will die young?"

Dharmapāla laughed again and said, "O noble āchārya! You don't get me. We are always conscious of our religion. We protect it with all our might. We never go against the doctrines of the Scriptures. We follow them. We are always humble, speak humbly, help others and serve the guests and the needy to the best of our ability. We keep distance from unscrupulous persons. Death can't be unjust. It can't kill the young. We protect religion and religion protects us." He was full of confidence for he had ample faith in his and his family members' pious deeds.

The āchārya had to accept the truth. He said, "You are perfectly right. Your son is alive. I was testing you."

Think and mentally calculate the deaths of young men after independence and also during the slavery of one thousand years. The difference in living and attitude will come out to light. It will definitely open the eyes.

(While thinking about the modern and metropolitan and mixed culture one should keep in mind the fact that there are three types of Indians today: Westernised Indians, true Indians and Indians hovering between the two.)

Lively Hindus

Hindus are full of the beams of *joie de vivre,* as they love handling interactions with other people. Their lively, short, meaningful and intimate exchanges – of affection, news, views and independent ideas – make the immediate time and the closer vicinity lively and pleasant. Grandparents, parents, parent-like persons, children, friends and distant relatives are all parts of their personal and social life. They get greater scope and larger area to live and work in. The relations and greetings or salutations vary from person to person. Of course, there is a definite law, set pattern and known tradition but the variations are also there. They can touch the feet or greet with folded hand, hug them or lift them up, pat them or even beat them or take them on their back or shoulders. There are varieties of ways to show the pleasure, the ecstasy. All the ways are accepted and followed. They entertain them, amuse them, talk to them, carry messages to and fro, and communicate with them in their idiosyncratic ways on each occasion that they meet. They keep them engaged, entertain them, feel involved and get energy in lieu there of.

Hindus have a keen desire to get more out of life, an incident or an article; collecting, keeping, assimilating and making use of all that they get. In that they seldom break completely, the broken relations. All the rituals, festivals, *yagyas* give them opportunity to mend their mistakes or come to a compromise or heal up the wounds or ease out the anger or forgive the errors committed by others or to accept the mistake and make the angry or displeased elders agree to participate in the function. Particularly, at the time of the marriage of a girl many blunders are easily forgiven on the pretext that the girl has done nothing wrong and she must be blessed since she is going to live with some other family at some other place. They have big, gentle and humble heart. Often they spend beyond their capacity just to show their love and liking. The have the solace, "I'm not doing anything wrong, God will be just and help me." Two of their popular quotes are that there is delay but poetic justice will be done; (der hai, andher nahin) and that he will face the music for he was at fault; (usane kiyā hai, wah bharegā). These quotes are repeated whenever one is willing to forgive others or one is being lured to forgive another person.

It's not only about possessing, keeping and maintaining relation. The same philosophy is vehemently applied to old and used up articles also They hardly throw away used up articles, including jars, cans, bottles, sacks, bags, worn out clothes, etc., they use it again, change shape and use for different purpose. They can use an old freeze as 'store-well'; an empty paint container as a bucket and so on. They use things in different ways till the last. In that they show their imaginative quality and ingenuity.

Belif in Karma

Hindus rely a lot on their skill, adaptability, and slow but steady pace. They see their hands first thing in the morning and pray:

Karāgrebasati Lakshmi karmadhye cha Saraswati,
Karmule basate Brahmā prātah karadarshanam.

कराग्रे बसति लक्ष्मी करमध्ये च सरस्वती ।
करमूले बसते ब्रह्मा प्रात: करदर्शनम् ॥

(The Goddess of Wealth lives at the top of the palm and the Goddess of Knowledge in the middle of it. At the very synapse (beginning) of palm and wrist lives the Creator, so look at your palm first thing in every morning.) It's nothing but the assertion of work and use of hand. The Hindus believe in the theory of *Karma* (deeds) but they very wisely, adroitly (and to be psychologically free from anxieties and a sense of depression, and as a part of their habit); shift the responsibility of all failures and calamities on to gods, fate and luck. Their most common dialogues are: 'It was not acceptable to God' (yeh bhagwāna ko manjur nahin thā); 'It was written in fate' (yeh bhāgya mein likhā thā); 'Time is all powerful' (samaya barā balwāna hai).

The most important among them is: 'We get what is written in fate, neither more nor earlier' (samaya se pahale aur bhāgya se jyādā kuchh nahin miltā).

It may seem to be contradictory but their faith and work are both aimed at 'upward mobility'; through the least available means and through narrower footpaths, (*pagadandi*) in literal sense, not in the sense of the footpaths of cosmopolitan cities; through vales and fields; crops, gardens, forests and other barren or grassy lands.

Preferences of Hindus

They are separated but they don't live in isolation (totally cut off from others like hermits). They create and maintain relationships, both in general and personal interactions. So, they have numerous brothers, sisters, uncles, and aunts, irrespective of caste, creed, faith, community, religion, work culture or standard of living. They turn more and more to family, to other families, congregations, friends, unknown persons for romance, recreation, integration, entertainment, as pursuit or hobby or interest or simply for passing idle hours, particularly, the time of 'waiting' for something or someone. It's their strength that has emerged out of the unity in diversity.

As a result, there are thousands of Indians in almost every region that have not visited a cinema hall, a theatre, an art-gallery, a library or a museum or a zoo even for once. Among the Indians, some visit such places as they feel that one should visit it at least once; some are forced to visit such places; some are regular visitors but they too don't visit all the places mentioned above; and don't relish visiting any.

These places are alien to them. Despite the fact that their number has grown and such new things are under construction at many places yet it has failed to attract them. They prefer *satsang* (congregations) to cinema. They prefer an ordinary function in the open than an important function in a hall. The poorest, oldest and the weakest among them would prefer to visit difficult and dangerous places of pilgrimage with meagre sum of money and scanty clothes.

Hindus don't fix deadlines; if fixed by chance or force then, they keep on changing it on this pretext or that; they don't think of pending matters nor attempt to review the things. In its place, they review the deeds and misdeeds, achievements and failures, tales and rumours of others. They set flexible goals and take many changing stances in life. Ironically enough, they are always free and always preoccupied. Modern metro-Hindus are exceptions. They are not a part of this general evaluation.

On every happy-unhappy-strange occasion they will turn towards their homes, family, community, etc for sharing it or for reinforcement, etc.

Hindus know that nothing clicks perfectly and things don't come easily. So, they are mostly interested in constant effort and pursuit. They beat heart but not at each failure and never for long. They have fixed days to mourn and they get busy in work even before the ritualistic mourning is over.

They move on without waiting for rewards, appreciation or recognition. They accept them if they get on their way forward, they don't lose heart when they don't get any of them. They deserve and that is enough consolation for them. They prefer to be the key or the hinge and not the treasure without thinking how they are kept waiting or how many times they are made to move unnecessarily. Their accomplishment and satisfaction is their treasure.

Hindus are Tied to Roots

Hindus try to remain tied and united to their roots by re-reaching it, cleaning, strengthening and by putting needed manure to the roots for they are sure that only roots provide strength to branches, leaves, flowers and fruits. Because of being tied to the roots and sucking energy from the source and transporting it to the top they flourish from inside often, in different directions. That results in giving them a balanced attitude. An average Hindu knows and is skilled to do more than one work with ease and competence. They exhibit their skill and give full expression to their creative instinct and ability. They strive for greater personal and spiritual liberty and self-expression. Even ladies and teenagers exhibit it through *alpanãs* (decorative flowers and other forms created at doors, etc., with flour and colour) to wall-paintings; doll-making to creating bunch of flowers and fruits inside a bottle; making utensils from straw to weaving caps, mufflers, scarves, shawls and sweaters and many such things.

They care a lot about their duties but are hardly conscious of their rights. They seldom press for it. They try to sharpen their communicating skills and use different ways and techniques of expression: traditional, modern, unique, subtle, mysterious and very personal.

The paradoxical counterpoise directly taken from Nature and society, cosmos and Scriptures mingled with introspection and socializing continues and flourish in their lives. It builds them, binds them and helps them in living a full and satisfactory life: playful childhood, energetic young age, busy mature age and tension free old age.

After spending the three distinct phases of life, known as *āshrams: Brahmcharya, Grihastha* and *Vānaprastha;* they wish and strive hard for the 4th, i.e. *Samyāsa.* But the number of persons opting for *Vānaprastha* and *Samyāsa* is going down under western influence. It is being replaced by 'Old Age Homes' that can be a solace for a metro-man but not for an average Indian. It is being exceedingly painful to lead a retired, workless and aimless life. The unhealthy modernity has sucked them dry. The children are not getting their childhood; late marriage and job-settlements have taken out youth and life from both the young men and women; the mature age is wasted in getting a house constructed, giving education to children, their marriages and settlement and the old age has turned to be more painful with none to take care of, none to share emotions, no work and no inspiration for doing something worthwhile. The older people are suffering a lot in all the ways: financially, socially, physically and spiritually. They must return back to their old paternal, traditional and tasted ways and engagement, for discharging moral and social responsibilities, for getting solace and peace in working for others, away from the growing family tensions and for happiness and bliss.

It was possible because Shri Krishna declared in the Gitā "to forget about the result and do only the duties. To act is under human control, the result and effect of that action is not up to them:

karmanyāwādhikarstu ma phaleshu kadāchan.

☙

Faith and Illusions

Faith: Hindus have immense faith, unbelievably deep and both on sublimity and triviality. It can be safely said that they are incarnations of faith; *Faith Incarnate*. One extreme example may enlighten and entertain others.

One day, a person lost his one leg. He repeatedly thanked God; 'O God! You're very merciful and kind. One asked, 'How can God be kind and merciful when he has taken your leg?' His answer was plain, 'He is powerful and could have taken both my legs but he is kind and merciful, so, He has taken only one.'

After a few years, he lost the other leg. He thanked God for his mercy and kindness. When asked, 'How can God be merciful and kind when he has taken both your legs?' His reply was the same, 'God is powerful, he could have taken my hands too but he has mercy and kindness, so, He took only legs.'

It so happened that in another accident he lost both the hands. Again he thanked God for being kind and merciful. When asked, 'How can God be merciful and kind when he has taken both your legs and both your hands? Now, you can do nothing.' He was un-shattered. His reply was the same, 'God is powerful. He could have taken my life but because he is kind and merciful so, He took only my hands.' It's the climax of faith, an example of extreme faith. Hindus have it.

Faith is the strength of Hindus. It's the faith that gives confidence, and helps them in sustaining during duress and extremely painful situations and conditions.

Hindus believe in themselves and others. They are not abnormal; neither extremists nor litigants;

Hindus are never in dilemma. They have clear concept of every aspect of life. It's the gift of great seers and saints. As a result even the illiterate and ignorant can tell the hidden meaning behind an event or a statement. They easily reach to the real intentions of the people. They can gauge a person's intentions from a mile.

The Hindus take their decisions at leisure after deliberations and consultations. They are not in a hurry. They are mostly friendly with Nature and Time. They hardly work against Time. So, they have ample time for everything. They may start searching a suitable groom for their daughter from a very early stage. They may take five or six years in searching a groom. This way they are able to arrange the marriage in time.

If they have to visit a pilgrimage they may start the preparations some two years in advance. There slow preparation will include meeting the people that have visited that holy place, collecting information regarding the religious and spiritual advantages, nearby places to be visited on that tour, etc. If they have vouched or decided to perform a yagya; say a 'Lakharaon' (the highest worship of Lord Shiva), they may start making a list and collecting the materials from the day one. So, they get time and do the things in leisure or very truly, leisurely. They don't wait for the day to arrive then hurriedly make preparations, and somehow perform it. Among the Hindus too there are certain exceptions that by nature delay the things and leave many unfinished works.

Hindus have little illusions, for their forefathers taught that the world is an illusion. We are all illusions; and money, *māyā* or lust for luxury and pleasure are the greatest illusions. This makes them free from illusions. *There is an incident. These above facts were taught by a rishi. He laid stress on the illusoriness of the world. His pupils were impressed by his philosophy, examples and suggestions. One day, the young daughter of the rishi died. The rishi started weeping. One of his favourite and most intelligent pupils went to him and said, "O learned sage! You have taught us that this life is illusion. Everything that we see is illusion. Hence, we should not feel attached to worldly possessions. Then, why are you weeping at the death of the illusory daughter?" The rishi replied without waiting to think, "O! You don't realise. This weeping and these tears too are illusions."*

Hindus Love Truth

Hindus prefer Truth, they don't practise falsehood but they keep mum and refrain from speaking the truth that may result in disaster.

Satyamabruyāt priyam bruyāt, satyamapriyam kathamapi na bruyāt. Speak the truth but only the truth that brings no harm. Don't speak the truth that may bring ruins.

It was the usual practice of Shri Krishna and under his instruction, of the Pandavas, to visit Kuaravas every evening during the great battle of Mahābhārat and to serve the wounded soldiers. During that visit Krishna used to gather information; who would be the Commander-in-chief the next day and how would he be killed. One day, he came to know that āchārya Drona will lead the army the next day and he would stop fighting if his only and great warrior son Aswatthāmā is killed. It was tough. He was the most accomplished warrior. So, Krishna planned the things in his own way.

There was an elephant (kunjar) named Aswatthāmā. He asked Bhima to enter between its forelegs and hindlegs. It would be his shelter and kill that elephant by incessantly hitting his stomach hard. It was done and the elephant was killed. Krishna spread the rumour that Aswatthāma was killed. It reached Dronāchārya. He wished to get it confirmed. He had faith in Yudhisthir. He asked him, 'Has Aswatthāmā been killed?' He had his son in mind. Yudhisthir said "Aswatthāmā hato naro wā kunjaro", (Aswatthāmā was killed but which Aswatthāmā: man or elephant.) Before Yudhisthir could utter the word 'kunjaro' Lord Krishna played on his great and famous conch 'Pānchjanya' and Dronācharya could not hear the most important word 'kunjaro'. As promised he laid down his bow and arrows and stopped fighting. Arjuna got an opportunity and killed him.

This is known as the half-truth spoken by one that was accepted as an incarnation of Dharma. Fingers are often raised against him because the 'half-truth' resulted into the death of the great guru and great warrior (Mahārathi) Dronāchārya. The Hindus, the Humanists and worshippers of truth, have not forgiven him for that 'half-truth'.

Hindus Prefer Sweetness

The Hindus love sweetness, from sweet dishes to sweet speech. They like sweetness in sound, music, and sweet rhythmic movement in dance and at work. They love to watch the men and women moving their feet in rhythm with a load on their head or shoulders. They prefer recitation to reading. The sweetness of tongue is the most praised thing. The girls and women with rough and cacophonous sound are summarily rejected. That is the worst demerit in a woman. They love mellifluous sound. They like sweetness in look. The eyes must project sweetness, if otherwise, the person is not friendly, gentle and human, he is a crook. They practise and find rhythm in sitting, standing and moving. Yoga has taught them and they teach their children. That is the reason that they pray:

Madhumanme nikramanam madhumanme parāyanam,
Wāchā vadāmi madhumad bhuyāsam madhusandrishah.
मधुमन्मे निक्रमणं मधुमन्मे परायणम् ।
वाचा वदामि मधुमद् भूयासं मधुसंदृशः ॥

(One should try to become 'sweet' with all his might. There should be sweetness and rhythm in movements, sitting and standing; sweetness in study; sweetness in tongue; sweetness in looking and sweetness in behaviour. He is like honey whose each organ has sweetness for others.)

Hindus are unique in their faith. Their faith is unshakable. They may discuss and may face tough logic but it will not shatter their faith. They may prefer to keep mum and continue to live with the faith that they had. If they have faith in someone or something it's almost fixed. The quality and height of a Hindu depends on the quality and depth of his faith. If one shows faith in a stone, divinity appears in that; if not then divinity will disappear. They have their fundamental *Mantra* of faith:

Mantra teerthe tathā dwije bheshaje gurou,
Yādrishi bhāwanā yasya siddharth bhawati tādrishi.
मंत्र तीर्थे तथा द्विजे भेषजे गुरौ ।
यादृशी भावना यस्य सिद्धर्थभवति तादृशी ॥

Inner Growth

Hindus aim at growing from inside. Even physical growth comes from inside. This habit gives extra energy and doubles the strength of their organs. Concentration is one way to increase it.

Samkalpo wai jayate karmamulam;
Determination is at the root of all actions.

So, they are able to live a complete life and feel perfection. They are taught: "I'm perfect. I'm indivisible. My soul is one and indivisible. The power of my eyes can't be divided. I possess eternal energy. My *Prāna* (inner living being) is united with the Prāna of the Absolute. My breaths are united with His breath. My soul is not separated from the Soul of the Absolute God. With Him my whole being is united and inseparable." They get courage, energy, concentration and determination from that assertion:

Yayuto   ahamuto   me   ātmāutam   me
chakshuryutam me shrotramyuto me prānoyuto
me apāni ayuto me vyāno ayuto aham sarvah.
Atharva Veda 19:51:1

अयुतोऽहमयुतो मे आत्मायुतं मे चक्षुरयुतं
मे श्रोत्रमयुतो मे प्राणोऽयुतो मेऽपानीऽयुतो
मे   व्यानोऽयुतोऽहं   सर्व: ।

Moreover, they are free from different weaknesses or at least, they try their best to free themselves from: Doubt, Anger, Cruelty, Sycophancy, Anti-social-ideas, Ego, and Lust, etc. For freedom from these weaknesses they have been taught and advised:

Ulookayātum shushulookayātum jahi swayātumuta kokayātum,
Suparnātumuta gridhrayātum drishdeva Pra mrina rakshaIndra.
उलूकयातुं शुशुलूकयातुं जहिश्वयातुमुत कोकयातुम् ।
सुपर्णयातुमुत गृध्रयातुं दृशदेव प्र मृण रक्ष इन्द्र ॥

[Get yourself free from lust and doubt that is there in owl; (for them *sansayah ātmā vinashayati*: doubt ruins the soul); set aside anger and the will to attack that is the nature of wolves; get rid of sycophancy and the wish to steal that is found in dogs; throw away anti-social ideas that is with ruddy-goose (*chakawā*); be humble and free from ego that is seen in eagles; and finally, free yourself from lust that is the livelihood of vultures.]

Mantras

Mantras are simultaneously scientific inventions and truth, and spiritual revelations; and have psychological effect. The name of *Devatā* clarifies the subject matter as that Rishi was engaged in Research on a particular topic. The name of Rishi shows the direction of research. The name of *Chhand* clears the algebraic and symbolic significance. The number of letters and their arrangemnent determines the extent. One can get at the bottom of a Mantra with the help of Vedic Dictionary and deep meditation. That way the symbolic meaning will be clear. The apparent meaning is not the real meaning. Rare scientific theories are hidden in the Mantras. Their psychological and healing effects worked as ads for them. So, people remembered and used them.

When modern man tried to create Mantras, he could create only slogans for selfish ends but in the name of general development. As it's the age of advertisement through placards, boards, hoardings, pamphlets, banners, mike, radio and TV, So, both the electronic and print media are engaged in advertising persons, places, products, rates and ideas, etc. So, anything can become popular and anything can be relegated to the backseat or thrown into darkness or oblivion.

The *Mantras* are constantly, deliberately and with prejudice, being backlashed; and slogans are in the forefront. Often a fortune is invested to popularize a person or a thing.

Anyway, *Mantras* can't be replaced by anything else. They are very important and eternal. It's our weakness that we don't know the meaning, benefits and different great uses. *Mantras are not needed if one does not know their meaning and uses but Mantras are essential for pleasant living and higher growth.*

Mahāmritunjay Mantra

The Hindus have one great shield in the form *Mahāmritunjay Mantra*. They believe that it frees from the fear of death. Simply by chanting the *Mantra* they become bold and fearless. Most often, most of them simply recite it because chanting of *Mahāmritunjay Mantra* is a very tedious task. Only the experts can do it, because it has been given three forms by adding *Pranava*, i.e. AUM and two sets of three Vyāhrities, i.e. *bhuh bhuwah swah* and *haun junn sah*. The original Mahāmritunjay Mantra is:

Trayambakam yajāmahe sugandhim pushti vardhanam;
Urvā rukmiva bandhanān mrityor mukshiya māmritat.

 त्र्यम्बकं यजामहे सुगन्धिं पुष्टिवर्धनम्।
उर्वारुकमिव बन्धनान्मृत्योर्मुक्षीय मामृतात् ॥

—शुक्लयजुर्वेद ३:६०

(We worship three-eyed Lord Shiva. He is and makes others free from the cycle of birth and death, fills one with divine fragrance and gives health and prosperity to His devotees. As cucumber is naturally separated from the creeper, He should free us from death.)

Gāyatri Mantra

The Hindus have another great shield in the form of Gāyatri Mantra: *muchyate sarvapāpebhyo gāyatrayā chaiwa pāwitah.* Whatever is higher, sublime, divine, worth worshipping and pious is Gāyatri Mantra. It's the essence of the Vedas. Hindus have the faith that it protects them; and it protects. It's the most famous *Mantra.* More than 80 % of male, female and children know it, have memorized and chant it with needed accent. It has been repeated and repeatedly talked in all the four Veda Samhitās. It's claimed that he never commits a sin (or sins never touch him) that chants the Gāyatri Mantra everyday: *Gāyatrim yo japennityam na sa pāpena lipyate.*

Gāyatri is both a *Mantra* (Hymn) and a *Chhand* (Metre). It has three *pāda* (pauses) of 8 complete letters each, so, it's often called *Tripadā Gāyatri.* It is said, and the Hindus believe in it that Gāyatri came out of AUM (the Absolute Brahman); from Gāyatri came out Sāvitri and from Sāviti Saraswati came out; from Saraswati all the Vedas and Veda Mantras came out; from the Vedas the Universe was created and at the end came life.

Maharishi Viswāmitra is the rishi of Gāyatri Mantra. But it is also said that each of the 24 complete letters has its separate rishi. It means the Gāyatri Mantra was envisioned by 24 rishis. Maharishi Viswāmitra is the rishi of its last letter. He completed it, so he is deemed to be its rishi. It's so sacred that when Maharshi Vālmiki composed the first epic of the world he started the first letter of each 1000 shlokas with a letter from Gāyatri. His Rāmāyana contains 24,000 shlokas. When the first letter of each one thousand shlokas, are taken together, we get the complete Gāyatri Mantra.

AUM bhurbhuwah swah tatsaviturvarenyam bhargo devasya dhimahi.
Dhiyo yo nah prachodayāt.

ॐ भूर्भुव: स्व: तत्सवितुर्वरेण्यं भर्गो देवस्य धीमहि ।
धियो   यो   न: प्रचोदयात्   ।

We meditate on that Absolute Sun God that pervades the Earth, the Sky and the Heaven. He will guide our mind to sublime deeds.

Rebirth

Hindus believe in rebirth, in life after death. For them the soul is immortal. It takes form and is born again. This way the soul grows. As the soul is abstract, so, it can't grow on its own. It needs a body to fulfill the unfulfilled desires, to accomplish all that was not accomplished in the previous life, to pay for the wrong deeds and to do good so that the next birth will be better and this way it can attain perfection or near perfection and be freed from the eternal cycle of birth and rebirth.

Hindu Dharma teaches immortality of the soul. It does not propound that this is the first and last birth. The human soul is also a beginning less and endless entity which undergoes evolutionary process in the human form. It leads to oneness with God – the ultimate purpose of life.

According to Hindu *Dharma* the soul's journey does not come to an end with this life. Spiritual progress continues to be made through reincarnations. In one life alone, which sometimes is very short, the soul cannot gain perfection. Therefore it takes many births before reaching *moksha* (liberation). By its teaching of Re-birth Hindu Dharma gives one hope in one self, in one's faith and for a bright future. Reincarnation is the means to the fulfilment of religious life, that is, to attain moksha.

The most important aspect of the concept of rebirth is the immortality of Soul. Indians accept and are sure that their body is mortal and hence, perishable but the soul, the living inner self is immortal and never dies. They get consolation that what they have failed to fulfill in this life, they will get another opportunity in the next life to fulfill it. In this regard the Gitā holds the key. The announcement of Lord Krishna is the most quoted shloka of the greatest and most concise book of philosophy and theology. Krishna says that the soul is immortal; that no weapon can cut it; no fire can burn it; no water can wet it and air can't dry it out:

Nayanam chhindanti shāshtrāni nayanam dahati pāwakah,
Na chayanam kledayantāpo na shoshyati mārutah.

नैनं छिन्दन्ति शास्त्राणि नैनं दहति पावक: ।
न चैनं क्लेदयन्तापो न शोषयति मारुत: ॥

गीता २:२३

Law of Karma in Rebirth

Another equally important aspect is the 'Law of Karma.' Every birth is ruled by the karma of the previous life. Accordingly the soul is designated the *yoni*, and are given the choice to select the time, place and body. It's indirectly proved by the stories of the births of different cursed souls.

In one body, the soul can make limited progress and it has to exist for an unlimited period. Naturally therefore, the soul must change the body. Most of the accidental deaths occur because the body was not suitable for the soul. It's also said (and it has no proof) that the soul selects the body by watching the couple. It may miss in its selection because the body grows under the influence of the parents and ancestors. The souls have their different unknown objectives, and follow different ways, adopt different means to make needed progress towards salvation. So, it changes body. Krishna says in the Gitā (2:22) that as we change our old and worn out clothes and replace them with new ones; in the same way the soul changes the body and takes birth in another new and fresh body:

Vansānsi jeernāni yathā bihāya navāni grihnāti naro aparāni,
Tathā sharirāni bihāya jeernānyanyāni sanyāti nawāni dehi.

वासांसि जीर्णानि यथा विहाय नवानि गृह्णाति नरोऽपराणि ।
तथा शरीराणि विहाय जीर्णान्यन्यानि संयाति नवानि देही ॥

Hindus believe that the birth as a human being is not the first birth. There were many births in different *yonis* (zoological families). One may take many more births. If one is able to purify the self then one can get better life, if attains sublimity then, one may not return back to the earth, but if otherwise, one may take birth as a non-human being, a vile creature or as an insect according to the deeds in this life. This belief comes from the Vedas:

Awa srija punaragne pitribhyo yasta āhutashcharati swadhāmih,
Āyurvasāna upa wetu sheshāh sang gachchhatām tanwā jāta Vedah.

अव सृज पुनरग्ने पितृभ्यो यस्त आहुत श्चरति स्वधामिह: ।
आयुर्वसान उप वेतुशेषा: सं गच्छतां तन्वा जात वेद: ॥

ऋग्वेद १०:१६:५

(O Fire God! Create again for ancestors the person that accepts for you the form of different offerings. O Omniscient Fire God! Complete the remaining part of his life, so that he is enriched in life element and gets a healthy and strong body.) In this Mantra the rishi says that after the death when the five elements merge into the cosmic energy then soul remains. This soul gets another body. It's a request to give a strong and healthy body when a person takes rebirth.

Ā yo dharmāni prathamah sasāda tato wanpushi krinushe puruni,
Dhāsyur yonim prathamah wā wiweshā yo wācham anuditām chiket.

आ यो धर्माणि प्रथम: ससाद ततो वपूंषि कृणुषे पुरूणि ।
धास्युर्योनिं प्रथम: वा विवेशा यो वाचमनुदितां चिकेत् ॥

अथर्ववेद ५:१:२

(The first life, that performs religious deeds, gets many lives. He, that hears the not so clear sound (probably of Brahman and AUM) and yet wishes to get wealth, gets the rebirth from the starting point.) The Rishi says that the soul takes on itself the resultant effects of his vices and virtues. He takes a refined or crude body according to those virtues or vices. A person, doing wholesome deeds, gets better and more refined and developed 'family' and others with unwholesome deeds are born in the family of animals or insects. That is the reason that in Yajurveda 40:15 the Rishi gives an advice to remember all the deeds at the time of death:

AUM krato smar. Klive smar. Kritang smar.

ओ३म् क्रतो स्मर। क्लिवे स्मर। कृत ॅ स्मर ।

This belief in birth and rebirth comes from the Gitā too.

Na twewāham jātu nāsam na twam neme janādhipāh,
Na chaiwa na bhabishyāmah sarve vayamatah param.

न त्वेवाहं जातु नासं न त्वं नेमे जनाधिपा: ।
न चैव न भविष्याम: सर्वे वयमत: परम् ॥

गीता २: १२

(In reality, it's not that I was not there in some era or you were
not there or these kings were not there; and it's not that they will
not live in remote future.)

dehino asmin yathā dehe kaumāram yaunam jarā,
tathā dehāntar prāptih dhih statra na muhyati.

देहिनोऽस्मिन्यथा देहे कौमारं यौवनं जरा ।
तथा देहान्तरप्राप्तिर्धीरस्तत्र न मुह्यति ॥

गीता २:१३

(As the body grows from childhood to youth and to old age, in
the same way it gets another body. So, the solemn men don't love
their body.)

This concept of previous life and the life or lives to come, make
and keep him conscious. He tries his best to do only good things.
He is not jealous of others that have got better life. He accepts that
they must have performed wholesome deeds in the previous life
so they are well placed in this life. Hindus faith in gods, Scriptures
and religion comes out from there. It endows him with devotion
and dedication. His tolerance comes out from that belief. He thinks
that he must have done wrong to others, so he is living a life of
downtrodden; if he repeats the similar acts and shows similar
character, he may fall into lower yonis.

An incident will illustrate reason behind the strong belief of the
Hindus in rebirth. Once, there was a debate what the nām-jap (recitation
of name) can do. A Rishi (at some places Lord Shiva himself) asked
his disciple (devotee) to go to a creeping insect and say 'AUM Namah
Shivāya'. He said so. The insect died. The disciple wondered, 'Why
did the insect die when it heard the purifying name?' Then he was
asked to say the same words to an earthworm. He went to it and said
'AUM Namah Shivāya'. Instantly, the earthworm too died. Then he
was asked to repeat the same words to a butterfly and a sparrow. The
results remained the same. They died. When the sparrow heard 'AUM
Namah Shivāya' and died, a deer appeared there. The disciple thought

that he had killed at least four living beings. But the Rishi explained that each of them died and were reborn taking the body of another. The earthworm was immediately, reborn as a butterfly and so on. The latest is the deer. It has been transformed from the sparrow. The Rishi said, "What you took as a certain death was a rebirth. It was the effect of the pious and divine 'AUM Namah Shivāya', that gave them a new body and new life. The body is not important, it's the transformation that is important."

According to Shri Krishna in the Gitā, the soul carries all the senses, their growth and developments, character and ingredients, with it from life to life. The new research on DNA amply proves that all directions for the development of the cells are written on DNA. The last balance of the last life is carried over to the new life. The new life takes a start from there on with that balance. The soul, then, spends and re-stores the resultant effects of the deeds and misdeeds of the new life through the sense organs. Krishna claims that only the wise know this fact. The ignorant have no inkling to it. Those, that have not purified their inner self, don't know this soul. These facts are evident in the following shlokas from the Gitā 15:7-11:

Mamaiwānsho jivaloke jivabhutah sanātanah,
Manah shashthāni indriyāni prakritisthāni karshati.

ममैवांशो जीवलोके जीवभूत: सनातन: ।
मन:षष्ठानीन्द्रियाणि प्रकृतिस्थानि कर्षति ॥ 15:7

The soul in the body is my eternal part and it, steadied by the *triguna* (three qualities, tamoguna, rajoguna, and satoguna), attracts the five sense organs.

Shariram yadwāpnoti yachchāpyut krāmati iswarah,
Grihitwai tāni sanyāti wāyuh gandhāni wāshyāt.

शरीरं यदवाप्नोति यच्चाप्युत्क्रामतीश्वर: ।
गृहीत्वैतानि संयाति वायुर्गन्धानिवाशयात् ॥ 15:8

As the air takes the fragrance from a fragrant place, in the same way, the soul takes away the senses from the body at the time of departure and enters a new body with it.

Shrotram chakshuh sparshanam cha rasanam ghrānam yewa cha,
Adhisthāya manashchāyam vishyānupasevate.

श्रोत्रं चक्षु: स्पर्शनं च रसनं घ्राणमेव च ।
अधिष्ठाय मन श्चायं विषयानुपसेवते ॥ 15:9

The soul in the body takes, enjoys, absorbs or experiences (the worldly truth, pain or pleasure, etc) through the five sense organs: ears, eyes, skin, tongue and nose.

Utkrāmāntam sthitam wāpi bhunjyānam wā gunānwitam,
Bimudhā nānu pashyanti pashyanti gyāna chakshushah.

उत्क्रामन्तं स्थितं वापि भुज्आनं वा गुणान्वितम् ।
विमूढ.ा न‌नुपश्यन्ति पश्यन्ति ज्ञानचक्षुष: ॥ 15:10

The ignorant don't know the soul leaving the body, or living in the body, or experiencing different things, or living in all the three states. Only the wise know the soul with their wisdom-eyes (eyes of wisdom).

Yatanto yoginashchainam pashyantyātmanwaiwasthitam,
Yatantoapya kritātamānonainam pashyantyachetasah.

यतन्तो योगिनश्चैनं पश्यन्त्यात्मन्यवस्थितम् ।
यतन्तोऽप्यकृतात्मानोनैनं पश्यन्त्यचेतस: ॥ 15:11

Even the wise yogis know the soul living in them with deliberate effort. They. that have not purified their inner self, don't know it even after persistent effort.

By mistake some people take rebirth (*punarjanma*) as reincarnation (avatāra). It's not so. Both are different phenomenon. Rebirth is common to all. Each soul has to take rebirth for further purification and inner growth. Reincarnation is limited to souls that are free from the eternal cycle of birth and death. Out of their will and for specific purpose and time, the godly, sublime, liberated and enlightened souls come to the earth as human being or in other form as they desire. It's reincarnation.

☙

Strength and Weaknesses
of Hinduism

Hindus are spiritually and philosophically very rich, the richest. They have both simple and complex ideas. The climax of it is that they can turn the most simple into the most complex, and make the most complex look simple, trivial and commonplace.

In the same way, the Hindus have common weaknesses and rare strength. What appears to others to be a weakness is their real strength because their strength is mostly subtle and imperceptible. Others wonder, what is there in them that the poorest may be the most revered figure, and the richest may be despised with for his numerous misdeeds, a person without depth and value. The reason is very clear. Hindus have a wish to accumulate wealth but they have least regard for material wealth. On the other hand they have utmost respect for inner qualities. For them, character and morality is meaningful; because wealth easily changes hands while character endures. They claim that a wise enemy with strong moral character is far better than an ignorant and arrogant friend.

That is the reason, that in the whole history of Indian culture and civilisation there is not a single example up to the Middle Ages when written tests were taken for examinations or competitions or for appointments. In India, only character and wisdom was tested. They valued the fact whether the knowledge of a person is a part and parcel of his nature, character and living or not.

Two incidents can prove it well and illustrate the points. They are not exactly stories but they are usually told in the form of a story.

When an ãchãrya finished his convocation address his pupils requested him to ask for the dakshinã (gifts given in lieu of the teaching; it is usually said or translated to be fee, by the modern men but dakshinã is different). At first the ãchãrya refused to take anything but when his pupils insisted then he said, "Don't ask anybody to give anything. Take something when no one is looking. Bring it on the next full-moon day.

On the full moon day, there were so many things before the ãchãrya. His pupils were talking about how they befooled others, how they took this or that article when no one was looking. Ãchãrya heard all and then sharply looked at one pupil who had come empty handed. He asked, "When all these pupils have brought so many and so costly things why have you come empty handed? Why were you not interested in paying guru-dakshinã?"

With head down that pupil said slowly but confidently, "Guruwar! I could not find a thing when no body was looking?"

Without changing the tone he asked again, "When all these pupils got things when no one was looking then how and why did you not get a single thing?"

With head down that pupil said slowly but confidently, "Guruwar! I tried my best to pick something up when there was no one else there. But whenever I stretched my hand I realised that every time I was looking at the article. I left them there because you had asked to bring articles when no one was looking. I agree, no one else was looking but I was looking."

The ãchãrya was happy. He announced, "Only he has passed the examination. Now, he can go home but your study is not complete, you will have to stay back for learning more. The lessons are useless if not followed in life. "

The incident or the story is small and simple but it brings forth the intention of the Guru and the inner character of the pupil. There are numerous such instances in Indian Scripture and Literature.

A king started facing revolts and unrest from many areas after the death of his Chief Minister. He tried his best to search out a worthy replacement, but failed. So, one day, he made an announcement: "He; that will bind the central pillar in the king's main reservoir without entering it; will be appointed as the chief minister."

It was a very big pond away from the palace. The cetral pillar was in the middle. at the very center of the reservoir. It was at equal distance *from the boundary in all sides. Many strong men came to try to bind it. Some came with very thin rope. They made coils and hurled the coil towards the pillar but it could not cross even the one-fourth distance. The king got tired of the numerous trials. People realised that it was impossible to bind it without entering the pond, so, they dropped the idea of trying. Some secret efforts were made but all proved futile. Five years passed. He could not get the chief minister. In the absence of the chief minister he was losing one region after another.*

One day, a young tapaswi came. He was a fresh graduate from a famous Gurukula. He announced in the court to bind the central pillar without entering the water. A date was announced. It was surprising news for the people after a couple of years. It was the biggest crowd ever that had gathered to see the tapaswi performing a rare feet. Will he succeed or will he not? It was the common question and both positive and negative came the answers. But many people had the faith in the young man. They claimed that he is the person that knows something. He has brains. He can do it.

People were standing from all the sides. The king, queen and the courtiers came. The tapaswi was asked to bind it. He rose up with a peg in one hand and a wooden hammer in another. He pushed the peg in soft land after hammering it. Then, he took one end of the big and heavy rope and bound it around the peg. Then he took that rope. Placed it on his shoulders and started moving around the big reservoir. He was loosening the rope. After sometime, it was only his rope on each side of the bank or the pond. He came to the peg. He tied a loose knot with the rope there. Then, he started pulling the rope. The people understood it then. They, suddenly, realised that the tapaswi will tighten the rope and the pillar will be under the grip of the rope. They started clapping. They roared. The king smiled. Suddenly, life had returned to the silent crowd. In a chorus, they encouraged the tapaswi. Nay, he was the would-be chief minister. It was a matter of some more time and the tapaswi was successful in binding the central pillar without entering the reservoir or touching water.

The king came to him, announced his appointment but asked him to explain. The tapaswi said: "O King! There is nothing important to explain. I tried to associate the pillar, reservoir and chief-minister. I studied your problems arising after the death of the chief minister. It was obvious that you want your kingdom to be ruled from a central place. You need a person that can move to and keep an eye on the complete boundary and take it on his shoulders to bind the kingdom in unity. **O king, the peg is the central point; the movement around is keeping vigil, carrying rope is responsibility on the shoulders; and without entering the water signifies without war and blood-shed.** *After coming to this conclusion, it was easy to bind the pillar."*

The people gathered there roared in unison to welcome their wise chief-minister.

It's simply amazing that the kings and kingdoms have waited for such a long period for a suitable minister. Just contrary to that belief hundreds of ministers take oath of office on a single day. They must ask to themselves, are they able to do justice to their enormous responsibility? Can they think of the whole country, universe and living beings? Have they got rid of their lust, greed and anger?

One must try to understand deeply this great and original Human Religion before accepting any post of general responsibility. Truth must prevail. Justice must be done. Life is to be saved. Man has to pay the price of all the ills that he has been doing for a couple of centuries. Saving life and saving the earth means saving the riches of the earth for plants and animals too because the existence of man obviously depends on them.

A written test of 'selected questions' based on published syllabus will never produce men of character and morality. Man is man because he can resist temptations. Man is man because he can sacrifice his own life for saving the life of others. There are incidents when man has sacrificed his life for saving books of knowledge. The animals and demons or insects can't do it. So, they are insects, animals and demons, they are not men. Even gods wish to be born as men for further development.

A Chinese traveller was returning back from India. He was given thousands of books written on leaves. It was all loaded on a small ship. Besides the members of the crew, he was escorted by fifteen young tapaswis (research scholars). When they were in the middle of the sea, a hole in the ship was detected. It was just four inches deep inside the water. The captain suggested reducing the load to bring the hole above the water surface. They suggested throwing away the books to reduce the load. The tapaswis heard it. They looked at each other. Silently conveyed their decision. They saluted their gods and suddenly, all of them jumped into the wild sea to save the ship and the books. Not all, only such dedicated and sublime souls among Hindus can do such feet.

There was no exam and no examiner but they had passed the exam; the test of character, power to observe, power to absorb, to take decision and to implement it. Can the life of another 30 years that they had, equal it?

For the Hindus, the obvious is not intriguing. They concentrate at the ambiguities, try to understand its hidden meaning and essence, and then to teach. They apply mostly the indirect methods.

For the Hindus the 'intriguing', 'intricate' and the 'mysterious' has been important. And, it has lured them. They won't like nakedness. They prefer to imagine, see through, and bring out the veiled truth and hidden realities. They have specialized in it. Their ignorant children too prefer to play with such puzzles that sharpen their mind and thinking. Their pastime does not include stamp collection. They prefer to lie down in the open and ask about the cosmic bodies. They introduce them and tell tales about their origin. They saw life in them. That life element is gone. Modern science is bent upon proving that they are a mixture of dust and gas and their brightness is mostly borrowed. The Hindus too claim that we come from the dust and to dust we return. The life element makes all the difference. The scientist that proved "Plants have life", gave all the credit to the Rishis, the ancestors. The glow, the movement, the growth, the changes are proofs of life. Modern science declares the death of stars as pulsars but won't accept life in them. How the death occurred when there is no life?

This places the Hindus in a definite advantageous position. It's the reason behind their great potentiality and immense growth and progress in the field of knowledge. They knew the universe, the beings, the bodies, Nature and nature of things. It may be treated as their weakness that they won't say that there are 1800 species of turtle (Who did take the inventory and when?) but they know how a turtle can be reared up and saved.

Their practical wisdom (even in this age of science and medicine) is far superior to others. Each Hindu is skilled to perform more than one thing. They can prepare different medicines and cure many diseases with tamarind, onion, garlic, neem, basil leaves and barks of different plants. An illiterate village woman too recognises and knows the uses of hundreds of herbs.

That is the reason that thousands of penniless Indians survive in this material world when it's being claimed that money can buy anything. Of course, money is buying a lot: skin-trade is at its peak that was once limited to prostitutes and whores; organ trade is picking up fast (one wonders what has gone wrong with the formation of a healthy child inside the safest womb of a mother that organ transplantations are needed on such a large scale?), every country is in the arms race and trying to make their presence felt in the region of nuclear weapons, rich companies are bought and sold within hours, the men under oath are committing heinous crimes for money, selling the secrets of countries and companies are very popular; and 'rights' too are being sold. (What can the "Duchess of Malfi" do after selling her soul?)

Money is not buying a good moral character and morality for a rich person, successful married life for a couple, freedom from terrorism for the world, peace, solace, health, happiness and blissful life for human and non-human beings. There is some fowl play somewhere that the human mind gets degenerated. *It may be the effect of wine, drugs, junk and stale refrigerated food that the perversion in thinking is so common. Or, it may be the natural outcome of unnatural life and living habits and milieu.* One thing is sure, natural freshness is nowhere there. People try to get freshness and refresh themselves by spraying fragrance and deodorants, chewing central fresh (to check the fowl smell of wine and junk-food), getting face-wash, cold-hot bath and applying different creams made out of the remains of foetus taken out during countless abortions which are necessary for the cream-industry to grow or survive.

Natural life is both the strength and weakness of the Hindus. They are happy with the least that they get from Nature. They know that refrigerated fruits and food remain fresh till they are in deep freezers but they rot fast once they are out for use. Natural ingredients and vitamins are easily lost and are vehemently attacked by bacteria. They often give rise to new or unknown bacteria. Those 20 to 30 minutes in usual lunch and dinners and one to two hours during feasts are important when the food is out from the freezer and served on the table.

Hindus distinguish wealth and health; knowledge and wisdom; literacy and education; information and knowledge; and machines and happiness.

Sant and Asant

In the same way the Hindus distinguish men from men by dividing them into two broad categories: *Sant* (Religious) and *Asant* (Ireligious) or we can say between good people and bad people.

The character and behaviour of *Sants*, the good people, is like that of *Chandan* (sandalwood) while the nature and deeds of *Asants*, the bad people are like that of an axe. The axe cuts the sandalwood; in return, it gives its fragrance to the sharp axe. As a result, the sandal is placed on the forehead and the axe is put to fire and hammered hard. Among Hindus the companionship with the *asant*, the bad people is strictly prohibited.

The good people do not love luxury and are not infatuated by physical pleasures. They share the pleasure and pain of others. They have no enemy for they are not jealous. They have no lust for they don't accumulate wealth. On the contrary, they acquire better qualities. They are simple and friendly, and kind and helpful.

On the opposite side are the bad people; full of pride, lust, jealousy, hatred and enmity. They won't like and tolerate the pleasure and prosperity of others. People deeply in pain will give them immense pleasure. They take shelter in lies, cunningness and deception. They possess anger, lust and cruelty in their worst form. They won't obey the elders, parents, teachers and Scriptures. They deceive those that help them. So, it's advised by all and for all to keep distance from such bad elements.

It's up to an individual to be religious and good or irreligious or bad. Hinduism is clear in its preference:

jeevatwam sammuthãnãya devatwam hetwah manushatwam grihitwã

For the progress of living beings and for becoming divine, be human.

The strength of Hinduism lies in Spirituality. Hindus possess cosmic and spiritual wealth: everything godly and divine, and spiritual and sublime. In the face of that possession the worldly wealth is like dust: *pardravyeshu loshtawat*. Fortunately enough, they acquire unlimited cosmic wealth with '*Karma*' as they believe that honest and true '*Karma*' is real *Dharma*, deepest devotion and it purges and frees:

Satkarmam drirtam mārgam satkarmena prāpnoti dharmam,
Dharmam dadāti moksham mokshena yāti devatwam.

सत्कर्मं दृढतं मार्गं सत्कर्मेन प्राप्नोति धर्मम् ।
धर्मं ददाति मोक्षं मोक्षेन याति देवत्वम् ॥

Understanding Hinduism

Hinduism is vast and immeasurable. It's deep and unfathomable. It's high and unattainable. Once a person remarked, "I don't want a religion that I possess, I want a religion that can possess me." After converting into another religion, a person starts possessing that religion and is not possessed by that religion. Hinduism possesses all. Hindus don't try to convert persons from other religions. All religions are acceptable to Hinduism. When a person comes in contact with Hinduism, he is possessed by it. He merges into its depth. He loses his identity. He is amalgamated. Hinduism is truly a religion that can possess 'all'.

Hinduism can be understood easily; if Brahman: the Absolute and Ultimate Reality is understood. Brahman is at once Reality (*Sat*), Consciousness (*Chit*) and Joy and Bliss (*Ãnand*). Brahman is the Reality that underlies the self (*ātmā*) as well as the World. One can realise God by realizing the Indwelling Brahman as the Self. By knowing 'Self' we can re-unite it with Brahman through moral discipline; by assuming and following certain qualities like harmlessness, truthfulness, non-stealing, self-continence and non-acceptance of unnecessary things; by self-study; reasoning and repeated contemplation on truth. These are regarded by the Upanishads as constituting the method of realisation. All other Indian Schools of Philosophy also accept them as the best method. There lies the Unity in different Indian Religious Sects.

Life is Death: Death is Life

Without understanding 'Life and Death', 'Death in Life' and 'Life in and after Death' one can't understand Hinduism in general and life itself in particular. Hinduism accepts and adds value to *ātmā*, and the Supreme God as *Paramātmā*. Both are Eternal and Deathless. Then what is death?

Death is only changing a body as we change clothes; throw away the worn out and take new ones. It is like the rejection of the worn-out and weathered one for a new, growing and healthier garment. Then and obviously, the body is a garment to soul. Just as a man casting off worn out garments takes new ones, so the dweller in this body, casting off the worn out, weak and old body, enters a new one.

It is the same in the case of Soul and Body. Death is the rejection of body by the soul. Some say that death is the separation of the soul from the physical body. In any case, the departure of the soul or the life element from the body is declared as death. Death brings new life. The birth, then, is like waking up.

It's the starting point as well as the finishing point. So, it's called a Chakra, a cycle. While in a Chakra it's impossible to point out the 'beginning and the end'; in other words, it's difficult to say whether it's the beginning or the end.

In India, like so many other things, it has also been illustrated symbolically, with pāyal or gorāi (Round silver ornaments worn at ankles by women. It's not so in vogue now as it was till some fifty years ago. Still, village women prefer to wear them.); with the trident and damru (a small drum, shaped like an hourglass) in the hands of Lord Shiva.

In gorāi two shapes are very common: one is a rounded pipe that has two conical ball-shaped endings. It is turned wide to open or create space at the time of wearing or taking off. The other one is a snake with open mouth and in single coil. The tail of that silver-snake is pushed inside the mouth to close it or taken off to create opening.

Now, the tail of the snake is in its mouth. From the tail starts the mouth and in the mouth there is the tail. It symbolically suggests that the beginning is the end and the end is the beginning; from there life begins where life ends.

The trident has three lance-like sharp conical edges that are linked together at a centre. In the middle is the present life while one side is the past and the other side is the future. There ends the symbol but the question remains unanswered that which one is the past and which one is the future? In fact, both the past and the future are linked to the present. Whose present, past or future can be answered but which past? It can't be answered.

Both the shape and sound of the Damru in the hands of the Destroyer gives a similar meaning. Its thin middle is the present life while the long and wider upper and lower parts represent the past and the future. It's the present life that is joined to the past actions and waiting and working to see and face the future happenings. Again, it's difficult to claim: this side is the past and that side is the future; and it's again impossible to answer: which present, past or future? The soul lives numerous lives till it is emancipated.

That is one reason that the wise men suggested to grow from inside and collect strength by leading a pure life to get that cherished and final salvation in this life of man in which there is a great opportunity to make tremendous progress towards spirituality, and there are chances that one can attain salvation in this life. So, they were pleased with their luck:

bare bhāga mānush tana pāwā:

It's a great luck that I got the body of human beings.

It is so because the Hindus believe that the type of body depends on the karmas or actions. Sukarmas (good deeds) will give body and mind of higher order along with the growth and achievements of that life. The savings will be carried forward. Dushkarmas will force the soul to take the body of vile creatures or insects with inferior mind. The pain and suffering, caused to others, would be carried forward and be felt by the soul. This way, only the soul knows what harm will come in future in this life or another life. So, the soul as conscience tries its best to guide one to healthy actions but only selected persons hear the inner voice of conscience.

All these symbols represent Time. Time is the factor that either determines or only shows the arrival and departure. In the course of our one life we can't be sure: how many times we have crossed over our own door while going in and out? To Hindus, through the Rishis, it's impossible to say, how many times we took birth, played our role and departed from the stage to come as a new actor to play another role among other actors to depart again. Life is a circle. We complete one circle in this life. The soul moves on in circle in order to complete that circle. The Hindu philosophy, Religion and Scriptures claim that the circle of the soul gets completion with the realisation of the Brahman and the resultant salvation.

With the birth of a person his/ her death takes birth; and with his/ her death it dies. The death of death indicates a new birth. It can be visualised in the falling of leaves and their subsequent appearance: green, fresh and rejuvenated.

Shat-vikār: Six Perversions

Kāma (sex); *Krodha* (anger); *Mada* (pride); *Lobha* (lust); *Moha* (attachment); and *Dwesha* (jealousy) are six perversions. A few lenient people or shaky thinkers give little bit of latitude by calling them deformations. Some try to defend by claiming them to be inherent qualities. In any case or form or way, the ideas are expressed, through them one can't get peace, can't be healthy or happy, won't get love and respect; won't grow from inside. With such perversions in mind and life one can never think of happiness or salvation. Those that possess these qualities, even a few of them, and lack control over self and through self, over them, don't live at all. They die everyday.

Hinduism teaches to be free from them by controlling them, and thus to be free from the fear of death. Even western people came closer to this realisation when they learnt: Cowards die many times. It is obvious that they are cowards that succumb or surrender to these perversions. They only grow and live that control then.

Freedom has different meanings in different context. Freedom from death is one of them. Death is a natural phenomenon. To be immortal is a curse. In western thought: Lady of Cybil/ Sybil symbolises that curse when after getting the blessings of immortality she had only prayer and wish: "O God! I wish to die."

Hindu philosophy lays stress on the fact that **we have to live till we die. Hence, living is important, death is not important.** Then, why should one feed such deformities that are hurdles in healthy and happy living? Then why not opt for their opposites? Then, **celibacy, love, humility, detachment, kindness, compassion,** and **sympathy** will help in fuller living. These are virtues and help in fuller, healthier and happier living. Those, that possess these virtues, can easily understand Hinduism or Humanism.

With different prejudices, lust and jealousy in mind one can't understand Religion in general and Hinduism in particular. Such persons can't get satisfaction from any thing. They can't be happy. Happiness comes out of virtues, not from vices; by helping others and not by committing crimes: serious or trivial.

One can accumulate a lot more money than needed but won't get pleasure, satisfaction and much needed 'happiness'. What will the money do if there is no 'happiness' in life? In the known history of man *Indraprastha* had maximum of wealth. What happened to that wealth? Where is that wealth? In every country, every kingdom and every century coins of gold, silver, nickel, copper, etc. were minted. None can imagine the weight of those coins minted down the ages. Where are they? Did they make man better? We may not dare to say but we all realise, rather know that these perverted qualities forced man to fight: small wars or big battles were fought; countless men, women, children (patriots will prefer to say 'warriors' or patriots) were killed; wealth changed hands and was destroyed. What to say of money; there is no trace of numerous kingdoms and towns.

On the other hand, those that preferred knowledge and penance; donated their wealth or left their kingdoms are still alive and respected. Most of them are worshipped.

Hinduism provides ways and means to get rid of those inhuman, unhealthy, irreligious maladies, ideas, perversions, sins and actions. It provides ways to purify the inner self and grow from inside to attain salvation. The reason behind the survival of this religion and such religious people is the possession of the virtuous qualities.

By discarding religion and losing grip over self; by showing disrespect to God and turning away from pious deeds we have lost the value. As a result life has no value in modern era. It has become meaningless; as we have no objective before us other than earning money. We earn even by illegal, immoral and spurious means. We prefer to show that money by spending huge amounts on wasteful articles. Manufacturing and selling spurious drugs is the most heinous crime that we are committing. It's most heinous because we don't know who will be declared dead after taking that medicine; and we definitely have no enmity with that unknown old, young, child or a pregnant lady. We have lost all sense and all values.

We need a lot of money to waste in showing that we are moneyed people. One example will be enough. Three land line phones and three mobile phones are a very common sight on the tables of higher executives that have no time to attend to phone calls. Personal secretary or assistants usually receive the calls. When a man is unable to talk on one phone what is the meaning of six phones? The answer will invariably be 'to impress others.' Do the visitors don't realise the meaning and intentions? Are they so knave? On the contrary, his ego and ignorance are exposed to the visitors that may not be on the equal footing. The assistants would have ignored his previous calls. In the style of a sycophant some may show that he is doubly impressed by the office and the officer. Are we religious in deceiving others? Is it wise to indulge in unethical practice to meet such unnecessary expenses?

That is the way life is being lived nowadays; rather, life, time, strength, energy and resources are being wasted in umpteen ways. The powerful and resourceful executives could and should have done a lot to facilitate matters, help others and make the society a better place to live and work in. The environment may have become soothing and secure; healthy and pleasant; the visitors or the needy may have felt relaxed and confident.

❧

Misconceptions Regarding Hinduism

Polytheism

A popular misconception about Hinduism is that it's polytheistic, that Hindus believe in many gods. Hindus have a different system. At the helm is the Absolute Brahman. When he had intense desire to multiply he created the Trinity: *Brahmā, Vishnu* and *Mahesh*, for further creation, sustenance and destruction, so that the process can continue. He entered all that was created later on by Brahmā and remained hidden as a small entity like the thumb. That way he pervades all. The creation grew vast. The Trinity took reincarnation in different forms at different times. They were all replicas of the Absolute God and were accepted as gods. Then, whatever matter or element stood for any of the three: Creation, Sustenance or Destruction: became god for the human beings. Thus they kept on growing and at present, by a rough estimate, there are more than 33,000 gods. They include, the incarnations of Brahma and Shakti, of Trinity, of other gods on the one hand, on the other, Natural Phenomenon, Forces of Nature, Birds, Animals, Plants, Cereals, Forests, and so on. They also include personal gods, family gods, village gods, gods and goddesses of crops, forests, marriages, health, and many sublime souls that contributed a lot for the welfare of living beings, etc. When the Hindus worship the God of Village (grāma Devatā/ grāma Devi) he becomes the Supreme God and others are accepted under him. It happens whenever they worship one god or another. In this way, Hinduism includes everything that human mind can think of as a god. All religious 'isms' and 'ists' are a part of this Eternal Human Religion, popularly or mistakenly called Hinduism.

Aum purnamadah purnamidam
purnāt purnamudchayate;
purnasya purnamadāya
purnamewavashishyate .
Aum shāntih shāntih shāntih.

ॐ पूर्णमदः पूर्णमिदं पूर्णात् पूर्णमुदच्यते ।
पूर्णस्य पूर्णमदाय पूर्णमेवशिष्यते ।
ॐ शान्तिः ! शान्तिः !! शान्तिः !!!

(ईशावास्योपनिषद् शांति पाठ)

What is the whole? This is the whole. He is the whole. The whole has come out of the whole and yet the whole has remained whole. It's the riddle that can be revealed only in deep meditation to pure conscience in a trance-like state of pure consciousness that gives ecstatic pleasure.

Vedas, the eternal source of knowledge, are perfect. Perfect knowledge of 'one', 'some' or 'many' can be taken out of it, yet it'll remain perfect. Thus both will remain perfect.

The essence of this verse is that the Infinite can't be expressed in mathematical terms or be measured as geometrical shapes. It's immeasurable and unfathomable. It's beyond the human experiments, tests and discoveries in tiny laboratories for it's infinite and beyond the concept of mind. The mind is a small fraction of that whole and yet each mind is a whole. They can't see the whole tree in the seed. It can only be expressed in subtle riddles. That Infinite God can be represented in Infinite ways: manifest or un-manifest. The Hindus have preferred all the propounded theories and known ways. That 'One' Brahman is represented by and in multiple forms and every form is Perfect and the Whole, at least in their eyes and mind. So, Hinduism is not a lake, it's a perennial river, like the Ganges, that comes out of the Himalayas and races towards the sea to become a part of the infinity. It becomes as deep and wide as the seven seas.

That God (or His Fraction) is everywhere, as a whole. It means that He is as much as and as wide as the unknown infinity, in all its known and unknown dimensions. In this sense, Hinduism is monotheistic because of That One Absolute God. He may be without qualities or a body but the Hindus visualise the Infinite because they have been taught:

yat brahmānde tat pinde: whatever is there in Cosmos is there in our body. So, in a calculated manner and with all knowledge and confidence they announce:

aham brahmāsmi. It's equality with the unknown in quality and essence; not in physique and performance.

But that God has many incarnations and numerous forms. So, wherever or in whomsoever the Hindus found Brahman's qualities they accepted it or him as God. They can compare one with *Brahmā*, the other with *Vishnu* and yet another with *Devādideva Mahādeva*. The numbers grew. Now, they have countless gods. Thus Hinduism is polytheistic. Among them some are atheists and some believe in such gods that are not generally, accepted as part of Hinduism. So, they are Pagan or they follow heathenism or therianthropism. Because of the word *Dharma*, that has infinite connotation, they cover the unimaginable width and heterogeneous ideas. Hindus are all. It's another proof of Hinduism being the Human Religion. Human life and mind differs in nature, culture, civilisation, inner-self, outer surrounding; and affect life in many ways. All the ways are part of Hinduism. It has not taken from any other religion. It could not because it had its general philosophy and rules fixed myriads of years before the birth of any other religion. As a Religion for all human beings, it had and has to inculcate and possess every trend in human life. Hinduism possesses all.

Idol Worship

Another popular misconception is that Hinduism promotes Idol Worship. One must think over this phase of Hinduism because what is most apparent is not the truth. Truth is different. Hinduism does not promote Idol Worship. On the contrary Hinduism urges to transcend all physical aids in worshipping for greater spiritual progress. Realizing that it's impossible to visualise the Infinite. It may fill one with false hope. So, Hinduism urges one to slowly and steadily continue one's effort and keep on making progress in the pursuit of Truth. For such steady progress Hinduism suggests to start with physical aids such as Idol Worship, praying in Temples, keeping an image when in meditation etc. Hinduism declares that one can take whatever physical means one wishes to take and worship it. From mother, father, a patient, to a saint, mahātmā or god; a wood or a stone as a symbol because the Absolute Brahman pervades all, and each path, including *nawadhā bhakti*, will lead to the same 'union'. **Hence, Idol Worship in Hinduism is not an end in itself, it's a means to achieve final union with the Absolute and get Bliss and Beatitude.** With devotion, worship and surrender one can succeed in visualizing the Perfect One, in getting emancipation and final freedom from the cycle. It hardly makes any difference which path is followed: one of Saguna or Nirguna; what aids are taken: of a guru or god; of a temple or work; of an idol or an abstract idea.

It seems very pertinent here to quote Swami Vivekanand:

"If a person wants to drink milk, he uses a cup as he cannot drink it directly. For the quivering and unsteady mind, there should be a visible form or a symbol, the idol, so that it becomes a foundation for his adoration. The Idol form of God is akin to a vessel, which enables a man to drink the milk. Through the instrumentality of an aid, a devotee comprehends divinity."

Hinduism in the eyes of western people is the religious belief and institutions of billions of inhabitants of India and parts of neighbouring countries. They deny its universal appeal and its essence that it's for all human beings. The MacMillan Encyclopaedia (1981; page 575) writes: "Hinduism is not a religion with a formal creed, but the complex result of about 5,000 years of continuous cultural development." For them it's not a religion for it has no formal creed (while creed is at the very basis of Hinduism; it may mean that it has some informal creed. Is it so?). It is a complex result. On the contrary each aspect of Hinduism, each pillar, each belief, ritual and rites is crystal clear and well explained in different books by learned seers; One must try to see the whole that remain out of sight or deliberately kept in oblivion. Diversity, comprehensiveness and extensiveness can't be taken as complexity. Hinduism claims, from the very beginning that 'Truth' is one, the learned people express it in different ways: *yekam sad viprā bahudhā vadanti.*

Prejudices against Hinduism

It's difficult to comprehend how did it happen but the Encyclopaedias claim that Vedānta denounced Jainism and Buddhism; that the Brāhmins were against Buddhism. They may not have the sequence of happenings in mind (or they may be deliberately trying to create a rift among the Indians). What they forget is the fact that Vedānta, the Brahman Sutra was written by Veda Vyāsa, thousands of years before the birth of Bhagawān Buddha. They also forget that the first five disciples of Buddha were Brāhmins, his gurus were Brāhmins, all the important persons to spread Buddhism (even to China) were Brāhmins, and Brāhmins wrote 95% of the Buddhist Literature in India.

There is only one difference with Buddhism. Buddha kept mum over Brahman and Soul. He preached what he thought to be in the best interest of the people of that time in the language of his own kingdom that was incidentally the common language of the people. During the Middle Ages, around one thousand five hundred years after Buddha, Adi Shankerāchārya rose against all other religions including Buddhism to guide the people, to show them the right path and to save Hindus and Hinduism. In order to unite the Indians he got four *Peethas* as pillars at four corners of the country.

The Encyclopaedia adds, "It includes a number of extremely diverse traditional beliefs (as if they are not religious beliefs; they are only traditional) and practices and over the centuries it has influenced and been influenced by younger religions, including Buddhism, Jainism, Christianity, Islam and Shikhism." While the fact is that in some form Indian Scriptures were followed in devising and improving all these religions.

"One of the central concepts is that the necessary result of one's actions in life leads to reincarnation at a higher or lower level of life, a belief that has given rise both to the system of castes and to a deep respect for all forms of life." This belief, of rebirth according to karma, has not given rise to caste system, because the birth can be in the family of insects, animals or birds too. The caste system (in reality, *varna vyawasthā,*) was fixed separately in Manusmriti on profession and division of labour. Varna is the growth of an individual or a group of individuals, and acceptance of a particular profession by him or them. By birth all are Shudras. The body that has spent in the cell of a jail like womb of mother in the dirtiest and most poisonous liquid can't be better than a Shudra, hence: *janmanā shudro jāyeta.*

"The goal of the religion (Hinduism) is to find release from the cycle of rebirth and to return to the ultimate unchanging reality, 'Brahman'. Release may be sought through good works, devotion to a particular god, such as the popular deity, Krishna; (incidentally Krishna is not a deity but an incarnation of Vishnu, and the Absolute Brahman) or through various types of meditation and asceticism." That is not the only goal of Hinduism. There are many goals like inner growth and development, perfection, sublimity. The most important one is *niskāma karma*, action without attachment or expectation. Emancipation or salvation is the result of pious and religious deeds on the basis of the *Kārya-Kārana Sidhānta*, i.e. cause and effect theory.

Regarding the misconceptions that either crept in the mind of the people or were deliberately created to mislead the immature and ignorant majority of Hindus, one thing is very peculiar that all the misconceptions or controversies are there in strongest aspects of Hinduism, that are obviously needed all over the world in becoming civilized, refined, sublime and divine without bringing any harm to life and the living society. Most of such controversies are in the green and healthy boughs: Varna vyawasthā; Ashram Vyawasthā, Purushārtha and in Sculptural field of idol making and worshipping. Hinduism in fact, *promotes stratification of society under the so called caste system (while it's varna vyawasthā, management of people* (HR for the business world) *and discourages discrimination against the less fortunate.* There are provisions for each caste to be the most powerful 'entity' some day.

This noble division in society and a very wise social order and standard representation was misinterpreted, exploited and abused by many down the ages; leading to the indiscriminate creation of numerous castes and sub-castes, including upper caste, lower caste and creamy layer. Such reckless and multiple divisions will never give stability to society. It will not be a happy place for there will be no cooperation. They are to be divided only in four if they have to be strong pillars of society with equal opportunity, load and responsibility.

Misconceptions were created out of prejudices. Prejudices against Hinduism are, broadly speaking, prejudices against India, Indian people and Indianness. For the reasons mostly unknown or undeclared all have some prejudice against India. These prejudices are weathering out the country from within. It's now coming to the surface with the uncontrolled and unprecedented rise in crime: crime of every kind. Some Indians don't try to know India and Hinduism and some are stopped (in different ways) from knowing them. As a result, the whole system is in the grip of non-Indian; and most of us wrongly favour everything non-Indian: from ideas to eatables; from job to currency; from books to religion. Some people are realizing the mistake but are unable to change the mood and motto of the young generation that is vouching for everything physical. Physical comfort is alien to India. The divided country, the divided self, divided faith is weakening and will definitely ruin the country.

Hindus are Conscious

Indians have boldly and intelligently faced such situations in the past. There is a remote possibility that they will realise their mistake soon, turn away from the luxurious attraction and will try to regain the character and wisdom. It is their real wealth and great possession. With it they are still indispensable for the world. They are needed for they have wisdom, skill, intelligence and diligence.

Indians are still the richest. They have saved and retained all that was necessary for growth. Whatever the world or the journalists may say but the progress that India has shown against all odds after independence can't be matched. They are the only people that are in every field; that produce everything; and in almost all the fields they are among the top ten. It's only because they possess what their forefathers handed them. There are many small ills but there are two great ills that each of us must be aware of and check it. One thing is deforestation and pollution, and the other thing is junk food and foreign debt. If they can keep it under control then again they will be *viswaguru*, and rule over the world with knowledge, love and non-violence. When Sri Aurobindo declared that after the Third World War India will be at the top, then, he had the herbs, animal wealth and man power in his mind.

There are four great wealth of a country: Manpower, Animal power, Forests and plantation, and Natural resources. We are destroying all. Most of our manpower is lying unutilized because of unemployment, we have at present virtually no animal power, are dependent on electricity and machinery. We need around 63% forest and have only 17% left. All rivers, ponds and other reservoirs are polluted and with motor and pump we are sucking our earth dry, as a result the water level is falling fast in almost every area. We are not conscious of the crisis because we are interested in colour films, serial, TVs, photos, cars, riches, luxury; and never thinking about the matters and elements essential for life. This is not the Hindu way of living. It's not Hinduism.

Not only the elderly Hindus but also the young, and the prejudiced bureaucrats are conscious of the suffocating atmosphere and the tightening noose around their delicate and tolerant neck. They are alert and mentally ready to face the challenges and dangers as their forefathers had faced many times in the past. They will be victorious with sheer character and determination. They will protect Hinduism and it will protect them as it has protected all in the past.

In Hindu family grand sons are more important than the sons because the grand sons show the continuity of life. The elders take greater interest in them. **We have to ensure that continuity, and carry the legacy not on our shoulders but in our inner self.** Hinduism is our prized, spiritual, sublime and divine possession. It is the truth and one will have to believe.

India is the country of ageless art, timeless religion, borderless culture and endless human values. Hinduism is the religion of endless faith, numberless gods, ageless worshipping, timeless devotion and strain-less living. Hold them and carry them forward. Stick to them, they will save all from total destruction.

☛

Hindu Darshan: Indian Philosophy

(One)

In Wider Perspective

Hindu *Darshan* is always mentioned in English as 'Indian Philosophy'; for it helps others to show the division because they can't see the philosophical and spiritual unity. It's beyond the perception of a selfish, lustful materialist to dive deep into Hindu philosophy and collect the big, bright and shapely pearls. It is translated as Indian Philosophy but in India it has been only philosophy like Religion as our forefathers used the words: Dharma and Darshan. Basically, only two subjects were taught: Sāhitya (Literature; that included all creative works and most of the Scriptures) and Darshan (Philosophy; that included all other subjects from Cosmology, Cosmogony to Meteorology; from geography, Botany, Zoology to Geology; from Physics, Chemistry, Astronomy to Astrology; from Architecture to Weaponry).

Hindu *Darshan* is always mentioned in English as 'Indian Philosophy' (because many people, mostly non-Indians treat Atheism, Buddhism, Jainism and Sikhism different to Hindu philosophy. There is no so called Hindu or Indian that will not salute Buddha, Mahāvira and Guru Nānak. Separation may be artificially created but the unity is there. Indians can't miss that philosophy of Unity, Oneness and *ātmavat sarvabhuteshu*: I'm like all. All are like me. At least, by deliberately not recognising Hindu *Darshan*, people view it in a wide perspective; yet they fail to give its due wider perspective as Human Philosophy or in its widest perspective as the Eternal Truth. Whether we say it or not, accept it or not but Hindu Darshan possesses and shows the TRUTH: **Satya**; and all the three: *sat chit ānand:* through *Sachchidānanda.*

Indians have the same respect for all the prophets and Gods. They show that respect and talk with respect. They may have enmity with a person but not with a religion. Those that have or show enmity may have lost their mental equilibrium.

Indians have deep respect to different branches of their philosophy and the philosophy that have originated in other countries. The result is that they show more maturity and greater balance in their feelings, dealings and expressions.

Very few people can feel the real reason behind it. In India, Philosophy is not a subject of teaching others it's an integral part of life. It's lived and followed here. What is lived and followed is called philosophy. It's the way to make adjustments with natural forces, other living and non-living beings and for inner growth without damaging others.

It's a truth that Indian philosophy is respected in all the countries of the world. It makes no difference if some scholars negatively analyse them and vehemently criticise them. Criticisms die, philosophy lives. It has survived like Hindus under adverse conditions and has the strength and immortality to sustain and remain immortal. The reason is that they are born out of thousands of years of research or after great deal of thinking or after visiting different places and collecting different facts or after great penance. And, it has survived and will survive also because Indian philosophy is natural, original and for all. There is no prejudice against anyone. The four original social and professional divisions have already crossed the 400 mark and are steadily growing. The 'split' is easily visible and the ruinous effect is before us; and known to all.

The people say, Indian philosophy is respected everywhere in the world. It makes no difference (whether people like it or not) to the most immaculate philosophical tradition. The rich and varied tradition will always guide 'all human beings on the earth' and teach them the best way to lead a contented, happy, blissful, healthy and growth oriented life. It will never come with extravagant and luxurious life without physical labour; it will not come with misery worthless and workless days and nights; it will come with a balanced and positive approach, frugality and by burning excess fat and sugar through adequate physical labour. Incidentally, only physical labour can keep one healthy and only healthy person can live a full life and get all: healthy body, sublime mind, happy family, friendly and co-operating atmosphere, non-handicapped healthy-happy children, honourable living and respectable death. That person (or such persons) will be a human being/s. The good moral character and only virtuous deeds; patience and perseverance; kindness and helping attitude; wistful helping hands and the kindred souls are enough to keep all free under great and grand limitations.

A Few Fundamental Concepts

The limitations are cosmic, natural and essential. Except the Unknown Brahman, each creation has to live, move and work under certain limitations; and to follow a system, a cycle; may be many systems and many cycles. Just in order to remain alive one will have to apply control, have *sanyam*: the greater the control the happier is the person (living being or a phenomenon).

This is a fundamental concept in Indian or Hindu Philosophy, all beings are free under certain limitations. The wise men since time immemorial have been teaching it and asking the people to have control, to control the senses in order to be free from the illusions and ignorance. That freedom through meditation and penance and the resultant purity and pure deeds pave the way for emancipation and salvation. Modern man will not accept it; then, modern man will not get peace, and can never be healthy and happy.

With that concept the wise men allowed utmost freedom for inner growth and for expressing the views; pain or pleasure and other likes and dislikes. Indians have been very liberal, tolerant and have preferred frugality to extravaganza or miserliness. They have maintained the balance and knew (were sure inside) that others will follow the suit. So, they gave utmost freedom; accepted all and assimilated and synthesized all.

Such freedom is real freedom; anarchy or terrorism or dictatorship or creation, sale or distribution of destructive instruments, weapons, poisons or even insecticides are not freedom. By snatching away others' freedom and security none can remain secure. In the security of the mass lies the security of the selected or privileged few. None can feel and be secure under guards; inside forts; behind high boundary walls, if other places are shaking under bomb-blasts and bullets are being shot at others. If all are secure, healthy, happy and living fearlessly then I, too, am enjoying them because I'm one of the "ALL." That is one of the major reasons that those wise men chanted the Mantra: *sarve bhwantu sukhinah sarve santu niramaya*.

This brings us directly to that great concept: *Ahimsa* non-violence. That is the only way to survive. Survival of the fittest is a partial truth. The real truth is a society without fear from fellow beings. Can modern man and society think of that security and fearlessness? No. Simply in order to force others to live in constant fear, from scientists to astrologers are working hand in glove and in unison.

As an act of balancing, there was and is freedom of ideas and expression but there have been definite restrictions on *karma*, action. Purity in action is preferred to anything else. The action must be for *bahujana hitaya* and *bahujana sukhaya*: in the larger interest and for the happiness of greater number of beings. A person's pleasure and survival has least importance. The action of a person must ensure safety, security, survival and sustenance of many or maximum. The persons that acted in 'self-interest' or lost an opportunity to help someone or that could not act in time were not forgiven. *Bhishma Pitamah*, the greatest personality in Mahābhārat has not yet been forgiven as he maintained silence in the court and did not try to save Draupadi; Dronāchārya, the greatest guru in that greatest battle asked for the thumb from Ekalavya in a moment of weakness and has not been forgiven. In action, Indians may not punish (for punishing others is not their right) but they won't forgive misdeeds. From *mama* Shakuni to Jaichanda there are numerous such examples. The jealous and lustful are despised with or at least, not liked by any. A person here will feel injured if and when he is said to be a Shakuni or a Jaichand. It's certainly degradation in human values and in the eyes of others.

On the contrary, a just action, a helping hand, a sacrifice for the survival of others has been praised. Such men have been given higher place: treated as heroes, mahātmās and devatās. They are divine and godly figures. As a result, Indians have sacrificed all for others: life, sons, wealth and family members. *The intention behind an action and the resultant effect in favour of life in general adds value and meaning. A life must be meaningful and a person is elevated if he/she acts for common good and welfare.* As only the action is under our control so we should act only after thinking the pros and cons, and only when the action is profitable for others. That way, a person keeps and establishes individuality and works for the community.

This brings not only to wholesome deeds but also to dutifulness. Be honest and sincere to duties; the duties are *dharma*: religion; perform them, save religion; religion will save: *dharmo rakshati rakshitah*. It can be analysed and explained in many ways. *Dharma* stands for or symbolises all 'good deeds' done towards other creatures and life giving and preserving elements and objects. Using the same pattern we can say:

Save crops; crops will save you;
Save fruits; fruits will save you;
Save trees; trees will save you;
Save air; air will save you;
Save parents; parents will save you;
Save children; children will save you.

Brahman Satya Jagat Mithyā

One of the greatest concepts in the Hindu Philosophy and Religion is the assertion of the fact that the projected world is illusion. The only Truth is the Absolute *Brahman*. Three examples are given to prove the point: (i) a piece of rope is taken to be a snake. It's an illusion. The appearance is false and misleading. (ii) The inner part of an oyster is accepted as silver. It's illusion. The appearance is not the truth. (iii) The mirage in a desert is taken as water and not only deer but wise men also follow that mirage. What appears to be true is just an illusion. Thus, the world is an illusion, and the universe is the greatest illusion. It's a dream, an endless dream or a series of dreams. What we know to be true is not true; and we don't know the Truth. The Truth is the Absolute *Brahman*.

The illusion is created not because of our ignorance but because of our knowledge. We know both the rope and the snake and there is a sort of physical similarity that creates the illusion. It's called the power of *Māyā*, the illusory force. They get a form in mind.

Forms are created in abstractions. The concrete form of matter is the result of our mental thinking. All the three are the projections of that Brahman. There is no difference in quality and non-quality. The visual world has no existence. It's only He that exists. It is the dubious creation and equally dubious explanation of the illusory force.

Growing Crisis

Modern psychology and modern philosophy give no space to 'life,' 'living beings,' or even human beings. They have the 'self' and that is all. They are vying for 'micro family'; taking oath to remain childless. Naturally, they are using condoms to stop the fertilization; and killing embryo if per chance the egg is fertilized; kill the new born in many ways; the easiest way is to give spurious medicines; if it survives then he/ she will be lulled into becoming a drug-addict so that they discard the society and live on and for only physical pleasure. They will be slaves in many ways and sense and work in that direction. They must commit crime and engage in killing; otherwise there is no sense in making arms, weapons, sophisticated weapons and sell or offer as gift. The universal conspiracy is very clear that there should not be a single man or woman that is not a criminal. Only criminals and demons will support other criminals. They will be the hero and guide others. They will be worshipped and Satan's wish will be fulfilled. All the honest, humble and human souls must be killed.

To sum up: **Modern man is Godless and Faithless; has no doctrine; follows no system and no philosophy; and has no Religion**

Life is a different phenomenon. It can't be lived full and well if one is not friendly and human towards others. The point is that we need a clear and human philosophy. *It's the philosophy that makes the character, shapes the personality; fixes the attitude and aim, paves the way or does the opposite; it makes or mars, creates or annihilates.*

Modern man has no philosophy; at least not a human philosophy. Materialism is a known and accepted philosophy nowadays. We all forget that materialism is apparently a part of living and surviving; it's not a philosophy. It was there when there was no language, no world like *bhautiktā* or materialism; it will remain even when we don't mention it. So, it's safe to say that modern man has no philosophy; more so because one changes one's so called philosophy everyday and every now and then. They don't stick to their words.

In this context the reading and analysis by Radhakrishnan opens the eye (An Idealist View of Life, 38): "Scepticism does not cost us much. It is faith that requires courage nowadays." May be it is faithlessness that has turned modern man unfaithful.

Indian philosophy clearly states that the sceptical people that lack confidence and change their stance are disbelieved. It makes it very clear: They are ideal men (great souls, *mahātmā*) that say what they have inside and do what they say; and there are demons (bad elements, *durātmanām*) that think something else, say something else and do something else:

Manasya ekam vachasya ekam
karmanyekam mahatmanām,
Manasanyad vachasanyad karmanyad durātmanām.
मनस्येकं वचस्येकं कर्मण्येकं महात्मनाम् ।
मनसन्यद् वचसन्यद् कर्मणन्यद् दुरात्मनाम् ॥

On the contrary, even in fast changing milieu, a reasonable percentage; still and truly follow Indian Philosophy and the dictates of the Scriptures. The reason is that Indian Philosophy and Scriptures possess all and show all, and strangely enough to all. That is the reason that it's Eternal.

Inflicting physical or mental injury and giving pain to others: human or non-human; is not in Indian Philosophy. During those Ancient Times Veda Vyāsa summed up all the teachings of all the eighteen Purānas that are integral parts of Vedas, Upanishads and other Scriptures; and declared: "In all the 18 Purānas Vyāsa has said only two things: **to help others is virtue and to give pain to others is sin:**

Ashtādasha purāneshu vyāsasya vachanam dvya,
Paropakārāya punyāya pāpāya parpidanam.
अष्टादशपुराणेषु व्यासस्य वचनं द्वै ।
परोपकाराय पुण्याय पापाय परपीडनम् ॥

The Only Saviour

Indian philosophy is against it. It values each living being including the lowly insects. It advocates that some eatables be given to others every day. It's charity; it's not begging. The *Brahmachāries,* the āchāryas, the *Sants, Sādhus* and others were not beggars. They had the responsibility of guiding, uplifting and keeping the society healthy and happy. The society (the *grihastas*) had taken the responsibility of feeding them. It was a healthy life of mutual faith and collaboration, co-operation and of interdependence. Each *varna* was dependent on other *varna.* Modern man has an empty heart, the Empty Canvass; bored at the physical pleasure and dissatisfaction; needs adventure and seeks that from war, death, killing and blood through weapons. He can't digest or tolerate the health or pleasure of others, so the divorces, murders, killer-instruments and only crimes are being shown on the channels. It's perversion. It's claimed that the people like such 'perversions'; then most of the modern men have turned into violence loving demons. The rest are fast moving on the right track. **Naturally, all the governments of the world have failed to check terrorism and crime. It's growing everyday. Its culmination into the successful attack on the Trade Tower and Pentagon is not enough to open the inner eyes of modern man. Man has eyes, heart and mind but has lost vision, feeling and wisdom.**

Indian Philosophy is the only way to take man out of this suicidal situation. Whether one likes or not but one must read, know and follow Indian Philosophy for Survival, Peace, Health and Happiness. It will salvage all from the brink of guaranteed disaster and total annihilation. It can emancipate and give salvation. Only Indian Philosophy and Indian Way of Living in Frugality and in the generous Lap of Nature will ensure 'Continuity of Life.'

(Two)

Indian Philosophy is Human and Eternal. It's Eternal and Universal, so it has branches, sub branches, boughs, etc. It admits that Brahman thought: 'I'm one, I should become many.' *Yeko aham bahushyām.* One Indian Philosophy became many as One Supreme Brahman became many. But the division of Indian Philosophy in Pro-Vedic and Anti-Vedic is highly objectionable. It has already poisoned the mind of even Indians. They may have taken something from Vedas and have left something untouched; that does not mean that they are Anti Vedas. It is a fact that no one has opposed Vedas. Mahāvir or Buddha or Chāravāka or Nānak has never uttered a word against Vedas. Social excesses are different maladies. The available speeches or sermons in the form of writings are proofs. Moreover, Indian Religion, Life and Philosophy has given freedom of speech, thought and to a certain extent of action, provided that it's in the larger interest of the living beings. Any stray incident can't be a rule. The difference may lie in their ways and moving on different ways does not amount to opposition. All the philosophical systems in India "insist upon a common pattern of intellectual, physical, and moral discipline, which stamps them all as Indian."

Shat Darshan: Six Principal Branches of Indian Philosophy

Philosophy deals with the creation, cause, effect and continuity of life and shows the meaning and purpose behind every object and being. It has been divided in six main divisions; and each of them has been divided in many sub-divisions because of the āchāryas who taught them. A slight deviation from the original in its perception and delineation gave birth to a different branch of philosophy. They are 1. *Vaisheshika Darshan* 2. *Sānkhya Darshan* 3. *Yoga Darshan* 4. *Nyāya Darshan* 5. *Poorvamimāmsā Darshan* 6. *Uttarmimāmsā Darshan.*

Vaisheshika Darshan

Vaisheshika Darshan establishes that God and Life are realistic elements. The duty of a Being is to follow its duties, the religion fixed for it, through its physical construction and mental aspirations. **It is Religion that gives prosperity and creates virtues and good fortune.** There are seven Elements: *Dravya* (matter substance); *Guna* (Quality); *Karma* (action); *Sāmānya* (general); *Vishesha* (special); *Samawāya* (multitude or concomitant); and *Abhāva* (Deficiency).

There are nine Matter Substance: Space, Water, Fire, Air, Earth, Time, Directions, Soul and Mind. There are 24 Qualities: touch, beauty, sap, smell, number, quantity, separation, synthesis, division, opposition, non-opposition, pleasure, pain, wisdom, desire, jealousy, effort, weight, liquidity, love, culture, religion, irreligion, and word. There are seven types of colours; six types of sap; two types of smell (fragrance and bad odour) and two types of mind (doubtful and determined).

The unity in elements is their general quality while there is a rare quality in atoms that separates them. It is their special quality.

Vaisheshika Darshan propounds a realistic pluralism, emphasizing particularly, a realistic epistemology with an acute logical analysis of language and the different processes of thought. It developed an algebraic logical terminology for precision of statement.

Sānkhya Darshan

In *Sānkhya Darshan* Maharshi Kapil has explained Nature transcending the atoms. The explanation of the world has reached its ultimate height in this branch of philosophy.

Sānkhya propounds a dualistic metaphysics of souls and Nature and the possibility of the liberation of the soul from its bondage to Nature by discrimination and detachment.

Sānkhya accepts two Eternal Elements called *Purusha* and *Prakriti*. In the world there are four types of matter: natural, artificial; natural-artificial and both-different. Nature is not anyone's act; so, it's Nature. A great system or element is created out of Nature; Ego comes out of it and from Ego five *Tanmātrās* are created that give rise to five Natural Elements. These are natural-artificial in substance Sense Organs, Work-organs, Five Gross Elements and Mind are deformations or artificial. Living beings are both — different or common. It is detached.

Prakriti, Nature is the balanced state of the three qualities: *raja, satva,* and *tama.*

Purush is conscious and Nature is non-conscious or unconscious. Because of closeness with *Purush* Nature becomes conscious. With the wisdom of *Prakriti* and *Purush* the knowledge of one's detached form is the way to salvation.

Yoga Darshan

The *Yoga Darshan* of Maharishi Patanjali is in fact, *Sānkhya Darshan.* They don't differ in philosophy. *Yoga* accepts the 25 elements of *Sānkhya. Purush Vishesha* has been declared as the 26th Element. *Yoga* aims at giving a practical solution to different worldly ailments and agony.

Ignorance, attachment, jealousy, ego (vanity) and desire are five causes of pain. God as knowledge is different to them. The world is not a worthy place because of the desires and attachments. We get united to God when we win over the causes of pain and affliction.

Yoga Darshan is also based on a metaphysic that is similar to Sānkhya. It goes deep into the psychology of meditation, attention and concentration; and lays down a practical path to liberation of the gradual concentration of attention on the nature of soul, aided by physical culture, moral discipline, and meditative exercises. The eight parts of *yoga*, known as: *Yama, Niyam, āsan, Prānāyāma, Pratyāhār, Dhāranā, Dhyāna* and *Samādhi*: will help one to achieve union with God and salvation if practised with purity, devotion and concentration.

Nyāya Darshan

Maharishi Gautam propounded *Nyāya Darshan* that laid stress on 16 deformities and suggested that one should consciously and judiciously be alert from them and be free from them for inner growth and prosperity. He has expanded the atomic form of matter leaving behind their physical form and qualities.

Nyāya too propounds a realistic pluralism, emphasising particularly a realistic epistemology with an acute logical analysis of language and the different processes of thought, and developing an algebraic logical terminology for precision of statement. This became "the language of Philosophical Discussion world over." It paved the way for the symbolic logic of the west. The later philosophical schools of India followed it and the west took directly from there while they wrongly claim it to be their original invention. They have mostly taken a part of one school and developed that to claim a 'new school of their own.'

The real, balanced and complete knowledge of the following sixteen is final freedom or salvation: *Pramāna* (proof); *Prameya* (desire); *Sanshaya* (doubt); *Prayojana* (purpose); *Drishtānta* (examples); *Siddhānta* (principles); *Yavayai* (organs); *Tarka* (logic); *Nirnaya* (Judgement); *Vāda* (isms) *Jalpa* (prattling); *Vitandā* (anamoly); *Hetwābhās* (fallacy); *Chhala* (deception) *Jāti* (genus, quality) and *Nigrahasthāna* (restraint, repression).

Pratyaksha (direct); *Anumāna* (hypothesis, *deduction*, analogy); *Upamāna* (object of comparison); *Shabda* (word) are the four means of knowledge. Mind is an achievement of knowledge and is eternal. The knowledge is the only cause of salvation.

26 Doctrines (Logic/Judgements) in Hindu Philosophy

Maharishi Gautam wrote his *Nyāya Shāshtra* in Sutras. The following are his 26 doctrines that are separately talked mostly in rural areas while the urban populations knows little about these great doctrines that give an insight into the personal, social, political and religious behaviour.

S.N.	Nyāya	Doctrine
1.	Andhachataka Nyāyah	A partridge in the hands of a blind.
2	Andhaparaparā Nyāyah	Blind Followers
3.	Arundhati Darshan Nyāyah	Arundhati-Tārā Philosophy
4.	Ashokavanikā Nyāyah	The doctrine of Ashoka trees
5.	Ashmaloshta Nyāyah	Of stone and mound of soil
6.	Kadambkoraka Nyāyah	Of the buds of Kadamb trees
7.	Kāka tāliya Nyāyah	Of Crow and Palmfruit
8.	Kāka danta gaweshan Nyāyah	Of Searching crow's teeth
9.	Kākākshigole Nyāyah	Of the round Crow's eye-balls
10.	Kupayantraghatikā Nyāyah	Of well and water-wheel
11.	Ghatkutiprabhāta Nyāyah	Of Sunrise at the Toll
12.	Ghunākshar Nyāyah	Of letters created by insects
13.	Dandāpupa Nyāyah	Of staff and bread
14.	Dehalideepa Nyāyah	Of lamp at the threshold
15.	Nripanāpitaputra Nyāyah	Of king and barber's son
16.	Pankaprakshālan Nyāyah	Of washing away mud
17.	Pishtapeshana Nyāyah	Of grinding the grond corn
18.	Beejānkur Nyāyah	Of seed and sprout
19	Lohachumbak Nyāyah	Of iron and magnet
20.	Vanhidhuma Nyāyah	Of fire and smoke
21.	Vridhakumārivākyavarnyāyah	Of old lady's one sentence blessing
22.	Shākhāchandranyāyah	Of moon on a tree
23.	Sinhāvalokan Nyāyah	Of lion looking back
24.	Suchikatāh Nyāyah	Of couldron and needle
25.	Sthunānikhanar Nyāyah	Of digging soil for pillar
26.	Swāmibhritya Nyāyah	Of master and servant

Purva Mimāmsā Darshan

Maharishi Jaimini created *Purva Mimāmsā Darshan* to discuss and elucidate different actions. He held the view, in the tradition of *Sānkhya* and *Yoga*, that good deeds are essential components for ethical knowledge. *Yoga* paves the way for those that can detach themselves from lust, ego, desires, etc. and go for hard penance, but those that prefer indulgence in worldly affairs can take refuse in Purva Mimāmsā Darshan. It is based on pure deeds and takes indulgence in worldly life and pleasures into consideration and hence it's also known as *Loka Darshan* and *Vedānta Darshan*.

Mimāmsa is very often and deliberately termed simply as a 'philosophic justification of Vedic Rituals.' But the fact is that 'it enters deep metaphysical and epistemological discussions aiming to maintain a pluralistic and realistic position.' It accepts Vedas as eternal and essential. Action is discussed along with religion with a clear aim to grow respect and dedication towards Scriptures and to turn the mind towards religion and religious deeds.

Uttar Mimāmsā Darshan

Uttar Mimāmsā is the real *Vedānta Darshan* based on the *Brahmasutra* written and propounded by Brahmarishi Veda Vyāsa. He declared Brahman to be *janmādyasya yatah*: creation, sustenance and delusion are in Him.

It is based on three books famous as *Prasthāntrai*. They are the starting point of all philosophy that man created. They are: *Brahmasutra* (*Nyāya Prasthān*); Eleven Upanishads (*Shruti Prasthān*) and Gitā (*Smriti Prasthān*). Initially, the schools came into being only after writing commentaries on these great creative writings.

Vedānta Darshan

Vedānta Darshan: *Vedānta Darshan* was re-propagated and re-established during the Medieval Period by Shankara. It's the most influential school of philosophy. Shankara emphasized the transcendental aspect of Brahman as the highest Reality; the world as appearance and the self as really and absolutely identical with Brahman. The creative, personal and immanent aspects of God are regarded as secondary conceptions of Brahman while these qualities were given adequate importance in the Brahman Sutra or Vedānta. Worship of God is helpful as a step to the realisation of the transcendent aspect. It's the knowledge of the identity of the self and the Brahman that brings about final union and salvation. Later on, in the eyes of the Western Critics, the Vedāntic philosophy changed into 'realistic pluralism.' It's difficult to understand the coinage. Though it seems to be attractive but it's difficult to feel pluralistic becoming realistic or reality turning to be pluralistic.

Vedānta laid stress on non-injury to life in any form that became and remained the basis of all schools of philosophy and sub-divisions of Religion in India. Around 10th Century AD and afterwards, Vedānta, under unknown and non-clarified influences and reasons, changed or developed into different types of Metaphysical and Epistemological theories and many schools were established.

Advaitavāda

The projected world is just a replica, an appearance and an illusion. It's so, because of ignorance. There is only one conscious entity that has no quality, no form, no attachment and no desire. The projected world is not different. It is in the *Brahman*. All appearances disappear, as they are temporal. He is the one that envisioned them. Known too is a form of the unknown. The world is nothing other than a name and a form. Illusion is indescribable. Though it's without a beginning but it ends with knowledge, so, it's non-existent. Only Brahman is true.

Dvaitavāda

The philosophy of *Dvaitavāda (Dualism)* propounded by Mādhwāchārya during the middle ages to save the religion from complete collapse due to the numerous attacks on it from different corners and in different feigned forms; is accepted as perfectly wise philosophy. He and other saviours of Hinduism had one and only one intention to save the religion and Scriptures at any cost and to stop the Hindus from accepting other religions. For this they claimed that whatever is one trying to get or search out from other religions, are alredy present in our religion: Saguna, Nirguna, Brahma, Shiva, Vishnu, Ramā, Krishna, and many more.

According to the claims of different scholars his *Dvaitavāda* is perfect. It's perfect because it takes both the Creator (*Brahman*) and His Creation and *Jeeva*, (being) into consideration and takes them to be separate entities. *Jeeva*, a being is atom and slave while the *Brahman* is with quality, specialty and free. It's a crime to see and claim similarity between the two. The appearance is inseparable from the truth. Despite the changes the world is not an illusion. Knowledge is under knower and known. Knowledge needs coordinates. There are two abstract matters: Conscious and Unconscious. Devotion, Sacrifice and Meditation are the ways to be followed for salvation.

Dvaitādvaitavāda

Sri Nimbakāchārya assimilated and synthesized the two opposing branches of philosophy and propounded a third one known as *Dvaitādvaita: Dvaita* and *Advaita*; Dualism and Non-dualism. The World is caused by the Brahman and hence, it's not mutilated. *Brahman* is Omnipotent. His qualities have prominence. The Brahman created and creates the World and the Living Beings. They are separate as well as non-separate from the *Brahman*. *Brahman* has no quality in Non-worldly form. Atom is the form of Beings. The Being that enjoys freedom feels Oneness with the World and the *Brahman*. Devotion and worship is the only way for salvation.

Shuddhādvaitavāda

Through *Shuddhādvaitavāda*, Sri Ballabhāchārya denied the illusory concept of the world and established devotion and worshipping. He accepted Sri Krishna as the *Brahman*, as *Nirguna, Nirvishesha, Kartā, Bhoktā, Nirvikār, Gunāteeta*, the shelter of all opposite religions, beyond worldly religions and the saviour of the world. The world is a creation and true. It's an inseparable outcome. Matters appear and disappear. Beings are like atoms and are pure. The best way for the Beings is to love and worship the God. *Brahman* can be explained and elucidated only through Scriptures and classical literature.

Vishishtādvaitavāda

Sri Rāmānujāchārya propounded the philosophy called *Vishishthādvaitavāda*. It showed some deviations and many specialties. He declared that we could be freed, only by His grace. If and till we are under His domain we would be punished for all the wrongs that we commit. Brahman is all the *chit, achit* and *vishishtha* elements combined together. Beings came out from the conscious self and Nature from unconscious self.

The Absolute God Nārāyana is the Lord of both the sentient and inert existence. The Sentient Beings know. Knowledge is their religion. It is not known that has no specialty. Beings and the Creator are different. One can attain salvation only by taking His shelter. Worshipping is the main aim.

Achintyabhedābhedavāda

The assertion of Sri Chaitanya Mahāprabhu that Sri Krishna is Truth, was given a philosophic concept by his followers. He declared Srimad Bhāgwat to be the real commentary on the Gitā, Upanishad and Brahmasutra. Without a commentary this school of philosophy became famous as *Achintyabhedābhedavāda*. God, Beings, Nature, Time and Action are five elements. The God is known only through the Scriptures. Sri Krishna is the Absolute God. He possesses all the qualities and blesses the Beings with Beatitude and Salvation. Nature is manifestation of Brahman. It has three qualities and is mortal.

Like other *Vaishanava* schools of philosophy it too aims at devotion and worshipping of the Absolute God.

Shaiva Darshan

India is a country of multiple and fertile thinking. The thinkers got the three ready things to start with and move on. The first one was the creation, the second included the Scriptures and the third one was the congregation where the opinion were well expressed and exchanged. It had a background to help and a foreground to work on. Because of parallel and deep thinking the thinkers faced enlightened audience and challenging question. This helped theology and philosophy to grow.

The fertile mind was like a sea: very restless on the surface and completely serene in the depth. It became the characteristics of Indian thinking. Incidentally, all the theories were tested judiciously before turning into a school. Parallel schools also got strength. The beauty in thought was the fact that each school was complete and had a plausible answer for each inquisitive quarry.

Hence and thus, along with *Brahman Darshan, Vaishanavanism* and *Shaivanism* got acceptance. Later on, *Saur Darshan, Shākta*

Darshan and *Gānpatya Darshan* developed and the root went deep and crept up all around. These were accepted both by *Dvaitites* and *Advaitites*. Surprisingly enough, Brahman was and is there everywhere. It is mute declaration of His Omnipresent and All Pervading quality. In every instance, Vedas are the final authority.

The Indian Scriptures are further divided as *Nigam Granthas* and *Āgam Granthas*. The devotees that worshipped Shiva as the *Par Brahman Parmeswar* followed the *Āgam Granthas*. Brahman's specialties were accepted and Shakti was given importance. It is very difficult to say 'all important' in Indian context but Shakti is often treated as 'all important'. In any case, among the Goddesses she is the supreme and all other goddesses are apparently her different incarnations and creations.

Shavaites are openly in favour of the *Āgam Granthas* and follow them. They give little importance to *Nigam Granthas*. Out from *Āgam* they have accepted both the *Dakshināchāra* and *Vāmāchāra* traditions of performing poojas and rites and rituals.

Shivādvaita Darshan

It's the contention of the *Shaivites* that Shiva (Maheshwar) is the *Brahman* and hence, He is to be worshipped. Religion is in His worship. By working without desire and with detachment one is able to be cleansed of sins. When such a sinless mind is purified then it gets knowledge. One can achieve perfection and salvation only by acquiring knowledge and performing wholesome deeds. It's acquired only with the blessings of Shiva. Worshipping results in salvation.

Pāshupat Darshan

Pāshupat Darshan, the philosophy pertaining to Shiva, believes that there are three perpetual and constant matters: *Pati*, i.e. God; *Pashu*, i.e. *Jeeva* or Living Beings and *Pāsh*, i.e. net, noose or snare that traps a being and forces to indulge in immoral acts. There are four nets or snares: *mala* (impurity); *karma* (action); *Māyā* (illusion); and *rodha-shakt* (opposition in creation and delusion). The being trapped in the snare of impiety is called *Vigyākala*. With devotion and penance one can become *Mantreswar* even before all impiety is cleaned while he becomes *Vidyeshwar* after getting fully purified. Religious and irreligious are snares of action. The being trapped in that net is called *Pralayākala*. They are freed after the maturity of the trap. The beings caught in all the traps are called *Jeewasakala*. *Karma-rodha-shakti* is the trap that brings hurdles in the way of creation and delusion. Those trapped in that take birth as different species of living beings. They get a body with 26 elements.

Lakulish Pāshupat Darshan

Shiva created the universe without cause and without assistance. There are two ways to attain salvation from this world: either by cessation of pain or by getting the blessings of God. The latter is known as *Paramaishwarya* (the supreme wealth). It includes omniscience and fulfillment of desires. Unnatural acts like weeping, laughing along with smearing sacred ash over the body are the ways.

Pratyabhigyā Darshan

The form of Shaiva Philosophy propounded by Sri Abhinavaguptāchārya is called Pratyabhigyā Darshan. The knowledge of Shiva is *Pratyabhigyā*. It gives *parā-siddhi* or *mukti* (salvation) and *aparā-siddhi* (prosperity). The climax of wealth is the slavery to God. With the help of the Scriptures we are able to know God. We know Him with complete devotion when the Absolute God appears before the Soul. Nature is His natural power.

Shakti Darshan

Parā Shakti (spiritual power) called *Tripursundari* has created the world. Shiva is the Absolute power. At the quivering of *Shakti* Shiva entered as *tejas* (light/ heat) and a *Bindu* (point) was created. The union of *Shiva tatwa* and *Shakti tatwa* gave rise to *Nāda* (sound). Nāda and Bindu united to become *Ardhanariswar* (half man and half woman). Male power is white and female power is red. It's known as *Kāma* (sex). *Kalā* was created out of these two. The creation was completed with the union of these four: *Bindu*, *Nāda*, *Kāma* and *Kalā*. In every development of the creation that Shiva tatwa is present. His *ajā ādyā Shakti* is Nature. Seven deeds are there for the salvation of a being: *Veda*, *Vaishanava*, *Shaiva*, *Dakshina*, *Wāma*, *Siddhānta* and *Kula*.

For worshipping there are ten forms of the great Eternal Power called *Mahāshakti*: Mahākāli; Ugratārā; Shodashi (Tripurasundari);

Bhubaneshwari; Chhinnamastā; Bhairavi; Bagalāmukhi; Mātangi and Kamalā.

Along with them there is the tradition to worship ten male counterparts Mahākāla; Akshobhya; Purush; Panchvaktra Rudras; Trayambaka; Kabandha; Dakshināmurti; Ekavaktra Rudra; Matang; Sadāshiva and Vishnu.

By following the dictates and worshipping the *Shakti* a Living Being gets emancipated and attains that *Shiva-tatwa.*

Bhakti Darshan (and others)

There are many other schools of Philosophy including that of *Nārada* and *Shāndilya*; and also Āyurveda (excluding the medicinal parts) that teach devotion and pave the way to God, Bliss and Salvation.

Not only Āyurveda but Chemistry too has its philosophy. The fundamental concept behind the union of *Shiva* and *Pārvati* is that they pervade the creation on the form of *Pārada* (Mercury) and *Abhraka* (Mica). Mercury is the expression of ecstatic pleasure. Mercury is the sap, the juice. It is called *pārada* because it transcends the creation. With the adjustment of mercury the body wins over old age and death.

In the same way Indian *Jyotish* has its own school of philosophy. It holds the view that the actions and reactions in the world are based on the movements, rays, and effects of the celestial bodies. What is expressed as action and matter on the earth is expressed as constellations in the space. Every action and every form is fixed from a very early stage. The being living in it changes its place. They are always created and continuously perish.

In the same way Indian Grammar (*Vyākaran*) also has its school of philosophy. (These are the real wonders for the people of other countries and also the westernised Indians. But Indians are lucky that at some stage in their life they are informed about these schools of philosophy. In fact the philosophy is mentioned or taught and the school is not declared simply because the modern egoist youth are not in contact with their soil and their Darshan.)

The philosophy that the great Pānini propounded is called *Sphotavāda* or *Shabdādvaitavāda.* For him word is everything. Word accompanied with sound is eternal and has no beginning as it was there before the creation. It is explosion (sphota) and birth of sound that is at the root of the creation of basically space and then others. It was taken up by those that initiated and expanded the theory of "Big-Bang'; of sudden expansion and explosion.

Panini in his philosophy says that word is beginning-less, end-less and eternal. The appearances are imaginations or ideas or their shadows. The outer world is unreal. Knowledge without word is not light. Word and knowledge are inseparable. The memory of word is behind breathing and other actions. Word possesses such powers that can't be explained. The world is created out of meaning. Word gives the knowledge of the world. The root and climax of word is *Pranava, AUM. AUM* is the root cause of the creation of the world. The world is name and form. The world is not the parināma (result) of Shabda-Brahman but its *vivarta* (falsity). The relation of word with meaning is not imaginary but eternal.

The sound of expressed word appears as *Parā* in the *Mulādhāra Chakra* (i.e. Perineum; between genitals and anus and represent sexuality and survival); as *Pashyanti* in the *Nābhi* (i.e. navel and associated with personal power); as *Madhyamā* in *Anāhat Chakra* (in the center of chest, associated with acceptance, love and compassion); and as *Baikhari* in *Vishuddhākhya (Saraswati) Chakra* (in the centre of throat, associated with creativity and expression). The worshipping of AUM (*pranavopāsanā*); Yoga, Correct and Truthful speech (*Shuddha- Satya- Bhāshan*) are helpful in the realisation of *Shabda-Brahman*.

The Kundalini Yoga of *Shata-Chakra-Vedha* is also a school of philosophy. *Tantra-Sādhnā* is another school. They all are an integral part of Theism or Theist Philosophy. The fundamental truth and the basic aim of them all is the same.

Atheism and Theism:

Broadly speaking, there are two aspects of life: the things that we see (the obvious); the **physical** world that denies the God, as it needs no God, and is called **Atheism**; and the things that we feel (the abstract); the **spiritual** world that accepts the God, as it needs a God at every step. Faith and devotion is important for them as they wish and try to know that which we feel but can't see. It's known as **Theism**. Those that follow religion are Theists; those that don't follow it are Atheists.

It can be illustrated through an incident. The story may be treated as a reality or explained as a symbol. In both the cases the meaning will not be affected.

India as a whole is a country of positive thinking. The few negations that crop up are readily negated. As a result there have been very few atheists that easily mingled among the multitude of theists and lost their significance and existence. On the other hand, the Indians present such strong logic either for theism or against theism that the existence of Atheism can't be totally denied. Despite good deeds, in the present life, if and when a person faces adverse situation or is struck by some tragic event, doubt about the eternal justice and existence of God creeps in the mind. It remains there till a satisfactory logic is forwarded. Of course, doubt is thrown out, faith returns but that always alert doubt plays its role to perfection and sometime, each man has to face its disastrous effect. Hence, Atheism raises its head off and on; and has not as yet been obliterated. Under the growing influence of the west (unfortunately, the young generation is reading great number of meaningless, faithless and spiritless books from foreign writers) positive outlook is at a decline. Doubt has started ruling in their minds. They don't feel and remember that there is a moral, spiritual and cosmic binding that the celestial bodies obey the rules and system. It is also true to human and non-human beings. Non-human beings follow the rules and dictates of Nature and natural system, only man particularly the modern man is not following that moral, natural, and spiritual binding. So, Modern man is the worst atheist and definitely in pain.

The greatest pain is seen in the trains in India. If perchance, an officer or a rich man happens to travel in general sleeper class then he feels himself to be the most wretched creature. While people travel even in unreserved compartments too. They are not aggrieved. The faces and tone of a man in three tier A/C is aggrieved for he is not in the two tier A/C. It happens in plane journeys also. There too are distinctions on the basis of classes. The 2nd and 3rd classes have been abolished to make all appear equal. But equality has been eluding. It's 'class conscious' or 'comfort conscious'. The comfort of a few hours and the comfort that can be bought in a few thousand are playing havoc in the minds of modern men. It will ruin (or perhaps has already ruined) them. They forget that comfort is not in the compartment it is in the 'attitude;' that there will not be any positive gain with negative attitude; that fate will not work (or will deceive one day) if there is no purity in deeds. The thief that gets success for thirty days is caught once and loses social recognition. Theism will always rule is amply supported by the fact that thieves or criminals still don't relish the black mark of criminal or thief on their faces.

Indians have enjoyed positive and moral outlook because they lay equal stress on *Karma* (action) and *Bhāgya* (fate). The final and lasting effect of all these schools and varied ideas is that **all Indians follow a mixed philosophy for they think that by doing so they can easily maintain balance.**

Chārvāka Darshan:

The Philosophy of *Chārvāka* : (of physical pleasure)

Physical pleasure is just and the only pursuit for the persons that follow *Chārvāka*. He advocated physical pleasure and luxury, and only physical pleasure at any cost. He said 'take loan if needed but enjoy refined butter. i.e. the best that is available.' *Rinam kritwā ghritam piweta*. He said that inner conscious is not a different entity. It's a part of the body and it perishes with death. So, he laid stress on maximum enjoyment of the sources and resources.

When did *Chārvāka* appear is not important as such materialistic philosophy has been there, since the creation of man because man had to live and procreate. For sustenance food is/ was required and sensual pleasure is/ was essential for procreation. It's needless to state that such stress on physical needs and pleasure will always be there in some form. It is not materialism if indulgence in everything or many things for physical pleasure is under control and in balanced form, shape and content. Excessive indulgence in physical pleasure, lust and luxury; and the concentration of all the efforts for that end is materialism or *Chārvāka Darshan*.

It was outrightly rejected and it is mentioned to make a joke of others or to teach someone a few lessons about consciousness and conscience. On the contrary, the whole world is following the same philosophy without mentioning his name. It will be difficult to search out a person from the towns, cities or metros that has no loan against his name. The moneylenders too take loans. The best person that detests loans takes a loan from at least PF account. The luxury items must be in the house. People are ready to pay any coast for it. The climax is that a son can murder his father for a motorcycle and a husband or a wife can kill the spouse for something trivial, though, very important in their eyes.

Jain Darshan

Jain Darshan was given by Teerthankar Mahāvir but its tradition begins with Bhagawān Rishabh. It started with a simple assertion that if the deeds are temporal, then the doer must be temporal. He, that performs one act, remains no more in a temporal world. Then, who will take the outcome of that did? It does not happen so. Hence, neither the deeds nor the doers are temporal. One that tastes or faces the outcome remembers that he is getting results of his previous deeds. That establishes his immortality. Soul is immortal. The world has no beginning. Truth is not temporal. It's beyond birth and destruction.

Jain school of philosophy further declares that there are two elements: mind (the faculty of reasoning) and non-mind (devoid of sense). Balanced knowledge of these two is wisdom. To use other matters for our own sake is the act and proof of mind; the opposite is the non-mind. There are five *astikāyas* (the elements that exist) in the world: Beings; Sky; Religion; Irreligion; and Gross Elements (*pudgal*). Sky gives leisure, and religion emancipates. Irreligion is hurdle in the way to final freedom. *Prthvi, Jala, Wāyu and Teja* are four gross elements. There are other things called *Sambar* that help in achieving salvation. They are: *Gupti* (controlling body from doing inferior deeds); *Samini* (Non-violence); *Nirjarana* (to destroy the effect of past deeds with penance).

There are three paths of salvation known as *Samyak Darshan* (Balanced Philosophy); *Samyak Charitra* (Balanced character); and *Samyak Jnāna* (Balanced Knowledge). In Jain Philosophy a lot of stress is given on Penance.

Bauddha Darshan

All the schools of philosophy in India, including *Bauddha Darshan*, preach Salvation. This one factor gives great unity to all the schools of philosophy. This was accepted and advocated by many sects in other continents too. It is the proof of the universality of Indian philosophy.

Bauddha Darshan was first divided in three groups called: *Heenayāna, Mahāyāna* and *Vajrayāna.*

Buddha thought and gave his four cardinal teachings: that there is pain and suffering in the world. There is a cause behind suffering. There is cessation of suffering, and there is a path leading to this cessation. Suffering can come to an end. Wholesome deeds are the ways and salvation is the aim. This represents, in a nutshell, the basic common attitude of all the Indians.

Buddha said nothing about the soul. He maintained silence whenever this questioned was raised before him. He explained his stand to Ānand, "I can't say there is soul because the people will accept that there is soul. I can't say that there is no soul because people will believe that there is no soul."

Buddha accepted Deduction and Induction to be the proof for the truth beyond the appearances. Bauddha philosophy is divided in four kinds known as: *Madhyam Darshan; Yogāchār; Sautāntric* and *Vaivāshika.*

Complete Bauddha philosophy is collected in *Tripitaka* (Three Cannons): *Vinaya Pitaka* (Code of Conduct); *Sutta Pitaka* (Discourses); and *Abhidhamma Pitaka* (Higher Doctrine; Philosophy and Psychology).

According to Buddha there are six *Āyatana* (spheres, internal spheres): eyes: the visible form; ears: sound; nose: odour; tongue: taste; body: tangible things; and mind: ideas, thought, conceptions. He held *panchakkhanha* (five aggregates) to be important: matter; sensation; perception; mental activities and consciousness.

The most important thing in Bauddha Darshan is to become an *Arhant,* one that is free from all fetters, defilements and impurities through the realisation of *Nirvāna* (salvation) and thus he is free from rebirth. For achieving it he asked his followers to follow *astāngamārga* (eightfold path): (i) *samma ājiva* (right livelihood); (ii) *samma ditthi* (right view); (iii) *samma kammanta* (right view); (iv) *samma samkalpa* (right thought); (v) *samma sati* (right mindfulness); (vi) *samma vācha* (right speech); (vii) *samma vyāyāma* (right effort) and (viii) *samma samādhi* (right concentration).

Buddha advised his followers to achieve *Upekkhā* (equanimity) a calm state of mind, neither angry nor upset; in order to become an *Arhant* and get *Nibbāna*.

(Three)

Unbroken Continuity

Dynamism, change, growth and development; and true devotion are the real reasons behind the survival of Indian Scriptures and Indian Philosophy. The world has taken a lot from it yet it has grown because its tradition was not broken. It has been fostered with care, diligence and intelligence. It is alive even today after more than one thousand years of slavery when there was pointed attack on the knowledge, religion, culture, Scriptures, philosophy and civilisation of India.

The west has annihilated most of the Indian-ness in the modern Indians of towns and metros that are reading a lot of western philosophy and the least from India and they wrongly feel proud of knowing western thought. So, whenever they are writing, they are simply quoting and analyzing western thought. Yet, everything has not been lost. The 'unbroken tradition' still continues and those (of course, only a handful) dive deep in the treasure land of Indian thought and Scriptures and bring out bright and benevolent ideas for they have variety in store and the depth is unfathomable. They are already steps ahead in evolving out a 'World Philosophy' for they are directly connected to the roots of Universal Philosophy. It saw a renaissance in Sri Rāma Krishna Paramhansa, Vivekānand, Rājā Rām Mohan Roy, and Swami Dayānand Saraswati. Sri Aurobindo assimilated all and Dr. S. Radhakrishnan worked as a very functional and strong link.

Sri Rāma Krishna Paramhamsa gave the advice to repeat the prayers of the Upanishads:

"God is the Ocean of Mercy. Be His slave and take refuge in Him. He will show compassion. Pray to Him: Protect me always with your compassionate face. Lead me from the unreal to the Real, from darkness to Light, from death to Immortality. Reveal Yourself to me and protect me always with Your compassionate face."

Swāmi Dayānand Saraswati in his 'Light of Truth': *Satyārtha Prakāsh*) took most of the things from the Indian Scriptures and added a few innovative ideas of his own. According to him: God, soul and matter are eternal. There are three causes – the efficient cause, the material cause and the ordinary cause. God is the efficient cause while matter is the material cause of the universe. Souls are ordinary cause. Brahman, the Supreme Being, by His efficiency creates the world out of its material cause *Prakriti*, the matter.

Sri Aurobindo declared it in 'The Life Divine' (Human Aspirations) in modern western language:

"To know, possess and be the divine being in an animal and egoist consciousness; to convert our twilit or obscure physical mentality into the plenary supermental illumination; to build peace and a self existent bliss where there is only a stress of transitory satisfaction besieged by physical pain and emotional suffering; to establish an infinite freedom in a world which presents itself as a group of mechanical necessities; to discover and realise the immortal life in a body subjected to death and constant mutation; - this is offered to us the manifestation of God in matter and the goal of Nature in her terrestrial evolution."

While trying to search out 'Substitutes for Religion' in his 'Idealist View of Life' Dr. S. Radhakrishnan comes to Humanism but he wants God at the centre and not man in that Human Religion: There is no conflict between religion and a reasonable humanism. The truly religious act in this world; the inner feeling of the relation between God and man is bound to issue in the service of humanity. While what matters is works or fruits of religious life, its social productivity, the most efficient servants of society are those who cultivate anxiously the interior life. "A religion whose centre is man not God is never a strong one." He is indirectly in favour of the Human Religion of Hinduism that has God at the centre and from there all through the periphery.

Ever-growing Thought and Consciousness

Hindu or Indian Philosophy has not as yet come to its full circle. Indians have not stopped thinking. There is no cessation to ever-growing ideas. They have a very rich written tradition full of varied ideas that have covered all the phases and all the aspects of Living Beings in general and Human Beings in particular.

No philosophy has nor can have so much. Despite the fact that western and modern 'wise men' claim that there was and there is conflict and opposition in many schools of Indian Philosophy. The presence of diverse elements and different thought is no proof of infighting. All the major classes of philosophy are collected here in their most shortened form but the fundamentals are all there. This was done deliberately with a purpose to show the readers 'the whole'. Only the names and schools will not change the prejudices. It is a different matter with those persons that are by birth prejudiced and whose philosophy and political and religious necessity are against Indian Philosophy and Indian-ness.

Difference of opinion is a different matter but the only country that practised and preached tolerance can't be intolerant and violent even in the expression of ideas; and above all, the country that did never attack another country and has survived under several attacks; that the people that follow one code of conduct can't get strayed and drowned by the sweet but poisonous conspiracies. The Indians have great 'Oneness' despite the differences in the means adopted here and there; many ways of worshipping; and divisions in faith. There is nothing in India that has no separate philosophy of its own. In this Indians are millenniums ahead of others. The integration of imagination and thought, and the basic philosophy of synthesis have ensured 'Oneness'. It's the strength of its philosophy that empowers a country to sustain numerous attacks down the ages.

That 'Oneness' can be seen in the amalgamation of all the branches of knowledge in a single subject called philosophy. Except the British system of education in India all the subjects are combined here in Darshan. In other countries, Religion, Politics, Economics, Philosophy, Psychology and Life are different subjects taught in every school and university. In India Philosophy is not only a subject of teaching but the basis and shelter of every region of life.

Aum; Hari Aum Tatsat; Aum Namah Shivāya; Brahma, Vishnu and Mahesh, sat, chit, ānand; satyam shivam sunderam, Jai Ganesh, Jai Matā Dee, Sat Sri Akāl etc. In general affairs these are mentioned and adored but not discussed.

Another cause of oneness is the common belief that true and effective knowledge cannot be attained by mere study. Moral and physical discipline (which is being searched in and expected from others) must accompany study, reasoning, intense concentration on, and repeated meditation of, the philosophical truths so that every thought, speech, and action in life may reflect them.

But those that don't have the prejudices can see the whole and will find 'unity' in all the schools. They have a lot in common. It's one factor that it's called Indian Philosophy and is a part of grand Indian Culture. The lustful and jealous can't see that strong current that flows, crashes to the shores, gets rejuvenated and returns back to come again at a greater speed and power.

Indian systems are more than theoretical discussions; they are ways of moulding life in accordance with different ways shown by the great wise men. Despite their theoretic differences, all of them insist upon a common pattern of intellectual, physical and moral discipline that stamps them all as truly Indians. **It is the unity of moral outlook. They believe that the constitution of the world is moral; that the actions of its beings determine the course of action and events in and of Nature as well as in minds; and that the moral worth of every action is preserved so that everyone gets his/ her due here or hereafter.** This belief is known as the law of *Karma* and accepted both by the theists and atheists and all the schools of philosophy in India in this or that form.

The turning point and the relief to the people is that the past deeds are not all in all; and will not determine the whole life. The life can be made better or one can fall in dirty ditches in this life with pure or impure deeds. It is accepted that one gets the *puraskār* of *purushārth* (the reward of good deeds) and the present life can be changed for the better by present effort. This attitude makes it clear that man is fully responsible for his/ her suffering and pleasure; for the rise or fall, for the poverty or prosperity, for knowledge or ignorance and for slavery to the cycle or for bliss and salvation. It's not the actions of others that determine 'mine' or 'your' life. **We are the makers or destroyers of our life.**

Grandeur, Sublimity, Humanness and Divinity are the inner characteristics of Indian Philosophy.

Brahman: Brahmā: Brāhmin: Brāhman (Grantha)

Brahman

Brahman originally means 'Sacred Word'. The secret and sacred word and sound 'Aum' represents Brahman.

Brahman is the Supreme Creator of the Universe, the Cosmos. He is the greatest find of Indian Eternal Human Religion that was taught by Bahman to Brahmā. Brahmā taught it to the Rishis and other wise men. They in turn taught it over to different wise men. Those that took on themselves to protect and spread it were called Brāhmans.

Brahman is the Absolute Formless and Changeless Unmanifest Supreme God that is the source (in the eyes of western philosophers; and creator (for the Indians) of the phenomenal universe.

Brahman is selfexistent, extra-temporal being, all pervading and infinite. For one that has achived Oneness and release, whose atmā is free: Brahman is both existence and life element.

For the Hindus the Brahman, the Absolute God is everything, and in every form or incarnation: *Brahman swaroopāya*: in the form of the Brahman. He is the father-mother, brother, friend, knowledge, wealth and everything and all in all:

Twamewa mātā cha pita twamewa twamewa
bandhuscha sakhā twamewa,
Twamewa vidyā dravinam twamewa twamewa sarbam mam deva deva.

त्वमेव माता च पिता त्वमेव त्वमेव बन्धुश्च सखा त्वमेव ।
त्वमेव विद्या द्रविणं त्वमेव त्वमेव सर्वं मम देव देव ॥

(Thou art mother. Thou art father. Thou art brother. Thou art friend. Thou art knowledge. Thou art wealth. Thou art all in all. Oh! God of Gods!)

Brahman is the Absolute and Ultimate Reality. Brahman is both Immanent and Transcendent. He is that from which the universe emanates and also that into which the world dissolves.

Brahman is at once Reality (*Sat*), Consciousness (*Chit*) and Joy and Bliss (*Ānand*). Brahman is the Reality that underlies the self (*Ātmā*) as well as the World.

Beings have the souls while the Brahman is *Parmātmā*: the Supreme Soul. Both can only be perceived, as both are body-less; hence deathless, decay-less, timeless, causeless and perhaps or so; space-less. The Paramātmā is the source and substratum for everything including the body. There is death for the body but the soul is eternal, hence, beyond time, space and causation.

Brahmā

It's difficult to understand or make others understand the actual creation because the first creatures are not there to testify. Even their presence would not have made much difference because we don't see how are we being created. We see and learn ourselves when we are fully grown up. In the opinion of some saints it's not necessary to know how were we created, it is important to know why were we created? If we know and feel the correct answer to this 'why' then our duties will be easily determined. This why has become dubious for it is said that God created us because he wished to multiply. Later on, it was added that man was created to look after the creation and ensure its safety and continuity. So, there is great responsibility on the mind and shoulders of man.

On the other hand man has a curious bent of mind and has unsatiated desires and wishes. The wish to rule is the worst among them. Whosoever is there and whatsoever work he or she is doing he/ she not only wishes but tries one's best to rule: not on the greater and more powerful but on the weaker and powerless. So, the theory of the 'survival of the fittest' came. If one is not strong one can't survive. This is not correct. The weakest survive easily. The cockroach, ants, whiteants, flies and mosquitoes are among the weakest and the strongest man has created many poisons for them, sprays and yet has not been able to abolish them. What is there in them? How have they been created that they survive? That gave another theory: *the humble survive and are respected.*

The elements of creation are the same. Yet, from where do the differences arise? It's inside. The power of every creature is in the creature, in the self, the inner self. That power makes the spiders to create cobweb, gives rise to musk in deer and empowers the bees to prepare honey. The power is inside. Those, that increase that inner power are known, those that fail to add to it, are forgotten; even perish. Only man is misled to believe that power is in money. That is the greatest illusion.

That brings us back to Brahman and Brahmā. Brahman thought to multiply. Remember the word is thought. He concentrated. What did he think and why did he concentrate?

The things are created first in mind. They take shape as an idea. Machines are made, pictures are imagined, shapes are thought out, poetry and story are created in mind. They are created first in abstractions, then, changed into reality. God concentrated, thought, imagined, drew a picture and gave the intricate system. It was the figure of unseen-unknown Shiva. He again repeated the act and gave a separate entity to the creative element. For that he thought of water and one drop of sweat increased to become a lake and now it's 71%. He concentrated at a point to give shape to creative force and the Hiranyagarbh appeared; and Brahmā came out of it. He had to be placed somewhere. The placenta was thought of and it came out of Brahman's navel; which was hardly able to keep the egg and the life in that egg. So, it was inverted and given a place inside.

Mind is also a creator and only mind can do it when there is the question of system or systems. All these things were taught to Brahmā who was given four heads to see everywhere and to keep everything in mind. Brahmā is our creator and Brahman is the Super Creator of the Universe and the systems. Brahmā too embodied that quality and as he was taught by the Supreme power so he too taught that to his creation. He placed that knowledge inside us for our development, growth and refinement. Our forefathers knew it and taught us. It's our mistake that we did not take their words as true. We should never doubt the scriptures.

We don't understand them, it may be our ignorance or weakness but there is nothing wrong written in the Scriptures. They are the divine words.

Brahmā has four heads and four arms. In the Trinity he shows the fourth dimension. Symbolically, the four heads and four arms of Brahmā represent: (a) Four Vedas (b) Four Varnas (c) Four āshrams (d) Four Yugas.

According to the Scriptures Brahmā is our immediate creator but the secondary one. After every delusion Brahmā appears to revive and re-create life.

Brāhmins

Brāhmins are those that know Brahman and Vedas:

Brahmano Brāhmanah (Yajurveda (30:5).

Brāhmans must know Vedas; be able to teach Vedas; they must follow them and behave as the Vedas ask them to. The moment they learn Vedas and know the Brahman they are endowed with teja and oja (brightness) known as Paramātma-teja (Celestial light) and Vedic-teja (Vedic light). Such Brāhmins must be respected.

(Brāhmins are embodiments of light and penance. By saluting the Brāhmins, the Sun has his place solidified in the sky.):

> Brāhmana hi param tejo Brāhmano hi param tapah,
> Brāhmanān ii namaskāraih suryo diwi virājate.
> बाह्मण हि परं तेजो बाह्मणो हि परं तप: ।
> बाह्मणान् हि नमस्कारै: सूर्यो दिवि विराजते ॥

Where have those Brāhmins gone? They were brutally butchered during the Middle Ages; and replaced by pseudo-Brāhmins. At least there is no trace of such Brāhmins in modern era. Now, there is a big question: Will they regain their wisdom and light with their character, penance, sacrifices and detachment? Rightly they are not getting the rights of Brāhmins; the respect and honour that they have been getting during the ancient periods. They are not growing from inside. A second and third line of such Brāhmins were seen during British period but it's claimed that most of the Brāhmins started accumulating wealth and turning towards politics after the first election in India in 1930s. It has neither helped them nor the country. Such Industrialists, Officers in Military or Governments; Managing Directors and Managers; Farmers, other Professionals or

Businessmen, Clerks or Peons or Guards are not Brāhmins, though they may have born in a Brāhmin family. They must possess the qualities of Brāhmins to be a Brāhmin. Buddha, too declared that "I take him to be a Brāhmin that has no lust; anger, desire; that is pure of heart and can tolerate abuses, physical pain and yoke, confinement and restrictions; that follows moral and ethical ways, has control and is like the leaves of lotus; that is wise, pure and does only wholesome deeds.

Those that claim to bear the legacy of Brāhmins must change their life, character and preferences to make the country strong by becoming strong. *Vidwān sarvartra pujyate*: Learned men are respected everywhere. They must realise that everywhere means everywhere, even in the courts of demons. The people from other *Varnas* should also come forward to take the status of real Brāhmins, not by birth but by accomplishments. Only then, India can re-claim its status as *Viswaguru*. Money and slogans will not win the areas where our forefathers ruled with wisdom, love, non-violence and other means taught by the great Rishis. They followed *Seva-Mārga*, *Rishi-Mārga* and *Sant-Mārga*.

Brāhman (Grantha) :

Only the word Brāhman is used to denote the Brāhman Granthas. The Brāhman Granthas are wonderful creations. They give the details of the ways the Mantrās be used and recited. The *Mantras* are dealt in detail in the Brāhman Granthas.

Some people claim that only the *Mantra Samhitās* and the *Brāhman Granthas* constitute the complete Veda. It seems to be an exaggeration, for other Treatises have so much to give that in absence of those great books the meaning of the Mantras can't be understood and the human knowledge will remain always incomplete. It is claimed that the *Brahman Granthas* were 1,131 in number. The following are the *Brāhman Granthas* available at present:

The Brāhman Granthās of Rigveda:

(i) Aitareya Brāhman

(ii) Shākhāyan Brāhman or Kaushitaki Brāhman

The Brāhman Granthās of Shuklayajurveda:

(i)   Shatpatha Brāhman (Kānvashākhā)

(ii) Shatpatha Brāhman (Mādhyandin Shākhā)

Published in three volumes the best and biggest Brāhman Grantha is Shuklayajuvedeeya "Shatpatha Brāhman". It has presented its subject matter in a complete and comprehensive way. It has 14 *Kāndas*; 438 *Brāhman*; and 7,624 *Kandikās* that are arranged in 100 Chapters. Because of the 100 Chapters it's called Shatpatha: *shatam panthāno yasya tatchchhatapatham.*

Shatpatha Brāhman meticulously describes different forms of Yagyas and all related and relevant *"Anushthāns"* (rituals). It lays great stress on *Agnihotra* and claims that an *Agnihotri* never perishes even after death. Fire is a boat for an *Agnihotri* to take him to heaven:

naurah wā yeshā swargyā yadi agnihotram.

Shatapatha declares Yajna to be the most important work in life:

Yagyo wai shreshtam karmam.

The Brāhman Granthas of Krishnayajurveda:

(i)   Taitiriya Brāhman

(ii) Madhyavarti Brāhman

The following are the four Brāhman Granthās of Sāmveda:

(i)   Tāndya (panchvinsh) Brāhman

(ii)   Shadvinsh Brāhman

(iii) Sāmvidhān Brāhman

(iv)   Ārsheya Brāhman

(i) Tāndya (panchvinsh) Brāhman

The name Tāndya Brāhman was given to it because it has 25 Chapters; and because it the largest among all the Brāhman Granthas, so it's called *"Mahā Brāhman"*. It deals with *'Audagātra Karma'*. In order to explain and illustrate its main theme the book takes the help of tales and anecdotes; for example we can take *"Veengak Sāma Gāna"* that tells the story how old Chyavan Rishi was metamorphosed into a young and healthy man.

(ii) Shadvinsh Brāhman

Shadvinsh Brāhman deals with the wonderful and unbelievable incidents that usually occur in our life basically with *"Smārta Yāga"* as for example, lightning falling on a house; tussle with officers; sudden deaths of horses and elephants; earthquakes; blood oozing out from trees and the birth of handicapped children, and other unnatural and supernatural events, etc. The descriptions of gods as *'chakrapānaye' 'dandapānaye'* or *'shoolpānaye'* is behind the idols of gods in modern times sculptured on these patterns with human body and some weapons in their hands.

(iii) Sāmvidhān Brāhman

Sāmavidhāna Brāhman is divided in three Chapters in which it's imagined and explained that the Almighty gave *Sāma* as food to satiate the hunger of man. The hunger was satiated with only the seven notes of the *Sāma Gāna*. But the time changed and man became a different creature.

(iv) Ārsheya Brāhman

Ārsheya Brāhman is divided in six Chapters and deals with the life and achievements of the Rishis related to *Sāma Gāna* only. In fact, Ārsheya is the name of Brāhman that gave the names of *Mantradrashtā Rishis* as the names of the *Sāmas*. The Chapter *'Devatādhyāyabrāhman'* gives the names of the gods of *Sāma* on the basis of *'Nidhāna'*. *'Nidhāna'* is a division of "Devotional Part." It has five parts in all.

The following are the remaining six Brāhman Granthas of Sāma Veda:

(v) Mantra Brāhman
(vi) Daivatādhyāya Brāhman
(vii) Bansh Brāhman
(viii) Samhitopanishad Brāhman
(ix) Jaiminiya Brāhman
(x) Jaiminiya-upnishad Brāhman

On the basis of the number of Chapters Tāndya Brāhman is named also as *Panchvinsha Brāhman*; and because it's the largest in length so it's known as *Mahābrāhman*. These Brāhmans represent *Audgātra Karma* that is in principle the songs sung in *Yāga* as

Stotras. The Brāhman Treatises have their specialty to use tales and anecdotes in the delineation of their main subject matter.

Only one Brāhman Grantha of Atharveda is available, and that is (i) Gopath Brāhman

The Brāhman Granthas are the *Prāna Tatwa*: 'living element' of the Veda *Vāngamaya*; as the Brāhmans are *Prāna Tatwa* of the Indian society; that must be made pollution free to enable India regain its Spirituality, Wealth and Status.

Hinduism: Purity and Brāhmin

Hinduism is purity in its purest form; it's virility in its basic form, and divinity in its true form. That is the reason that there is no dearth of Gods, demigods, Rishis, Saints, Munies, Mahātmās, āchārya, swāmis, gandharvas and pandits here. They possess a great soul. Hence, they are often neatly, separately and unitedly, expressed as Brāhmins.

Hinduism can't be understood without accepting and understanding Brahman, Brahmā and Brāhmin. Brahman is the Absolute God; Brahmā is a creation of Brahman for the sole purpose of creating other phenomenon, different things and living beings; and Brāhmins are the most enlightened souls that have developed from the lowliest state. They are the symbols of all the 'best' things in a human being. Continued degeneration and deterioration and degradation has affected the Brāhmins also, and it's difficult to get a true Brāhmin. Other persons are raising doubts against the integrity of Brāhmins. Such doubts were not there, a few centuries back.

Still, in Hinduism Brāhmin is a very sacred word and the Brāhmins are sacred souls. They are very honourable and respected figures. Brāhmin stands for great qualities, piety and sublimity. No one expects and accepts anything untrue and unethical from them. They have always stood for qualities.

A Brāhmin means an embodiment of all good qualities, pious soul and a philanthropist that lived for others and had no care for own physical needs. A man very conscious, a Brāhmin is a soul of pure conscience. According to Manu, Brāhmin means embodiment of piety, severe penance, austerity, detached from worldly needs and pleasure and pain. Brāhmin means one that has forgiveness, kindness, sympathy and pity, spiritual attainment, unearthly effulgence, renunciation of riches and acceptance of suffering for others. 'Brāhmin means to him an inflamed fire that burns to ashes all sorts of social ills, filths, sins, and whatever is undesirable for social health for the ultimate good of the society and its smooth running.'

Anyone can purge oneself and grow from inside to become a Brāhmin *Aitareya Samhitā* claims that the peasant or the householder that possesses all the eight characteristics of an ideal householder becomes pure as a Brāhmin, gets elevated in life and is freed from the endless cycle of birth, death and rebirth:

Yashchaitairlakshanyukto grihastoapi bhaweda dwijah,
Sa gachchhati param sthānam jāyate neha wai punah.

यश्चैतैर्लक्षणयुक्तो गृहस्तोऽपि भवेद द्विज: ।
स गच्छति परां स्थानं जायते नेह वै पुन: ॥

The Scriptures have very high hopes and expectations from Brāhmins. So, they failed to tolerate if and when a Brāhmin committed a sin or a crime. Manusmriti announces the most severe punishment to Brāhmins. It's most lenient to Shudras for their ignorance. The punishment gets harder with more refined members of the society. In Manusmriti 8:337-338; for a similar theft different punishments are announced, the harshest being against the Brāhmins:

Ashtāpādyam tu shudrasya steye bhawati kilvisham,
Shodashaiwa tu vaishasya dwātrinshat kshatriyasya cha.
Brāhanasya chatuhshashtih purna wā api shatam bhawet,
Dwigunāh wā chatuh pashtistaddoshagunahviddhih sah.

अष्टापाद्यं तु शूद्रस्य स्तेये भवति किल्विषम् ।
षोडशैव तु वैशस्य द्वात्रिंशत्क्षत्रियस्य च ॥
ब्राह्मणस्य चतु:षष्टि: पूर्णं वाऽपिशतं भवेत् ।
द्विगुणा: वा चतु: पष्टिस्तद्दोशगुणविद्धि स: ॥

(If a Shudra knowingly commits a theft, he should be fined 8 times worth of the stolen property; a Vaishya 16 times, a Kshatriya 32 times and a Brāhmin 64 times or 100 times or even 128 times.)

Lord Buddha's *'Dhammapada'* is a proof that Brāhmin always stood for qualities. The last Chapter of the book deals with 'Brāhmin Varga'. He has discussed in it, 'Who is a Brāhmin?'

"He is a Brāhmin that never commits sin, neither from mind and words nor from bod." (9)

"One can't be a Brāhmin by matted hair, gotra or by birth; he is pure and he is Brāhmin that possesses Truth and Religion." (11)

"I call him Brāhmin that meditates, is stable, does wholesome deeds, and achieved emancipation."

Out of jealousy or for selfish ends people started mitigating this word and defaming the Brāhmins; and with great success. Now, it's limited to people born in a particular caste, Brāhmin Varna. How can a man devoid of knowledge, intelligence, purity and good moral character be said to be a Brāhmin? It's indigestible. Hindus have as yet not digested it.

☙

Women Worshipped

Life is a very sacred thing in Hinduism; and a woman that gives birth to a child becomes greater in comparison to man. There are stages and time when great changes, almost metamorphosis, occur in the life of a woman: after marriage when a girl reaches an unknown family as wife and mistress; when she gives birth to the first child and when her menstruation stops after attaining the age of 55. She procreates, becomes a mother, helps man to be called a father; so a woman is great and respectable. For that very reason she should be worshipped. Kaikayee the villain mother of Lord Ram was excused and worshipped simply because she had given birth to brothers like Bharat and Shatrughna.

In Hinduism a woman has a great place. She is taken as an embodiment of purity, chastity, expert in behaviour and one that maintains the family, cultural and religious tradition. She is given preferences on seven different counts:

(i) The marriage shows a relation of many lives between that man and that woman;

(ii) Hinduism treats the palm of a woman as the most pious part and hence marriage is called *pānigrahana samskāra*;

(iii) The complete life of a woman is penance;

(iv) To give a girl in marriage is the greatest charity; a householder is not purged if he does not perform a *kanyādāna*. He, that has no girl child, requests others and performs the ritual of *kanyādāna* of their daughter.

(v) It's imperative for every Hindu husband to keep his wife happy;

(vi) A woman gets the status of a mother called: *jāyā pada* or *mātri pada*;

(vii) Equal status; and rights in property equal to her husband.

> *Janmāntareeya   sambandhastathā   pānipavitratā,*
> *Tapahpradhānā nāryashcha kanyādānasya shreshthatā,*
> *Striyah   prasādāya   kritih   jāyātwamekarupatā.*
>
> जन्मान्तरीय सम्बन्धस्तथा पाणिपवित्रता ।
> तप:प्रधाना नार्यश्च कन्यादानस्य श्रेष्ठता ॥
> स्त्रि: प्रसादाय कृति: जायात्वमेकरूपता ।

A son in India is wealth; a girl here is an incarnation of the goddess of wealth (*Mahālakshi kā roopa; Lakshmiswaroopa*). A man in Hindu society and culture is a worker, labourer to earn livelihood; a housewife is the queen (ruler) at home (*ghar ki rāni; grihaswāmini*). A girl child becomes a woman (*nāri*) the day/ night she is married. She becomes a goddess (*devi*) and rules supreme, the day she becomes a mother. A woman's body is not a filthy thing for physical play and pleasure; it's the most and sacred possession for creation. She is the power (*shakti*); able to feed all (*annapurnā*); half of man (*ardhāngini*) and makes a man complete. Without a woman a man is incomplete. After becoming a mother she turns into the most respected member of a Hindu household. In all parts, all younger persons must touch the feet of ladies; in some parts, older ladies touch the feet of girls. Among Hindus there is a ceremony in which girls are worshiped (*kanyāpujana*). It is imperative for a husband to take advice of his wife in taking all major decisions in general; and of purchase or sale of a property (animals/ land etc). A married woman, whose husband is alive, is a very powerful figure.

A woman must possess a pleasing physical figure for health and attraction. Both Rigveda (10:86:9; 2:32:7) and Shatpatha Brāhmin (10:86:8; 3:5:1:11; 1:2:5:16 describe her beauty: her shapely smooth arms and angular fingers; thick well-formed thighs and thin upper portion; thick long hair etc. Giving birth to many children results in ill-health and loss of shapely figure (Rigveda 2:20:3). The lady that maintains her body even after giving birth to many children has been praised in Rigveda 10:86:23. A woman should be attractive, pleasant, shy, sweet, soft and speak in mellifluous tone.

According to Rigveda (10:18:7; 3:58:8; 1:76:3 etc) a *sadhawa* (woman with husband alive) must remain healthy, decorated, wear good clothes and ornaments, be lively, pious, loving, committed to husband (*pativratā, patiparāyana*) and be wise. She is all in one: daughter, daughter in law, sister, sister in law, wife, adviser, mother, grand mother, aunty and man more.

India is a very strange place; and the mothers here are the most wonderful creations. They are so much engrossed in looking at, talking to and feeding their children that often they forget what are they feeding them? Does he/ she need water or anything else? Her children are full devoted to her. What of human child the great incarnations of Vishnu have adored and worshipped the mothers.

Krishna had gone to meet Vidur. Vidur was not there. He met his wife. As she was like a mother to Arjuna, so she was like his mother. He touched her feet. The lady was instantly overwhelmed by love, affection and pleasure. She had not expected such a sight in her lowly home. The arrival of the Lord was the last thing that she expected. She had no idea what to do? Where to make Him sit? What to give him to eat? She hurriedly went inside and returned fast with a bunch of banana. She unknowingly sat on the cushioned chair and asked Lord Krishna to sit at her feet. He did so. She was so much absorbed in love and was in such an ecstasy that she lost all feelings, all knowledge. She knew only one thing: Krishna was with her and she must feed him. He is a child. She started taking the skin (rind) off from the bananas. She was in heaven. She had forgotten the place and everything else. She, absentmindedly, threw the pulp and gave the skin to Krishna to eat. Krishna ate it. He enjoyed eating the skin. He said nothing. He only listened to her.

Lord Krishna went on eating the skin of banana, and did not look at the pulp that the overwhelmed mother was foolishly throwing away. He could not thought of saying, "O Mā! You're making a mistake?" She was the mother and always correct.

Then, Vidur came there and was full of wonder at what was happening there. He said, "O Krishna! Don't eat the skin? It's not healthy and digestible."

Lord Krishna smiled, "Mā is giving it. It's like nectar."

Krishna was like a son to the mother of hundred sons Gāndhāri. He has shown greater respect to her wish. She cursed him and he gladly accepted it as a mother had given it.

Krishna met Gāndhāri in the forest when the battle of Mahābhārat was over. He had lost her hundred sons. She was aggrieved. She was in agony. It got better of her and out of intense anger she cursed Lord Krishna: "As my family has fought among themselves and got destroyed; your family and the clan will be lost in the same fashion; and you will be killed by an ordinary vyādhā, hunter."

Lord Krishna bowed to Gāndhāri and humbly said, "O Mā! I accept your curse." It was then, that Gāndhāri realised what had she done. She said, "You could have denied the curse. You possess the power. Why did you accept it?"

"Because it was given by Mā." Krishna again bowed to her.

The Hindus treat the wives of other persons as mothers. In the wake of total criminaliation of the society, people are forgetting their best philosophy and falling down the non-westernised Indians treat: *mātriwat pardāreshu*: the other women as mothers.

Hindus are clear in their mind and hold the view that a mother can't be wrong or can't do wrong to her children.

Putro kuputro jāyeta mātā kwachidapi kumātā na bhawati: The sons may do wrong but the mothers can't bring harm to her children.

Unbelievably high honour is given to women. Manusmriti says that an *āchārya* is better than ten *upādhāyas*; father is greater than 100 *ācharyas*; a mother is far greater than one thousand fathers. (2:145)

Upādhyāyāndashāchāryaāchāryānām shatāmapitā,
Sahastram tu pitrinamātā gauravenātirichate.

उपाध्यायान्दशाचार्य आचार्याणाम् शतं पिता ।
सहस्रं तु पितृन्माता गौरवेणातिरिच्यते ॥

(मनुस्मृति–२/१४५)

Goddesses: Parā Shakti

It's difficult to count the Gods in India and it's equally difficult to count the Goddesses. As Goddess, *Parā Shakti* is the creator. She is half of the *Ardhanārishwar*. On that pattern all the married women here are called *ardhāngani*: half of their husbands. Man is treated as incomplete. One gets perfection only after marriage when the other half of his being meets him and is united.

Parā Shakti, the eternal mother, is worshipped mostly in three forms: Mahā Shakti; Mahā Saraswati and Mahā Lakshmi. The fourth is also added as Mahākāli. They have different forms and names: Gauri, Kāli, Tārā, Chāmundā, Kushamāndā,

Lalitā, Bhairavi, Dhoomāwati, Chhinnamastā, Durgā, Mātangi. Surprisingly enough, they are not called incarnations. Perhaps, that is the reason that they are worshipped in different ways.

Shakti, popularly known as Mātā Durgā, has other forms too. She is worshipped as: Shailputri; Brahmachārini; Chandraghantā; Skandamātā; Kātyāyani; Kālarātri; Mahāgauri and Siddhidātri. She is Shākambhari; Bhrāmari; Kunadalini and Yogamāyā. She is worshipped for nine days twice in a year during *Chaitra Navarātra* and *Aswina Navarātra*. She is projected with two, four, six, eight, ten, hundred and thousand hands. She is very kind and compassionate. She endows the devotees with effort, power, talent, wisdom, brightness, wealth and prosperity.

As Durgā she is an embodiment of power and killed worst demons like Raktabeeja, Shumbh, Nishumbha and Mahishāsura.

As Saraswati she endows with architectural, artistic and musical skill, talent, intelligence and wisdom, and knowledge and brightness.

As Laxmi, she is both Ramā and Rādhā. She came out of the sea at the time of churning. She selected Vishnu as her *Purush*. She resides either in Him or by Him In that form she is stable on lotus or eagle or airāvata or mammoth but when she is worshipped alone, she is restless and moves on owl.

Divine Women

It's only in India that women got status equal to great Rishis and are known as Rishikās. Very famous among them are Shachi, Gārgi, Mamatā, Viswavārā, Apālā, Ghoshā, Wāka and Suryā.

Gandharva girls and apsarās (nymphs) have created history. Some of them have taken human form and given birth to human beings with rare qualities and of extraordinary merit. Urvashi and Menakā head the list.

Ancient Indian History (Purānas) are full of great deeds of great women. They are not only honoured and respected, they are even worshipped. Ahalyā; Draupadi; Kunti; Tārā; and Mandodari are famous as *Panch Kanyā* (Five Damsels)

Some Indian women are always mentioned with reverence. They are oft quoted as they created a history and an example of a different kind. **Sati Sāvitri**, the daughter of Aswapati and the wife of Satyavāna fought against Yama, won over the lust and worldly-dual. As a result her dead husband got his life back. **Mahāsati Anusuyā**, the daughter of Maharishi Kardam was the wife of Maharishi Atri. With her love and devotion to her husband she got a wonderful distinction of feeding the Gods of Trinity as mother. Rām and Sitā too treated her as mother. She created a branch of River Ganges that is famous as Mandākini. Couples worship them for a pleasant conjugal life. **Damayanti**, the daughter of King Bhishmaka and Nala, the king of Nishadha were made to love each other by a Swan's description. Her love; for Nala without meeting the man; forced her to reject the gods and accept Nala as her husband in swayamber. On another occasion also she recognised him when they were separated for quite a long time. **Sita**, the daughter of earth and fostered by king Janak is the universal mother and fondly called 'jagat janani.' It was she that recognised and used spices, taught new ways of cooking, started the use of turmeric, used pestle to change spices into pastes and created many flowers and fruits. She taught new ways of agriculture too. As she had helped in procuring and preparing food so, she is like a mother to all.

Great Women

Because we know a lot about the last few centuries, so we have a big list of great women: devotees, household-ladies, Queens and Warriors. **Meera Bai** was the greatest devotee of lord Krishna that we actually know about. Our battle for independence from British Imperialism begins with **Lakshmi Bai**. She fought a fierce battle with an adopted baby tied on her back. The sad and valiant tale of **Sati Padmini** is fresh in every region. She gave her life along with many other ladies. They burnt alive on pyre but did not accept the nasty demands of the moghul rulers. They are adored for they have sacrificed, or served or shown character and determination. They have no peer anywhere in the world.

Modern Women

Like modern men, modern women too are at a cross section. More than anything else they have to reconsider their physique, physiology and health; and only then they can think of satisfaction, happiness and prosperity. Wealth alone is not prosperity. Prosperity begins with health and leads one to the final balance sheet of achievements. Whatever they possess they give it to the family and society. In return, they get something and have their demands also. They have nothing to think about what they give, because of their inherent power and capacity to give. They must think about what they get. Are they healthy? Have they retained creativity, sweetness, delight, fragrance and the power to foster well and maintain the family health? Do they still get respect from the elders, praise from the young and love from the children?

Retaining the qualities and possessions is key to health, happiness and prosperity. The losers and the persons under debt get none of the above three. Numerous murders, easy divorce, separation without divorce, imbalanced physical growth, prevalent diseases and other personal, family and social maladies are indications that a lot is wrong. Women will have to consider what is correct for their health and what is right for their happiness. How can the immense loss be regained?

Women are still a power to reckon; still responsible to insure continuity of life; still able to bring peace, health and happiness to family. Will they do it or will they be drowned in the flood of growing wishes and be swept in the storms of lust? They have to decide.

In every age Hindu women knew more than the men: about the seasons, climate, herbs, medicines, food, and even about celestial bodies. They conducted and directed the rites and rituals. At many places the same practices are being followed. But at almost all the places and milieu they are breaking away and feeling broken like a robbed merchant or pauper or like an extravagant wild child. The effect is seen, marked, discussed and cried for everywhere but no one is ready to know the root cause and uproot the very cause of ailment.

There are great examples of modern women too. The Indian Independence movement is full of the valiant deeds of Indian women. The scenario remained the same even decades after independence but the last two or three decades have seen a seachange in the outlook and life of Indian women. It is not healthy from any corner and any standard.

A good percentage of modern Indian women are following a superfluous philosophy and life. They are fast changing into just a body, and hence, a commodity. Unfortunately, they feel pride in keeping themselves only to physique. They forget that it's easier to take bath in the skin-shallow water; anyone can do it;

it's difficult to dive in heart-deep water. When their menstruation is finally stopped after 50 years of age, they suddenly *realise: tan ke teer tairnewāle mile bahut; man ke ghāta nahānewālā nahin milā:* (I met many persons that enjoyed the body but could not get a single one that can live in heart.)

In Hinduism, women have their selected field of supremacy and men can't interfere. They selected the fields with the help of the teachings of the Rishis that taught them the difference between a male and a female body. A male body has greater strength, a women's body has greater tenacity and sustenance. A girl child can survive in adverse situation and condition; a male child will need a lot of care for his survival. Most of the organs of the body are the same but a woman's body is more delicate, subtle and intricate than a man's body. The secretion of hormones is behind the creation of a separate and different body for a man and a woman. In fact, the difference between a man and a woman is in the secretion and uses of hormones and also in their effects.

Easy and light work will help in the secretion of female hormones. It will save their sweetness, delicacy, tenderness, elasticity and give them sustenance and durability. If and when they take on hard and heavy works of men, male hormones start secreting. That results into coarse voice, rough skin, under grown-breast, hair at unwanted places and irregularity in menstruation etc. The health and physical pleasure of a woman depends solely on the regularity of menstruation; the monthly cleaning and revitalization of blood. Once, it's disrupted they can't be healthy and happy. They are like males in construction not in constitution. They can do manly works but they have to pay (and definitely they are paying) a heavy price for it. They can do it at the cost of their body, happiness, health and everything womanly. Very loose and soft cloths (only either cotton or silk) were for them, as they need more air and oxygen for their organs; thick, coarse and tight clothes (that they are wearing in towns and metros are deadly poisons) are not for them. It's a great wonder that every grown up and mature lady knows it, yet they are destroying themselves; or running a destructive race.

Anyway, women can't be made to believe at present. They are in ecstasy and not in a mood to realise the crisis; and what powers, a tender body and rich soul they are losing. When the eunuchs (neither male nor female) will outnumber women only then they will realise that within the last 25 years eunuchs have multiplied many hundred times. It may take time but the realisation will come. They may not get enough time to regain some of those precious possessions.

It seems to be pertinent here to remind that the institution of marriage was not easily and unanimously accepted by a without a reason. *There must have been a time when almost every man and woman suffered with syphilis, gonorrhoea, and AIDS like sex and skin diseases. That must have been the time when blood was tested and the concept of 'nāri' was established. The physical relation between two similar blood groups were admonished, the laws of marriage accepted and one man and one woman relation was established. But it can't be established now as we have no proof and it's simple hypothesis. The cause behind the emergence of marriage institutions may be different. The fact that there is an upsurge in diseases related to sex and fertility, and also the birth of physically handicapped children that one is forced to draw such conclusions. Hence, the health of woman is more important than that of men. But we can't dare to ignore one for the other.*

Sadly enough, the elite society is breaking away from the rich and pious tradition, and doing away with the most refined culture. The women that were and are worshipped; and related to many in many ways are turning fast into a commodity under the 'world trade-treaty'; and because of the globalization. The indecent and indiscreet photographs and scenes in print and on electronic devices including Internet are proofs of degeneration and degradation and also of unrefined sensibility. Art and adoration is gone, the physique and physical pleasure has become everything. The influence of wine and woman is working as intoxicant and most of them are living and behaving as if they are constantly under the influence of deadly drugs. For proving to be human beings a balance is to be maintained in all the four common pursuits: *Dharma, Artha, Kama* and *Moksha*: by making them our 'constant pursuit.'

A decade back the unethical pictures of women were used in advertisements; now they are happily using such pictures for their own advertisement. They don't realise that these borrowed business ideas will caste them into or reduce them to be only a vamp or whore.

Diverse Elements

Different Aspects of Hinduism

There are different aspects, dimensions and facets of human life and Human religion. Hinduism shows them clearly and discusses them in detail. If the original writer has not given the details; then, they have added it that wrote the commentaries on those books. It had to be clarified and it was clarified. It had to be simplified and it was simplified. No further clarification or simplification is needed. Then, there can be a question 'Why was this book written?'

The answer is very simple: because people do not read them, neither the original Scriptures nor the Commentaries; and because all the aspects are not given or presented in a sequence at one place. If people read them and follow the path shown there, then there is no need of other books. But the world has become smaller (though, universe is growing) and the heart is reduced to an insignificant entity. People have lost health, life, morality and character. We are all living only for money to buy luxury and luxurious things to show others how rich we are; and to collect sympathy of others for our ill health and ill fate. We are responsible for nothing only fate is responsible, fate is responsible for all our failures; for fires from short circuit; for heaps of garbage accumulated, almost everything; for bird flu to stop us from having hundreds of poultry farms in every state and from eating chicken everyday; for the theft of kidneys that are transplanted to other persons whose kidneys are damaged or ill-formed as they ate only junk food. These are few examples. Oh, Yes! Fate is responsible for everything. Man is the wisest and the best creation and man has all the right to use and misuse all the things, life, minerals, vitamins, etc., available or created by Nature in millions of years. We are living a very fast life and consuming in a year what the earth metamorphoses, prepares and manufactures in millions or billions of years.

[The title to this part of the book may mislead one because it is "Different Aspects of Hinduism". The title is given so, because the book is about and on Hinduism but the readers must keep it in mind that it's actually Eternal Human Religion that has been simplified and clarified. Different aspects of Hinduism will be clear in the following pages. Hinduism is not flat. It has a round character, so everything is not visible in one glance. It has six dimensions and ten directions like a dice. One can't see all the numbers on a dice at one glance. It's essential to turn the dice. It's true to Hinduism. One will have to turn the leaves, open the doors and windows, clear the dirt of prejudices then can understand Hinduism. One great aspect is here.]

Human consciousness was at its best during the unknown period of the Rishis when they used to connect their physical electromagnetic power with the cosmic energy and become a living part of cosmic consciousness; yet the modern man claims that there has been gradual development of human consciousness. Moreover, the poetic diction of the Rishis has not been achieved in any other age. Hinduism, its Scriptures and the most ancient language Samskrit boast of the near perfect language; of unfathomable depth and immeasurable height. The command over sound, words, metres, and subtle use of symbols, similes and metaphor was never achieved again. It's the specialty and prized possession of the Hinduism that all the books of Knowledge, Religion, Art, Architect, Science (Math, Botany, Zoology, Chemistry, Astrology, Astronomy, Machine and Medicines i.e. Āyurveda); Sex, Philosophy, and Psychology, etc. were written either in Shlokas or Sutras.

Hindus believe that life is not a movement from imperfection to perfection, it's also retrogration from better to worse. The cosmic system works in opposition; and the opposites co-exist simultaneously together. It is not true when there is day then there is no night; when there is day then at some other place there is night; when someone has born here then someone else has died there.

Some say India is a country of philosophers, poets and poor people. They have only read about India. It's only a part of the truth. They have not seen India. India is the country of 'detached karmayogins'; of very rich people that are rich in inner power and skill; and of wise men that know their land, work and environment. They rise before the sunrise and take rest after the sunsets. These people know and believe that the works are not done in the office created and functioning on western pattern. Actually, works are done in the fields, on and by the roads, in and around the residences and about the markets. There were only a few markets in India. Necessary articles were transported to the consumers i.e. the householders, and their surplus was bought from there. They were not allowed to waste their precious time in the queues for kerosene oil or sugar, for fertilizers or diesel or for votes or ration cards. The works done in the offices are not productive. They either control or are engaged in distribution.

In India, all workers are not thinkers but barring the ultra-moderns all thinkers are workers. They thought, gained skill, perfected themselves to a greater extent, and performed the tasks to last long. Such men have not totally perished. They are the rare figures that live in all the three divisions of time: past, present and future. For thousands of years the invaders and rulers have tried to wipe them and India out but they have succeeded only in dividing it and raising doubts.

Yet, the Indians have shown that they can stand united and create faith, possess it and work together. This is the power of its religiosity and spirituality. It's the lasting achievement of the Eternal Religion, the *Sanātana Dharma*.

India can dominate once again through the ancient ways and means of Religion, Art, Culture and Wisdom; with the help of the glorious past by reviving it and by connecting the present aspirations with previous achievements. **India will not remain India if it ignores its past. There is no separate existence of today. It exists only in relation to the past and the future. One can't dominate today if one has no yesterday or no tomorrow.**

Brahman: The Absolute God

Hindus are religious; and that is all. Hindus are neither Monotheists nor Polytheists; neither Pagan nor Henotheists. They are all 'ists' and 'isms' or they are not 'ists' and follow no 'isms'; not even Hinduism, for Hinduism is a word deliberately given to them for the original and Eternal Human Religion. It's apparent from Hindu Scriptures where only 'Dharma': religion word is used without a suffix or prefix, without a word before or after. Dharma has in itself become both a suffix as in 'dharmāchāra' (religious conduct) or satdharma (pure religion). As Dharma has been repeatedly used so they are dhārmic; and Brahman, the Absolute God, is their Supreme God.

Brahman is everywhere, all-powerful, knows all and devours all. He is the Omnipotent, Omnipresent, Omniscient and also Omnivorous. He is perfect.

Sachidānand is Sat Chita Ānand

Prakriti and Purush

In the Taitiriya Upanishad (3:1) it is said that He is the Brahman that has created the Cosmos, Sustains it and Destroys it:

Yato wā imāni bhutāni jāyante yen jātāni jivanti.
Yatprantyabhisamvishanti.
Tadwijigyāsaswa tad Brahmeti.

यतो वा इमानि भूतानि जायन्ते येन जातानि जीवन्ति ।
यत्प्रन्त्यभिसंविशन्ति ।
तद्विजिज्ञासस्व तद् ब्रह्मोति ।

The Absolute God, Brahman pervades all and is present in all religions. God has been there from before the creation, from an infinite time and will remain for unknown and infinite time. He is infinity and infinity is in Him.

God said: 'mayi sarbidcm proktam maniganā ewa. (I'm present in the Universe as thread in jewels.)

One can claim each jewel to be a religion or sect or community and as a thread God resides in each of them. Vivekānad said, "The religions of the world are not contradictory or rivals. They are all abstract representation of the same immortal truth. This eternal religion has been the basic religion of the world since time immemorial."

Ishāvāshyopanishad says that God pervades all; whatever living and non-living forms exist in the world. While keeping that God with the self one should use and utilize the things with detachment. One should not get attached to anything. Wealth and utility articles belong to none.

Ishāvāshyamidang sarbam yatkinchid jagatyām jagat,
Tena tyaktena bhunjithā mā gridhah kasya swid dhanam.
ईशावास्यमिदँ सर्वं यत्किंच जगत्यां जगत् ।
तेन त्यक्तेन भुंजीथा मा गृध: कस्य स्विद् धनम् ॥

Ishāvāshyopanishad 1

Who is Brahman? Taitiriya Upanishad makes it very clear. It says, "He is the Brahman from That all the beings come out. He is the Brahman by whose existence others exist and sustain after taking birth. He is the Brahman in whom every being merges after death":

Yato wā imāni bhutāni jāyante yena jātāni jeevanti,
Yatprayautyabhisanvishanti tad Brahman.
यतो वा इमानि भूतानि जायन्ते येन जातानि जीवन्ति ।
त्प्रयन्त्यभिसंविशन्ति तद् ब्रह्म ॥

तैत्तिरीय उपनिषद् (३/१)

Then Brahman is 'All' and All are Brahman. Then everything possesses Brahman and possessed by Brahman. Then,

Annam Brahman: Cereals are Brahman.
Prāno Brahman: Life-element is Brahman.
Mano Brahman: Ego is Brahman.
Vigyānam Brahman: Knowledge is Brahman.
Ānanadam Brahman: Pleasure is Brahman.

Brahman generally means the Supreme Creator of the Universe, the Cosmos. Except the Supreme Brahman, all else are bound by endless cycle of change, birth, decay and re-birth. They have to follow the cosmic system and dictates. They are bound by the cycle; also known as 'transmigration'. The Absolute Truth and the Ultimate reality does not perish, even though, all others are subject to decay. Except the theory of birth and rebirth, all other findings, about the Absolute Brahman is accepted by others in this or that form.

The theory of *Bhumā* and *Alpa* is more mysterious but clarifies the Brahman in its own way. "It is *Bhumā*, where nothing else is seen; where nothing else is heard and nothing else is known. On the oither hand it is *Alp*, where something else is seen, something else is heard and something else is known. **The Bhumā is Nectar, Immortal, the Alpa is mortal.** Brihadākāranyaka Upanishad (2:4:6) *idam sarvam yayamātmā*: All these are souls.

It is repeated in a changed form in Chhāndogya Upanishad (7:25:2)

ātamaiwa sarvam: All are souls.

It asserts and declares that in the beginning there was only this Essence:

sadewa somyedamagra āsidekamewādwitiyam (6:2:1).

Kenopanishad goes one step ahead and says: What the world (people) worship is not Brahman. You must take that Essence to be the Brahman: *tadewa Brahman twam viddhi nedam yadydamupāsayate.* 1:5:8. As that Brahman Krishna in Gitā (10:27) declares that "O Arjun! I'm the soul living in the heart of all living beings: *ahamātmā gudākesha sarvabhutāshayasthitah.*

Yogis and others with extreme penance try to get united with that Brahman. This union or Oneness is called *Moksha* because during this union one loses his 'Self', Ego, Existence and is merged in Him. This Oneness is a state of mind where we are free from encumbrances, and indeed, the Brahman. '*Tatwamasi*', declares the Sāma Veda. It means 'I'm the Essence'/ 'I'm That'. We fail to realise that it's not only 'I' but we are all That Absolute Brahman or a part of it and both physically and symbolically represent Him. In Hinduism this Oneness signifies Oneness with other living beings also: *ātmawat sarvabhuteshu'*: all are like me. In this concept Hinduism has always been far ahead of all other religions. We transcend our individual 'Self'. And, it's all because of that Absolute Brahman.

Chāra Mahāvākya (Four Great Sentences): In Indian Scriptures four very small sentences are said to be the four great sentences. They are all related to Brahman and jiva. These are dealt in detail in the Rahasyopanishad written by Shukadeojee, the brilliant son of Vedarishi Veda Vyāsa. It's written there that Lord Shiva taught these most pious and secret Mantras to Shukadeojee. They all begin with ॐ AUM. They are:

(i) प्रज्ञानं ब्रह्म। *Pragyānam Brahman.* Knowledge is Brahman. That gives sense to the living beings; by that one sees, hears, smells, tastes and expresses are known as senses (pragyānam). That sense is also in me. The knowledge of all is Brahman.

(ii) अहं ब्रह्मास्मि। *Aham Brahmāsmi.* I am He. Man has the right to know the Brahman, the wisdom through which Brahman is known. That Brahman is said to be aham when he does appear in the body as apparent proof. Asmi means I am. So, this sentence shows unity with the Brahman. I'm like the Brahman.

(iii) तत्त्वमसि। *Tatwamasi.* You are that. Before the creation there was the Nameless and Formless Essence. That Essence is still like that. It is clear by the word 'tat'. In our body we possess that Essence. It's clear by 'twam'. We must feel the existence of God (that Essence) in our body. We are a part of that Essence. You are that Essence.

(iv) अयमात्मा ब्रह्म। *Yayamātmā Brahman.* This soul is Brahman. The soul in us, contained in *'yayamātmā'* describes the apparent form of Brahman as light and force. The greater essential force that exists in all apparent 'world' is Brahman. It's the light and life. My soul is that Brahman.

The body too is indicated and included in these great sentences but they deal mainly with 'Pure Consciousness'. Brahman is the Pure Consciousness that we all possess. **In a way, the Pure Consciousness does not create body but become its life and functioning force.**

Creation and Creators (Srishti aur Srishtikartā): In the very first Chapter of Mahopanishad, as at many other places, the creation is described in detail and in logical sequence.

There was only the Essence, the Brahman, Pure Energy, Pure Consciousness, Absolute Power, (or one can call Him with whatever name one likes for He was Formless and Nameless) before the Creation when there was nothing else: no space, no sky, no earth, no stars, no planets, no Brahmā, no Shiva, no water, no fire, neither Sun nor Moon. There was the solitary existence of Absolute Energy and Pure Consciousness. He didn't like to remain alone. He wished to multiply. His wish and determination is called the Great Yagya. During that determined meditation he created Fourteen Male Powers (*Purush*) in the form of Ten *Gyānindriya* (Sense Organs), (11th) *Mana* (Mind), (12th) *Aham* (Ego) (13th) Prāna (Life-element) (14th) Ātmā (Soul); and a Female Force (15th) *Buddhi* (Wisdom). Other than these *Panch Sukshma Tanmātrāyen* (Five Matters in Subtle Forms) and *Panch Mahābhuta Tatwa* (Five Gross Elements) appeared. That Essence, the Absolute Brahma entered them (in all the 25) and *Kāla* (Time) appeared and Space was created.

Trinity (Brahmā, Vishnu, Mahesh) Then, again He got engrossed in Meditation with different desire. Whatever His form may have been, in a trance, He imagined a figure and out came a tall shapely figure with three eyes and a trident in hand. He was *Eshāna, Mahādeva*, or as we know Him, our Lord Shiva. He possessed Purity, Morality, Ethics, Truth, Beauty, Aesthetics, Celibacy, Penance, Asceticism, Renunciation, Free Mind, Prosperity, AUM (*Pranava* and its uses), All the Four Vedas and all the *Chhandas*.

Brahmā

Then, again He got engrossed in Meditation with a different desire. The tension and intensity increased and a drop of sweat fell down. It spread out and covered a vast area. It became water. Then, He concentrated at a point in that growing water body and a bright golden egg appeared. It was called *Hiranyagarbha*. From that egg came out Brahmā. He looked towards east and meditated on *bhuh*, the earth, *Gāyatri Chhand*, Rigveda and Fire God; they appeared. He looked towards west and meditated upon *Bhuwah*,

Trishtupa Chhanda, Yajurveda and God of Wind; they appeared. He looked towards north and meditated upon *swah, Jagati Chhanda, Sāmaveda* and Sun God; they appeared. He looked towards south and meditated on *Mahah, Anushtupa Chhanda, Atharva Veda* and *Soma Devatā* (Moon God); they appeared.

(It is claimed by some modern thinkers that the Europeans divide human beings in Hemetic and Semetic. These words are the changed forms of Hiranyagarbha and Soma.)

Because he turned his head to look towards all the four directions, he got four heads. With that he again meditated on the Absolute God, Narāyana, That is Omnipotent, Infinite, Omnipresent, Transcendental (beyond all), Perpetual, Eternal and has the form of all or none. Brahmā envisioned that Absolute Brahman with thousands of heads and double number of eyes that pervades all, is both the cause and effect, is the welfare of all, is immortal, is the form of all or all the forms are in Him; He is the Universe, the Cosmos, the Cosmic Lord. He saw Him taking rest in *Ksheer Sāgar* (the sea of Milk). That Brahman, the *Akshar Brahman* appeared. He was making a sound incessantly. That sound was that of AUM. The stem of Lotus has risen up from His navel like an umbilical cord. Brahmā was shifted on to it. The manifestation of the Trinity was complete. Then Brahmā created all other sentient and insentient and animate and inanimate.

There are different variations but the original description is the same: Brahmā is the creation of Brahman and has the responsibility of creating all living beings. There are countless adjectives that are used for him.

Vishnu

In Hinduism Vishnu is accepted as Brahman. He is Nārāyan. He has the responsibility of feeding all the living beings.

Yasmādavishwamidam sarvam
tasya saktyā mahātamanah,
Tasmādevochyate vishnuvinshudhātoh praveshanāt.
यस्माद्विश्वमिदं सर्वं तस्य शक्तया महात्मन: ।
तस्म देवोच्यते विष्णुर्विषुधातो: प्रवेशनात् ॥

He has thousands of names. One can call him by any name or chant any that he/ she likes. He is very kind and tolerant. He shows great patience. He has a sweet tongue and musical speech. When Bhrigu Rishi hit Him on His chest he was not angry. Instead he smiled and asked: *Brāhman Devatā*! Did you hurt your foot? This is the climax of tolerance. The Hindus share that tolerance of their gods and Rishis.

Vishnu dwells in *Ksheersāgar* on the bed of *Sheshanāga*. Laxmi is always seen with him. He has his own world called *Vishnu Loka*. He has written a treatise known as 'Vishnu Smriti.'

Mahesh: Shiva

Shiva means good omen, lucky:

iyam shivyā niyateriwāyatih

Moral, ethical and prosperous:

shivāni bastirthajalāni kanchit

poised, stable; may your journey be peaceful:

shivāste santu panthānah

and whose end is fruitful and pleasant:

prayatnah kritsnoayam phalatu shivatātishcha bhawatu.

Shiva, one among the famous Trinity of the Hindus is called the God of destruction. On the other hand he is seen and is associated with numerous blessings: mostly of weapons and power. In showering blessings he is the most generous. He is pleased most easily. In anger, he has no parallel. In penance he has no peer. He has three eyes. The third eye, that remains mostly closed, is only fire and light. Once, Kāmadeva, the lord of Sex; known as *Manmath* and *Madan* or *Pushpadhanwā*, tried to disturb him in his penance. He opened his third eye and Kāmadeva was burnt to ashes. From then on the Lord of Sex has no body.

In the churning of the sea; first came out the poison. Shiva drank it and did not allow it to pass through the food pipe. It remained there and the colour there changed into blue; he became *Neelkantha*.

All the *Vidyā* and *Kalā* have come out of Shiva's great book known as *Maheshwar Sutra*. Man got most of the knowledge including that of Ayurveda and Dhanurveda from Shiva-Shambho.

He is called *"Devādideva Mahādeva'*: God of Gods, the great God; because he is the most powerful among the Trinity. There is hardly any human abode in India where there is no temple of Lord Shiva or a Shivling that symbolises him. The villagers worship him with 'Unique Shāber Mantras' that has not as yet been deciphered.

For his blessings a special and difficult fast is observed and water from the Gangā is offered and poured over him on the 14th day of *Phalguna Krishna*. Like Brahmā and Vishnu he too has his separate world called *Shivaloka*.

One Shiva does many things. He is the consort of Umā that became his wife again in another life of Pārvati. Shiva often tells stories to Pārvati or Umā or moves from place to place with either of them taking the men and women in danger out of the woods; or offers arms to gods, men and demons alike; or fights against his strong devotees to test their devotion. Tales about and of Shiva are endless.

Sri Ganesh and Kartikeya are his two sons.

Shiva is said to be without a beginning and He has no end; He is beyond comprehension. He is known by numerous different names. He is called Rudra and Neellohit also. In the Gitā Krishna has twice affirmed the same fact: *Rudrānāmashankerashchāsmi; Rudrānāma neellohitam.*

As Rudra Shiva has 11 forms called: Manyu; Manu; Manihasa; Mahān; Shiva; Ritadhwaja; Ugraretā; Bhava; Kāla; Vāmadeva; and Dhritvrat; and the eleven wives are respectively: Dhee; Vriti; Ushanā; Umā; Niyuti; Sarpi; Ilā; Ambikā; Irāwati; Sudhā and Dikshā. His eleven abodes are: Heart; Senses; Prāna; Sky; Air; Fire; Water; Earth; Sun; Moon and Penance.

Once, Brahmā asked him to create living beings. In right unrest he created beings of his personal liking: *Preta* (Phantoms); *Pishācha* (Ghosts); *Bhairva* (Dogs); *Vināyaka* (Eagles); *Yātudhāna* (Demons); *Dākini* (Sorceress); *Shākini* (Female Demons); *Kushmānda* (Pumpkins); *Vaitāla* (Minstrels) and *Yogini* (Female Ascetic Attendants). Brahmā was full of wonders at the unique creation. He immediately stopped him. He was given the responsibility to control his unique creation. All of them became Shiva's *Ganas*. Brahmā asked him to go for penance. Such creatures were not needed.

Body and Soul in Hinduism

Body

The Hindus believe in what the Rishis, the most ancient learned men said. Up till now, the modern science has not reached on equal footing. Slowly they are realizing and rediscovering the same facts. It's very apparent in the creation of foetus and the birth of a child.

According to *Maharishi Pippalāda* who wrote **Garbhopanishad** of Krishna Yajurveda our body is *panchātmaka* because it's created with the Five Gross Elements: Earth, Water, Heat, Air and Space. The solid matter in our body is earth; the liquid is water; the hot is *teja* or heat; that which moves and communicates is air and the holes are space. The five sense organs do their duty. The body can distinguish six different tastes or juice: sweet, acidic, salty, bitter, sour and astringent. It has or can produce ten sounds: *Shadaja; Rishabh; Gāndhāra; Madhyam; Pancham; Dhaiwat* and *Nishāda;* (seven sounds of Musical Notes); *Ist, Anist* and *Pranava*. A man can be born in any of the seven colours: *Shukla* (white), *Rakta* (red), *Krishna* (black), *Dhumra* (smoke), *Peeta* (yellow), *Kapil* (reddish brown or wheatish) and *Pāndura* (yellowish white).

When God created (in modern science 'fertilized') egg gets worldly matters or eatable materials; a juice is created inside. This juice is called *'shataras padārtha'* (six types of matters) that change into *rakta* (blood); blood helps in the creation and growth of *mānsa* (flesh), flesh gives rise to *meda* (marrow); marrow helps in the creation of *snāyu* (veins and artery); from it *asthi* (bones) are created; from bones to *majjā* (different marrow) and *shukra* (sperm) from it. These are seven types of *dhātu* (primary substance; a humour of the body; hormones or semen). The sperm from a man and blood of a woman give rise to embryo or foetus.

All these are contained in the heart (basically in blood) and reach each part through the blood. Inner heat is generated in the heart that creates gall that give rise to *vāyu* (gas) that helps in the creation of heart and this way, the foetus grows.

After the menstruation if conception materialises then in one night a *kalala* is formed with the meeting of blood and sperm; it becomes *budabuda* in seven nights; in a fortnight it becomes a *pinda* (gets a body); that hardens in a month; it gets head in two months; legs are formed in the third month; in the fourth month *gulpha* (leg-bones and joints), abdomen and waist get ready; *peetha* and *reedha* (the back bone) comes in the fifth month; in the six month *mukha* (mouth), *netra* (eyes), *shrotra* (ears) and *nāsikā* (nose) are formed. In the seven month the foetus gets life; gets completion in the eighth month. After the completion of the body with the five elements a conscious mind in the form of ॐ (AUM) enters the body and the sense organs are activated. This ॐ (AUM) creates eight *prakriti* (natural instincts like *prakriti*: nature, *mahat tatwa*: greater element, *ahankāra*: pride, and 5 *tanmātrāyen*: subtle forms of matter) and sixteen *vikārs* (change of forms like 5 *gyānendriya*: senses; 5 *karmendriya*; working organs; 5 *sthula bhuta*; solid matters and *mana*: mind) in that conscious body. Only after that the food-intake of mother starts reaching the child through *nāla* (umbilical cord). It remembers the previous lives and wishes to get free from the womb and to do only good deeds. After that the child is born in the ninth month. The moment it is touched by the worldly air of *māyā* (illusion) it forgets what he thought inside the womb and all the previous good and bad deeds turn away from his weakened mind.

How and why the *pinda* becomes or called a body? When the born pinda becomes a temple, it's called a body. Without taking the pinda as a temple it's not correct to say it to be a body. Almost all the languages say it to be body without knowing the difference. The presence of soul makes all the difference.

The soul is the *Yajmāna*, one that performs the yagya; mind is *Brahmā*; lust, etc. are animals; patience and contentment are *Deekshā*, the teachings; sense organs are *pātra*, (vessels/ respectacles); work-organs are *havi,* offerings; head is *kapāla,* destiny or begging bawl; hair are *durba,* sacrificial grass; mouth is *antarvedikā,* inner altar; head also works as *chatushkapāla,* four-shelters; and side teeth are begging bowls. The body has 107 *marmasthāna,* sensitive places; 180 *sandhi,* synapse; 109 *snāyu,* sinew, nerve or ligament; 700 *shirā,* veins; 500 *majjā,* marrows; 360 *asthi,* bones (during childhood); 4,50,00,000 *roma,* hairs; the heart weighs 8 *tolā,* i.e. 96 grams; tongue weighs 12 *tolā,* i.e. 144 grams; the bile in gall-bladder weighs 1 *sera,* i.e. 930 grams; phlegm or rheum weighs 2 ½ *sera,* i.e. 2.325 grams; semen or sperm 1 *pāwa,* i.e. 242 grams; and some materials to be excreted out of body. Their weight depends on food and water intake.

It possesses everything that needs cleaning and purification. It can be done if the body is a temple and *yagyas* are performed regularly inside it. The next body depends on the resolution of the soul at the time of death in this life: *manokrite nāyātyasminsharire.* (Prashnopanishad 3:3)

Protection of Body

Hindus believe that the development and the growth of the soul depend on body. It needs a body, as it can't grow in abstraction. So, body must be protected and kept healthy so that it can endure the rigours of life particularly that of austerities and penance. They follow many paths to ensure the health: Yoga, Fasting, Living closer to Nature, Herbal Medicines, Brahmacharya, Least indulgence in sex and worldly affairs, Detachment and so on. They prefer a life based on the geographical conditions, climate and seasons. Their food habits and clothes are all modulated on that pattern of adjustment with Nature and natural surrounding. That way they were able to lead a long life, *Purnāyu;* and remain healthy till the end as they opt for *Vānaprashtha* and *Samyāsa.*

Cremation of Dead Body

Hindus were first to realise that a dead body must be destroyed in some way. They came to the conclusion during that primitive period that a dead human body is totally useless, and it spreads diseases very fast. As they had enough of firewood they preferred cremation because it would be summarily destroyed and won't spread diseases. Yet in some parts and some sects other means of cremation is preferred. Hindus put the dead body on pyre after bathing and anointing with ghee, etc and then, preferably the elder son puts fire to mouth (known as *Mukhāgni*) and the whole body is burnt to ashes.

There was a chance that the people will not destroy the dead body, only on medical grounds so many religious, supernatural and spiritual bindings were deliberately added. The burning and thus the end of the body gave comfort and solace to the family members, friends and relatives of the departed soul. It was performed more for the living beings and least for the dead man or woman. The children, particularly the infants, are not put to pyre. They are placed in graves.

Shrāddha for Relieving the Soul and Relatives

Shrāddha is a thirteen-day procedure of various social customs, and religious rites and rituals to give complete relief to the bereaved family. It's a balanced mixture of mourning and showing respect to the departed soul; and making the family members and others free from the memories, and suffering. Because they have to perform different rituals so they forcibly check their emotional outbursts. That way they are able to get rid of tension and the resultant depression or psychological disadvantages. That is why performance of *Shrāddha* is indispensable for a Hindu.

Shrāddha is well mixed up with *Tarpan* (offering of water and rice, etc) and *Dāna* (gifts to Brāhmins and feast to all others). They feel that the water poured at the time of *Shrāddha* will soothe the feelings of all concerned. The yet unborn soul is felt to be very close to the vicinity as a *Preta*. When the *Shrāddha* is performed the members and others become mentally sure that the soul is satisfied and it will take re-birth and get a better body. The person performing the *Shrāddha* leads a life of penance and complete austerities as a *Brahmachāri*: eats selected things at prescribed times; wears least cloth and sleeps on hard bed. He is never left alone for the fear of nervous breakdown.

Soul

After the complete formation of the body with the five elements in the womb, a conscious mind in the form of ॐ (AUM) enters the body and the sense organs are activated. It gives three types of heat to body: *jatharāgni* (the fire of abdomen that helps in digestion);

darshanāgni shows the forms, shapes and colours; and *gyānāgni* that brings all wholesome and unwholesome deeds, vices and virtues before us. There are three places of Fire or heat in our body. *Āwāhaneeya agni* is in the mouth; *Gārhapatya agni* is in abdomen and *Daksheenāgni* is in the heart. The soul resides in a thumb-like organ in the head. The presence of the soul, the pure consciousness and the pure conscience makes the difference.

Why does the soul take a body? The soul enters the body because the body is essential for the soul. The soul can grow only in a body. The body functions and gives opportunity to the soul. The soul can't grow and develop in its abstract form. It can purify itself through benevolent deeds, by helping others and by gaining in better qualities like control, balance, devotion, egolessness, kindness etc. Only in a body the soul can get needed light, taste sweetness and enjoy fragrance; and only through body it can spread these three great and most needed qualities. It's not possible in the subtle form of a soul. A body, particularly a human body, is its greatest need. This is the reason that the gods too wish to get and long for a human body.

Mahāmahopanishad teaches us to think: 'I'm not the body; I'm not in pain; I'm not tied;' and it will free the mind. 'I'm not flesh; I'm not bone; I'm a different element than the body'. Such ideas strengthen the soul and kill the worldliness.

There are four types of decisions that the Soul takes:

(i)   "From head to toe my parents created me." This decision comes out of the lust and ties the soul with the illusory world.

(ii) "I'm more subtle than the top of a hair and different to worldly ideas, aspirations and things" is the second decision. It's very plain and pure decision.

(iii) I'm the soul of all worldly matters; I have the form of all and "am indestructible." This third decision makes one free from life; and that soul lives and plays in cosmic self. It becomes the cause of emancipation.

(iv) "I and the world are infinite void like ether" is the fourth decision. It liberates and the soul never again feels pain or agony.

One *Mantra* that is found both in the *Gitā* (2:20) and *Kathopanishad* (1:2:18) declares soul to be birth-less and deathless; it's neither created nor is destroyed:

Na jāyate mriyate wā kadāichnnāyam bhutwām bhavitā va na bhuyeh,
Ajo nityah shāshwato ayam purāno na hanyate hanyamāne sharire.

न जायते म्रियते वा कदाचिन्नायं भूत्वां भविता वा न भूय: ।
अजो नित्य: शाश्वतोऽयं पुराणो न हन्यते हन्यमाने शरीरे ॥

(गीता–२/२०)

[The conscious and wise soul neither takes birth nor dies; it has neither come out of anything nor anything comes out of it (it's neither cause nor effect). This birth-less entity, always remains in the same subtle form; it neither grows nor weathers; it dies not even after the peril of mortal body.]

Avatāras: Incarnations

As the Hindus believe in rebirth, so they believe in incarnations and re-incarnations of gods. It can be divided in four groups: major, minor, known and unknown.

Hindus believe that Sri Ram and Sri Krishna are the physical forms of the quality less Absolute God. This belief is at the root of Hinduism and popular since time immemorial or from the beginning of human life and civilisation. As matter takes form from the formless, in same way each body has been created or come out of the Formless Brahman:

avyaktādwayaktyah   sarvāh   prabhawantyaharāgame.
अव्यक्ताद्वक्ता सर्वा प्रभवंत्य हरागमे

Avatāras (Incarnations) Month Wise
(As in Panchāng)

S.N.	Avatāra	Month & Tithi	Time
1.	Matsya	Chaitra Shukla, 3	Evening
2.	Rām	Chaitra Shukla, 9	Noon
3.	Parashurām	Vaishākh Shukla, 3	Pradosh
4.	Narsingh	Vaishākh Shukla, 14	Dusk
5.	Kurma (Kachhap)	Vaishākh Shukla, 15	Noon
6.	Kalki	Shrāvana Shukla, 6	Evening
7.	Krishna	Bhādra Krishna, 8	Night
8.	Vāmana	Bhādra Shukla, 12	Noon
9.	Buddha	Āshwina Shukla 10	Evening
10.	Vārāh	Bhādra Shukla, 3	Noon

Matsyāvatāra

In order to emancipate the Shrutis and keep their musical and intellectual tradition alive Lord Vishnu took the form of a fish. It is known as Matsyāvatāra. Rajarshi Satyavrat took water from Kritmālā (The incarnation in a calm river fully suggests that life started in a river, and not in a sea or ocean, as claimed by the west.) in his palms for offering. A Hilsā fish came on to his palms and requested him to save it. It kept on growing fast and at last, Rājarishi brought it to the sea. Now he was sure of the incarnation and asked Him to explain the reason. The God in that incarnation informed that delusion is just a week away. He asked the Rajarishi to make preparation to save 'Life' on a boat. It was done and with the help of the Fish-God the boat was saved. The existence of this story in different forms and names in different religions is another proof of the universality of this Eternal Religion.

Kachchhapāvatāra

The defeated Gods needed extra power to regain heaven and survive. Lord Nārāyana suggested to churn the sea with the help of Rākshashas. When Mount *Mandarāchala* started sinking in the sea then the Absolute God took the form of a Turtle and gave stability to that mountain on His back and helped the completion of churning and finally the emergence of Amrit, Nectar. It is known as Kachchhapavtāra.

Vārāhavatāra

At the requests of Manu; as he was ordered to create living beings; and as the earth was submerged in the sea; the Absolute God appeared as a spot in the sky and within seconds became larger than an elephant and kept on growing. It took the form of a *Vārāha* and entered the sea. A demon rushed to fight against Him. When he reached there, He had already balanced the earth on his tusks. He ignored the demon; brought the earth out of water, stabilized it; then fought against the demon and killed him. (The dragging of the earth left a track of land inside the sea. It is now called continental plate.)

(The sudden and abnormal growth of *Matsya, Vārāha* and *Vāmana*; after getting three steps of land; has prompted the western thinkers to come up with the idea of sudden and abnormal growth of a point into infinity; octillions and octillions of times; within a part of a second.)

Narsingh

The subtle formless form of God took the body of a man and head of a lion and came out of a pillar in the evening and caught Hiranyakashipu, the father of the great devotee Prahlāda; on His thighs and opened his chest with His strong nails because he was blessed by Brahmā that he won't be killed by weapon, neither on the earth nor in the sky; neither during the day nor during the night; neither by man nor by animal. He thought himself to be immortal. Only a pure consciousness like the God could have engineered a way to get rid of that cruel demon.

Vāman

When Bali dethroned Indra and the Gods fled away from Heaven then under Shukrāchārya Bali, the grand son of Prahlāda, started 100 *Aswamedha Yajna*. After performing it he would become the Permanent Indra. Aditi, the mother of gods, requested the Lord to save the gods. In the form of a dwarf but as an enlightened and brightened Brāhmin the God appeared at the place of *Aswamedha Yajna*. He was welcomed by all. Bali requested the Brāhmin to ask for anything and promised to give that. Shukrāchārya alerted him by telling that the dwarf Brāhmin is none other than the Lord. Bali said, "I have given my word, I won't back out." The God asked for three steps of land. Bali happily agreed. Then, Vāman became Virāt, of unimaginable height. In one step he measured the earth, in the 2nd he measured the Heavens, etc. and then he asked, "Where should I place my third step." Bali bowed and said, "On my head." He placed His feet on his head. Bali had surrendered. The kind God was pleased and He blessed him to be the Indra in the next Manwantar.

Parashurāma

Paramveer Parashurāma was the son of Maharishi Jamadagni and Renukā. Jamadagni is the fifth star among the Saptarishis known as Ursa Major. *Haihairāja Sahastrabāhu* took the *Homadhenu* from *Jamadagni* by force. Parshurāma came to know of the incident. He alone, without any army, attacked Sahastrabāhu and killed him in the battle. He returned with the cow, Homadhenu. He was chided by his father and ordered to visit all the places of pilgrimage for a year.

Once when he returned home his mother Renukā informed him that the sons of Sahastrārjuna have beheaded his father Jamadagni, when he was under trance of meditation; and fled away with his head. Parashurāma vowed to wipe out the Kshatriyas from the earth 21 times. After killing them he returned with the head of his father; performed Yajna and joined his head. His father got his life back. Whosoever among the Kshatriyas became the king was killed by Parashurāma. Maharishi Kashyap asked the earth in Dāna and Parashurāma donated it to the Rishi. The Rishi then ordered him to leave the place. From there on he is living somewhere on the Mount Mahendra.

He is one among the 5 chiranjivis; the immortals. He is still alive and some pure and lucky souls, from time to time, claimed to have seen and met him.

Sri Rām

In order to free the earth from the demons, the Lord took birth as a human being as the son of *Dasharath* and *Kaushalyā*, and was named Sri Rām. He showed his *Virāt Swaroop* (the Infinite Form) to his mother when she asked to open the mouth. He lived and behaved like a man through out his stay on the earth. So, he is said to be *Purushottama*, the best man. Along with Laxman and an army of Monkeys and Bears he attacked Lankā to free his wife Sitā and killed Rāvana. He made Rāvana's younger brother Bibhishana, the king of Lankā. He returned to his motherland and kingdom Ayodhyā and ruled for a long time. Peace, health, pleasure and prosperity were his gift to the people. His governance is called *'Ramrājya'*; the best administration so far.

Sri Krishna

Sri Krishna, the most luminous and enchanting among the incarnations of Nārāyana, was born in a jail. Because of an airy announcement that the 8th child of his sister Devaki will kill him, Kansa imprisoned her and her husband Vāsudeva. They had promised to give all their newborn babies. Kansa killed six of them. The seventh was sent to the womb of Rohini by Yogamāyā and the 8th child was Sri Krishna. Immediately after his birth, the shackles were broken, the gate opened. Vāsudeva transported him to Gokul and replaced him with the daughter of Yashodharā. She was, in fact, Yogamāyā. When Kansa tried to kill her, she flew in the sky, got her eight hands and warned Kansa that the baby to kill him had already taken birth in Gokula. He tried his best to kill Him through *Pootanā, Shakatāsura* and *Vātyāchakra* but of no avail. They were all killed by baby Krishna. He was growing and playing and studying and side by side Kansa kept on trying to kill him through *Bakāsura, Vatsāsura, Pralamba, Dhenuka, Aghāsura, Mayaputra Vyomasura*, etc. but all were killed by the growing Krishna.

Krishna saved the people of Gokula from incessant hard rain by taking Mount *Gobardhana* on his fingers and keeping it there for seven days. At the age of 11 years and three months he left Gokula and never returned back. He went to Awanti as a pupil, completed his education and as Dakshinā to Guru, he gave life back to his drowned and dead son, after searching him out of the river.

Then he returned to Mathurā and killed Kansa. Jarāsandh, the father in law of Kansa attacked him seventeen times and was defeated. In order to give safety to his people he got a fort constructed in the middle of the sea at Dwārkā, and left that place when Jarāsandh attacked for the 18th time.

Lord Krishna is famous for *Rāsa Leelā* before he attained youth; and after that for marriages with 8 Queens and other sixteen thousand wives. He kidnapped his first wife Rukmini; he went in search of Syamantak Mani and brought Jāmbwati as a gift; his third wife Satyabhāmā was given to him by her father Satrājit; Kālindi got him through tough penance; he won the fifth one Laxmanā by correctly aiming at the fish in the swayambar; he tamed seven bulls of king Nagnajit and got his daughter Satyā; kidnapped again the 7th Queen Mitra Bindā and the 8th Queen Bhadrā was presented as gift by her father.

He went with Satyabhāmā to kill Bhaumāsura, that has taken the chhatra of Varun and kundal of Aditi. He killed him but there was a great problem of 16 thousand Narendra damsels that were imprisoned by the demon king. Krishna accepted and emancipated them. During that journey he brought *Kalpa taru* to Dwārkā by force. Indra started a fight and was defeated.

Krishna had to fight against Bānāsura, that had one thousand hands; he reduced the hands and killed him when he had only four hands left. Before the battle of Mahābhārat, he killed Paundraka, Dantavaktra and Shālva; and also Shishupāla. That great warrior decided not to take weapons during Mahābhārat, the greatest battle so far on the earth. He could have stopped the war but he had other intentions. Within the 18 days of the battle of Mahābhārat, all the weapons were destroyed and all the warriors except Pandavas were killed. Complete disarmament was achieved. From there on Indians were not allowed to create and manufacture weapons for mass destruction: bombs and missiles.

For this very achievement of making the people free from fear, Gāndhāri cursed him. He accepted the curse. As a result, the Yadavas fought and perished and an ordinary hunter shot an arrow aiming at his red foot. He thought it to be a deer.

In the temples Krishna is mostly seen with Rādhā and at places with either Rukmini or Satyabhāmā.

Buddha

There is an incarnation of Lord Vishnu as Buddha. The place too is Gayā, well associated with Buddha whose real name was Siddhārtha and he was the son of King *Suddhodan* in the Shākya Dynasty related to Lord Ram. But it has been made debatable; perhaps because it happened around two thousand six years ago (according to the modern calculations); and because the incidents described in the Purānas and Buddha's life are different. There are ample proofs that many Purānas were written and many were amended during the long period of slavery. Original Purānas are only 18 while the available Purānas are around 400.

So, Siddhārtha became Buddha and he is accepted as the 9th incarnation of Lord Vishnu. He is known as the Enlightened One and is worshipped by the Hindus. The Western writers falsely claimed that Buddhism was eradicated from the land of Buddha. It's a gross mistake. The Indians or (to be conservative) the Hindus need not be baptized into Buddhism for worshipping and following Buddha since they accept him as an incarnation of the Lord.

Buddha got Enlightenment at *Uruvellā* in Gayā, now the place and temple is called Bodhagayā or Buddhagayā under a tree, and for about 45 years moved from place to place and taught the people to be pure and indulge in only wholesome deeds for *Nirvāna* i.e. Salvation. His followers are called Bauddha or Buddhists. The kings, the rich men and the common people of the time bowed and listened to and followed Bhagawāna Buddha. The religion spread over many countries. It was the victory of and by love, compassion and wisdom.

Kalki

According to Indian Scriptures and Panchāng six times Kalki had appeared and every time there was delusion. Demon-like men were destroyed. Everything was purged for the *Satyug* to arrive. It's the period of the seventh Manu.

That Kalki Avatāra is awaited. Astrologically His arrival has been calculated. He is to appear in a village called Sambhala in the family of a Brāhmin named Vishnuyasha. The Vedas: Shrutis and Smritis; will disappear. The demonic man, without character and morality, will get a very short life.

It is claimed that Lord Kalki will be taught Vedas by Parashurāma; and weaponry by Lord Shiva. Because of His presence on the earth the new generation will become real human beings and really humane.

Besides these major incarnations Bhagawāna Vishnu has many different incarnations on his name. They are: (i) Nara-Nārāyana; (ii) Sanakādi; (iii) Kapila; (iv) Dattātreya; (v) Yajna; (vi) Rishabha; (vii) Hansa; (viii) Dhanwantari; (ix) Hayasheersha; (x) Vyāsa; (xi) Prithu; (xii) Hari etc.

Devatās (Gods)

As Human Religion and as Eternal Religion Hinduism possesses (some atheists may like to call 'devised') all the gods and goddesses or their equivalent that are worshipped by different human beings everywhere in the world. Naturally, these gods and goddesses cover each region that has one, a few, some or many gods and goddesses. In this way, they belong to different regions (a metropolitan man will like to call sectors). Even these regions can be divided in major and minor categories.

One tradition, in Hinduism, begins with the Creator Brahman (*Purush*) and descends through the trinity to their different incarnations, and the places where they reside; and also the 'beings' that live with and accompany them. The other tradition begins with Creative Female Force, *Shakti*, Eternal and Cosmic Energy, that takes different forms and names. This tradition includes Durgā, Laxmi, Saraswati, Umā and descendents to their different forms and incarnations, and the places they reside; and also the 'beings' that live with and accompany them. These belong to the major group of Life Giving Gods and Forces; and are very identical to Preserving Gods and Destructive Forces or the Gods that help in sustenance or destroy. Both Vedic and Non-Vedic gods and goddesses are worshipped.

Other than them there are many gods that help in sustenance, are associated with cereals, plants, food-world, animal words, birds and other super creatures. Then, the Elements and other allied gods are worshipped along with the gods that are celestial bodies. Natural Forces are also accepted as gods for they possess and endow us with power. There is a big region of health sector.

represented by Bhagawāna Dhanwantari and another of arms and ammunitions and supernatural power that includes war gods and the scientist *Rishis* and *Munies*.

Many persons, other creatures, birds and animals got the status of gods with their exceptional deeds or great devotion: *Bhaktas* became *Bhagawāna*; and also those that ensured victory of purity, truth, humanness, divinity over demons and demonic acts. Along with them there are personal and local deities based on the blessings received by a person or a place. The local deities include the forces and powers that helped and help in leading a healthy, happy and full life under their protection and blessings.

It's apparently polytheism but there is the underlying faith expressed in the Rig Veda that 'the One Real is called by different' names': *ekam sad viprā bahudhā vadanti*: the Truth is one, the God is one, the wise men call him by different names. This proclamation and assertion has given ample latitude to people to worship 'anyone or anything.' The Indians do enjoy that liberty or that Omnipresent Quality of the Supreme God. They identify with the God, the things of their liking or the things of their livelihood and worship them. So, an Indian in a profession will worship his tools: that includes from pen to screwdriver; from sickle to tractors; from oxen to carts; and from nail cutters to washing stones; from weighing balance to fish-net. Not a single businessman in India will start the day's proceedings without remembering, worshipping and bowing to his/ her business deity, i.e. (in all probability) Laxmi.

And, hence it's apparently monotheism because the form of That One is followed and worshipped. It's very plain in concept but it's complicated to those that don't feel such deep devotion and dedication. It's complete dependence on God; it's complete surrender to God. It's further expressed in the clear description of the Supreme God as the Supreme *Purush* (Person) pervading all beings as His parts and yet remaining beyond them. What is otherwise thought to be inert is living pure consciousness for Hinduism, they are pervaded by That Pure Consciousness. As a result; some claim that Hindus have 33 crores (in the opinion of others 33 thousand) Gods and Goddesses. It may appear exaggerated but for them it's real because they have adopted such a philosophy. *Ātmat sarvabhuteshu* (everything is like me) is also *brahmavat sarvabhuteshu* (everything is like the God); so a Hindu declares: *atithi devo bhawah;* (guests are god); *pitri devo bhawah;* (father is a god) *mātri devo bhawah;* (mother is a god); *gurur devo bhawah;* (teacher is a god).

It's all apart from the Trinity or Trideva (Brahmā, Vishnu, Mahesh) and their Shaktis (powers) Saraswati, Laxmi, Durgā); and Surya (the Sun) and Sri Ganesh. Each *yajna* and *poojā*, begins with the worshipping of Sri Ganesh; the *Bighnavināshaka* (that removes hurdles) and *Mangalkartā;* that changes the happenings into good fortune. There are *Asnta Lokapāla* (eight guards of directions); one for each direction: Indra; Varun; Kuber; Yama; Agni; Niriti; Marut; and Aryamā. Because they have their share in the offerings in *Yajnas* so Pooshā; Bhaga; Aswinikumars and Soma (Moon) are worshipped.

Deva-guru Brihaspati and Deva Senāpati (Chief Commander of gods' army) Kārtikeya are specially worshipped for their individual qualities and contributions. Apart from these every Hindu has his *Ishta Devatā* (his individual god whom he worships); *Kula Devatā* (the deity whom his whole family worships (the unmarried girls are not allowed to participate in that ritual for they are expected to worship the traditional deity of the family of their respective husbands.). For the fulfillment of different desires or even after the fulfillment of desires that deity is worshipped that fulfilled the desire. There is no intricacy in it. It's all very clear. The climax is that each major God is the King of Kings; the God of other Gods. It's Henotheism. As conclusion one can safely say that each God that man can think of, or has thought of, is worshipped by Hindus. On the other hand all Hindus don't worship all the gods. The family God of one will not be worshipped by the family of others if by tradition they don't belong to the same family. Members of one family tradition will worship the same deity. It makes no difference whether they separated and living apart from a few days back or for hundreds of years. Hindus definitely remember their family God when they start a new work. The extreme truth is that the known and declared atheists too do that.

Lord Chitragupta is the greatest example. Once, on the second day of the month of Kārtika Shukla; Brahmā was meditating upon the Absolute God, after finishing the work of Creation. During that deep concentration a very bright being of unique colour came out of his body with an inkpot and pen. When the trance of Brahmā was broken that bright figure asked him: "Who am I? What's my name? Where should I reside? What should I do? Please give me needed directions."

Brahmā said: "You have come out of my kāyā (body) so you are Kāyastha. Your name will be Chitragupta, according to your colour. You will keep the record of the pure and impure deeds of the living beings. You will reside in Yamapuri." Chitragupta bowed to him, followed his instruction and keeps the record. His descendents are called Kāyasthas. The kāyasthas among the Hindus treat him as their original forefather and worship him on every 2nd day of Kārtika Shukla fortnight.

Chitragupta

Chitragupta got nine sons: Bhatta; Nāgar; Senaka; Gaur; Shrivāstava; Māthur; Ahishtāna; Shakasena; and Ambashtha. Each among them has his separate descendents. Their Kula-Gotra is named after them. (In another version; Kāyasthas are divided in thirteen Gotras.) Their marriages are performed preferably in their Gotra. Each one treats personal family Gotra to be the best. That is the beauty of Indian spirituality: Each one is the best for in a way each one possesses the Brahman.

Dharma Devatā

Dharma Devatā (the God of Religion) is the mind-born son of Brahmā. According to Matsya Purāna (3:10) and Mahābhārat, Ãdi Parva 66:31 he was born out of the right breast of Brahmā to keep all the worlds happy and pleasant:

Stanam tu dakshinam bhitwā brahmano narvigrahah,
Nihsrito bhagawān Dharmah sarvalokasukhāwahah.

स्तनं तु दक्षिणं भित्वा ब्रह्मणो नरविग्रह: ।
नि:सृतो भगवान् धर्म: सर्वलोकसुखावह: ॥

(महाभारत आदि पर्व-६६-३१)

Dharma is all white; his colour is white; clothes are white; earrings are white and garland, etc. are all white.

According to Mahābhārat 1:66:14 Kirti; Laxmi; Dhriti; Medhā; Pushti; Shraddhā; Kriya; Buddhi; Lajjā; and Mati are the ten wives of Dharma:

Kirtirlaxmidhritirmedhā pushtih shraddhā kriyā tathā,
Buddhirlajjā matishchaiwa patnayo dharmasya tā dash.

कीर्तिलंक्ष्मीधृतिमेधा पुष्टि: श्रद्धा क्रिया तथा ।
बुद्धिर्लज्जा मतेश्चैव पत्लयो धर्मस्य ता दश ॥

(वही-६६/१४-१५)

But in the Srimadbhāgwat Mahāpurāna 4:1:8:48 the number of Dharma's wives is thirteen. Not only the number but the names too differ. They are Shraddhā; Maitri; Dayā; Shānti; Tushti; Pushti; Kriyā; Unnati; Buddhi; Medhā; Titikshā; Hring and Murti:

Shraddhā maitri dayā shāntistushti pushti kriyon natih,
Buddhirmedhā titikshā hringmurti dharmasya patnayah.

श्रद्धा मैत्री दया शान्तिस्तुष्टि: पुष्टि: क्रियोनति: ।
बुद्धिमेधा तितिक्षा ह्रीमूर्ति धर्मस्य पत्लय: ॥

(भागवत पुराण)

Dharma is said to have many sons but the numbers and names differ from place to place.

Indra

Indra is not a person but a post; the post of the god of gods and the ruler of Heaven. His throne is called *Indrāshana*. A ruling Indra is substituted by another one after every *Manwantara*. The great emperor that performs 100 *Aswamedha Yajna* is given that high post. In the running present *Manwantar Purandar Deorāja* is the Indra. Shachi, a *Rishika* and the daughter of demon king Pulomā, is his wife. They have a son named Jayant and a daughter named Jayanti.

Varun

The Master of Water and Water bodies Varun was the first to perform *Aswamedha Yajna* after defeating all the gods. He has his abode in the Western Sea. It's called *'Ratnapuri Bibhāwari'*. His main weapon is *Pāsha* (Net). His son Pushkar is always seen in his right.

Kuber

Kuber is the son of Vishrwā and Ilavillā. Brahmā appointed him as the Master of all the wealth. After penance he became the *Lokapāla* of North. He lives in the *Alkāpuri* near Kailāsh.

Yamarāja

Yamarāja is one of the two sons: Yamrāja and Shrāddhadeva Manu and a daughter River Yamunā. He is the judge of the pure and impure deeds of the living beings. He is the Lokapāla of South and lives in the fearful and strange place called *Samatamanipuri* that is full of bad omen. He is worshipped in his fourteen different names. He moves on a buffalo. He is worshipped a night before the Deepāwali, the festival of light.

Agnideva

Agnideva, the Fire God, is the *Dikpāla* of the Southeastern Corner. It's known as *Agnikona*. He took birth from Basubhāryā, the wife of Dharma but he got his origin in the mouth of the Virāta Purush. Swāhā is his wife. He moves on a sheep with *Shakti* and *Akshasutra* weapons.

Agni has many forms. In a body he resides as Jatharāgni; in the seas as *Barawāgni*; in the forest as *Dāwāgni*; in the Sun as *Divyāgni*; in the world as manifest and non-manifest simple Fire and in the clouds as *Vidyuta* (electricity). The worldly Fire has five forms: *Brāhman*; *Prājāpatya*; *Gārhastya*; *Dakshināgni*; and *Kravyādāgni*.

Nairarita and *Nirariti*

Nairarita used to save the travellers from the robbers in his previous life. Once, while saving a group, he was killed. He became a Dikapāla.

Nirariti is the Goddess of sin. She came out of Sea at the time of Churning before the appearance of Goddess Laxmi. So, she is the elder sister. On her request Lord Vishnu fixed her place in the banyan tree. On every Saturdays Laxmi goes to meet her at the banyan tree.

Marut

Marut are usually called Marutgans as they are 49 in number. These are the forms of air. There is an interesting story, strange but true, behind the creation of the Marutagans.

Lord Vishnu killed both the demons sons of Deva Mātā Aditi. She was angry with her son Indra for whose safety her two sons were killed. In anger she wished to bear a child that could kill Indra. She pleased her husband Maharishi Kashyapa. She conveyed him her desire. It was difficult for the Rishi to help in the birth of a child that could kill his own son. He suggested her to observe Punsawana Vrat. With sincerity and devotion Aditi started the vrat. Indra came to know of it. But he was unable to harm her as she was very alert and conscious against every eventuality. The day of the birth of the child was coming nearer. One day tired Aditi slept in the evening. Indra got a chance. He entered the womb and broke the foetus in 49 parts. It was the effect of the vrat that none of the part died. They all took birth. They were named Maruts. They are 49 in number. They are even called "Unchāsa Pawan". They are worshipped for health, perfection and prosperity.

Aryamā

Aryamā is the Master of forefathers. The forefathers are satisfied through him. His abode is in the *Uttar Phālguni Nakshatra*. He is the son of Kashyapa and Devamātā Aditi. Along with Mitra and Varuni he accepts *Swāhā habya* and in Shrāddha he accepts *Swadhā kavya*. He is worshipped for the continuity of family tree.

Pushā

Pushā, the god of animal wealth, is one among the 12 Ādityas. He is a part of the Solar System. He moves round the world on a fixed path and in limited time. He looks after the animals and helps in their survival and growth. He is offered crushed rice. He has no light of his own. He is lighted by the light of the Sun. It's said that once he had his light but Beerbhadra took away his light.

Aswini Kumārs

Aswini Kumārs are twin brothers: one is *Nāsatya* and the other one is *Dasra* but it is not known to most of the Hindus. These twins are famous as Aswini Kumārs. They know Āyurveda and are the Deva-Vaidyas.

They are the sons of the Sun and Sangyā. The latter, left the Sun because of the intense heat and left her Shadow there. She started living in a forest in the form of Aswini (a mare). The Sun came to know of her and went there in the form of a horse. The twins that were born are the Aswini Kumārs.

They move on airplanes especially built for them. They have performed great and strange operations. They were expert in the treatment of blindness and attaching the chopped up heads.

Chandra

Chandra Deva, the Moon, came out of the sea along with Laxmi, in the famous churning of the sea. So, he is her brother. And, since, Laxmi is the mother so, *Chandramā* is the *Māmā*; popularly called *Chandā Māmā*. That is also the reason that the sea-tides are associated with Chandra.

Maharishi Atri changed him into Soma. The medicines were created when the Soma dropped on the earth while Chandramā was taking rounds of the earth. They gave health to the living beings and changed their constitution. It was all the effect of the Soma. Lord Shiva made him the Master of *Chandraloka*.

Brihaspati

Brihaspati is the son of **Maharishi** Angirā. He is the best among all the planets. He is the Guru of the gods and saved them on many occasions. Maharishi Bharadwāja is his son. He wrote Brihaspati Samhitā. Brihaspati is called in almost every *yajna*.

Kārtikeya

Kārtikeya is the son of Lord Shiva. He got form in a forest. He sucked milk with six mouths and is called Shatmukh. He is the Commander in Chief of the army of Gods. He moves on peacock and has bow and arrow as his weapon. He wrote a treatise on *Dhanurveda*. He was married to *Brahmaputri Devasenā Shashti Devi*. He is worshipped with a wish to get a son.

Kāmadeva

Kāmadeva is the son of Dharma and Shraddhā. He is also said to be the mind-born son of Brahmā born out of Sankalp (Resolution). He has a younger brother called Krodha (Anger). He uses five arrows of pushp (flowers) made up of: *Neelakamal; Mallikā; Āmramaura; Champaka* and *Shirish* flowers. He moves on the chariot of parrots. He has a flag with the emblem of fish.

Prajāpati Daksha

Prajāpati Daksha came out of the right thumb of Brahmā. In another *Kalpa* he was born as the son of Pracheta. He married Asikni, the daughter of Prajāpati Veerana. He had cursed Nārad to remain restless. He got 53 daughters. Ten were given to Dharma; 13 to Maharishi Kashyap; 27 to Chandramā (that became his Kalāyen);

One to pitars; one to Agni; and one to Lord Shiva. He insulted Lord Shiva and his Daughter, the wife of Shiva named *Sati* burnt in her own fire. Shiva was angry. He created Veerabhadra that disturbed the *Yajna* and threw the head of Prajāpati Daksha in South Hawan. On the request of the gods Shiva gave back his life through a newly born goat kid.

Viswakarmā

Viswakarmā, the engineer and Architect of gods, is the son of Prabhāsa Basu and Mahāsati Yogasiddhā. He constructed great cities and forts, including the *Swarnapuri of Lankā; Dwārikā Dhāma; Jaggannath Sri Vigraha* and manufactured all the arms and weapons of the gods. He is known as Twestā also. His daughter Sangyā became the wife of Sun. On her complaint he divided the Sun in sixteen parts to reduce his brightness and heat.

Maya, the *dānava shilpi*; architect and engineer of the demons, was on equal footing with Viswakarmā. He has often surpassed him.

Sri Ganapati, Gajānan, Ganesha

Mātā Shakti collected the left overs of Ubatan (a paste to smear the body with) and created a figure. The figure had consciousness and power. He stood up, bowed to the creative mother and requested to give some orders. The mother asked him to guard the door and not to allow any one to enter inside as she was going to take bath. Shiva came and was stopped. The boy defeated all but could not be taken off the door. At last, out of anger Shiva cut off the head of that boy. Mātā came and saw the headless body of her son. She asked for the son. Lord Shiva got the head of a newly born elephant. He fixed that head on that child. From thereon he became *Gajānan*, the son of Lord Shiva. He was asked to look after the father's *gans* and he became *Ganapati*.

The God of Mangal, welfare, peace, prosperity and knowledge is worshipped first in every *poojā* and every *yajna*. He removes all the hurdles from the way and ensures smooth and trouble free comletion of an important work. He is the husband of Riddhi and Siddhi. He is very famous for taking dictation from Veda Vyāsa and completed the greatest epic Mahābhārat.

Bhagawāna Surya

The Hindus worship Surya, the Sun God everyday in the morning and evening; and two times in a year: in Chaitra and in Kartika since time immemorial. He gave the Hindus the theory of *Karma* and also of *Niskāma Karma*.

Surya is married to Sangyā, the daughter of Viswakarmā. He had two sons: Vaivawasta Manu (also known as Shrāddhadeva) and Yama and a daughter River Yamunā. Later on he got twins famous as Aswini Kumārs. During *Tretā Sugriva* and in *Dwāpar Karna* were born out of a part of Surya.

There are many Solar systems in the world. (Sixteen Divisions of The Sun by Viswakarmā is in iteslf a proof of at least Sixteen Suns. Either he actually divided or he had discovered them.)

Hindus worship him as *Bhagawāna Sri Surya Nārāyana*; a physical manifestation of the Absolute Brahman, *Nārāyana*. He came out of the eyes of the Absolute Brahman. During a year Surya Deva is worshipped by twelve different names as the rays make different impact on the life and plantation on the earth.

The Sun moves on a Chariot that has seven white horses and is driven by Aruna, the elder brother of Garuda.

(Indian *Rishis* and Astrologers claimed that the Sun moves but the Europeans declared that the Sun is stationary and the earth moves. In the late 20th century they realised that the sun too moves. The sun is not only a perennial source of energy but also keeps the cells at their position. If the sunrays will not reach the body the cells of skin will drop down as powders. The sun keeps us alive and healthy.)

(Happily enough; the position of India on the earth and the relative movement of the earth and the sun and the angle on the axis gives India an advantageous position. It's the only sub-continent or country in the world that enjoys six seasons: Basant; Grishma; Rainy; Hemant; Shishir and Sharad. Ironically enough, in every new book only four seasons are taught in India; although, all of us know that in India the seasons change after each two months. 15th November to 15th January, it's different and from 15th January to 15th March it's different and so on.)

S.N.	Gods	Wāhana (Transport)	Weapon
1.	Brahmā	Hans, Swan	
2.	Vishnu	Garuda, Eagle	Chakra, targeted missile
3.	Shiva	Bull (Nandi)	Trident, (Time & Destruction)
4.	Durgā	Lion	Lance
5.	Sri Krishna		Chakra
6.	Sri Ganesh	Rat	
7.	Kārtikeya	Peacock	Bow and Arrow
8.	Indra	Airāwat	Vajra
9.	Agni	Sheep	Shakti and Akshasutra
1o.	Brihaspati	Nitighosha Ratha	
11.	Kāma	Chariot of Parrots	Pushpāyuddha
12.	Yama	Buffalo, Bhairava	Gadā
13.	Shani	Crow	
14.	Pushā	Goat	Danda

Purpose behind Incarnations and Life

The incarnations of the God have/ had a physical form and a symbolic meaning. They had some specific purpose to achieve. That answers different questions but the greatest one is that each being has come to the earth with a definite purpose. All other religions have not as yet clearly decided on this point but Hindus have been striving hard to grow from inside because without ample growth in inner power one cannot achieve the goal and fulfill the greater purpose with which life was created.

The greatest boon that human being enjoy is the fact that the Creator kept us free for growth. We are bounded by the greater spiritual and cosmic system and are free at physical level to try to be free at all levels.

Hinduism proclaims that to make the body the central figure is to increase the bondage and to go beyond the physical self is the freedom. We make a big and beautiful house and spend a lot of energy in its maintenance and protection. Since we have collected and arranged many things of our personal liking and for our comfort and the use and comfort of the other members of the family so we are both physically and mentally attached to it. We boast of it. We are proud of it. We feel and claim to be richer and greater than many. That house becomes our aim in life. We live it behind when we die. Now, did the God create us so that we get a house constructed on the earth and live in luxury? The inventions and construction of houses are and were for shelter from intense cold and intense heat as well as heavy rainfall. Are we right in spending all our savings and taking loans from different sources to complete it? Unfortunatey enough, at the completion of the house and just by shifting there we feel that we have completed our purpose; that our life is successful.

We will have to re-think and concentrate at what our forefathers said building not a house but building character is the purpose in life; laying high, tall and smooth walls is not the purpose of life but to make the mind and the self big, tall and strong; not to live in the protection of a house is the purpose of life but to become stronger, larger and benevolent enough to give protection to others. In place of getting a fort constructed make your own self and being and mind a fort so that many are protected by it.

The outer forts were either destroyed or they tumbled down; the physical form will worn out; the body will not last long; it will be left and a new body taken for further growth. Hence, Hinduism makes us realise that outer reality and perfection is not needed; it's the growth from inside and the inner strength that is important.

It's very clear that the Great Wall of China was constructed with the purpose of saving the country from outer attack. It's existing still but its intial purpose is lost; it can't protect the country, the way the people are moving and attacking. There is no permanence in the physical and worldly matter and form. The spirit has the permanence; the soul is immortal; the spiritual self is to be made strong.

The Rishis had grown so very large and strong that they are still living; the physical body has perished but the spiritual self is present; that we are unable to surpass them. They lived without houses; visited places to know earth, life and plantation and learnt about medicinal plants to keep others healthy and happy. Had they lived inside the protected walls and glassed houses they would not have realised the truth. This can be and should be our aim to be fully purged and gain spiritual power. At least, the *Rishis* and the Incarnation amply suggests: kill the demons if in you or if outside; be victorious by attaining *sat*, *chit* and *ānand*. We are excessively indulged or made to indulge in physical pleasure and the demons, the enemies of life and good qualities are growing everywhere both in number and power. We are lulled into materialism and conscious of the safety of life and wealth. The demons are overpowering us. We are afraid of the bullets and bombs. The situation has grown worst. At playgrounds, at the places of entertainment and worship we are checked for safety, yet get killed. The buses, the trains, the planes are not safe because of the demons, famous nowadays as terrorists for they are from among us and like us in appearances. Are we, our women and children free and safe? No. The rapes, kidnappings, theft of organs and other numerous crimes are proofs that the demons have grown powerful; the gentlemen and the gods are defeated; dethroned and running for protection. Health, pleasure, purity and chastity, etc. are all gone and have been substituted by demonic trends and acts. Crime is the reality and criminals are the heroes.

The deeds of criminals and terrorists (the real demons) are shown on TVs and printed in newspaper or broadcasted on radio 24 hours. How can the common man and the pure souls survive? The gods and gentlemen are being forced to change their religion and turn into demons? Demons are making others demons through bribes, loans, wine and women. All the Surpanakhās are active and attracting the young Laxmans, all the Sitās are imprisoned in luxurious Ashoka Vatikās. Think of it and decide for yourself.

So far the purpose in life is concerned, Hinduism is very clear. It asks to go all out to achieve four *purushārthas*: and to make balanced progress in Dharma, Artha, Kāma and Moksha. Do your duty for living, sustenance and fostering the family; (unfortunately, it is now being called 'raising a family); adopt means to earn *artha* for that specific purpose; enjoy life not for enjoyment but to ensure the continuity of life by having children; and try hard to be pure, lead an ideal life to get salvation; freedom from the cycle of birth and death.

Mixed Hindu Society and Culture

𝒯he very idea and philosophy of *sarve bhawantu sukhinah* had to opt for a mixed society and culture and a united family. These things were there in the society when the theories were propounded. In India the theories have not created the society; the society has set examples for such theorization.

Indian society is mixed in many ways: biologically; geographically; psychologically; sociologically; and spiritually. *Ātmavat sarvabhuteshu* in a very natural way needed the presence and existence of all. There was no effort to wipe out one for the sake of others. So, all types of human and non human beings got a place here. It's the most heterogenous combination. The non-tolerant rest of the world will have to learn, adopt and follow some important lessons on co-existence from India and Indian Saints, Seers and Prophets.

The climax is shown with the Demons (*Rākshas* and *Daityas*). It's really a wonder that there was a continuous battle between the gods and demons; yet most of the important demons; were blessed by different gods. The greatest wonder is that as many as twelve demons move with the sun: Heti; Praheti; Paurusheya; Shukra; Varya; Vyāghra; Vāta; Senajit; Vidyuchchhatru; Arishtanemi; Brahmāpeta and Makhāpet.

Just on the opposite side are the sublime and divine *Rishis*, *Maharishis* and *Munies* that are most wise and most human. They lived a very decent life and taught the pupils and the people, including the kings, queens, prince, princesses; the best, healthiest and the most religious way of living, in which there is something very important for the people of each Varna and all ages.

The *Maharishis* (The Great Visionaries, Seers and scientists); *Rishis* (Visionaries, Seers, Inventors and Scientists) *Munies* (Seers) led a very pious life in frugality; eating only once the produce of non-cultivated land; and incessantly worked for 'life' and society. *Sanak, Sanandan, Sanātana* and *Sanat Kumār* preferred to remain a child of five for its innocence by the power of penance. Their *Sanatkumār Samhitā* is a milestone as a Scripture that teaches religious acts. The *Saptarishis* are in the space as Ursa Major with only their sublime deeds. Some of them are replaced by some other; in every *Manwantar*. In the present time the *Saptarishis* are: *Kāshyap; Atri; Vashisntha; Viswāmitra; Gautam; Jamadagni;* and *Bhāradwāja.* They bring those on the right path that have lost the path of piety. *Maharishi Dadhichi* gave his bones to prepare Vajra so that the demons be faced and the gods be saved. Yet the *Yoga* and *Dhanurveda, Āyurveda, etc.* were taught to the demons also.

In India there has been householders on one side and on the other the whole country has fostered the *Sant* (Saints) with care and respect. The *Sants* have been true teachers and have shown the right path. They have been greatly supported by the *Āchāryas* (Teachers) and *Mahātmās* (Great Souls) and *Swāmis* that have been spiritual and religious teachers like the Mahātmās. There is no dearth of *Yogis, Sadhus* and *Pandits*. They have contributed well in keeping the tradition, culture, civilisation and religion alive.

In the past, Kings played their role according to the Scriptures. Then, there was peace and prosperity in the country. Art, Architect, Music, Religion, *Yoga, Vairāgya,* Trade grew and India was a 'bird of gold' where milky rivers with pure water flowed. But the first doubt crept up in the minds of the *Kshatriya* Kings and *Brāhmin* Ministers. The kings started appointing *Kshatriyas* as minsisters and the *Brāhmins* started dethroning the kings and declaring themselves as the king. This weakened the kingdoms and thus the country. The seeds of doubt were sown by the robbers from other countries that came solely for the wealth of the country. The weakness grew. The doubt spread over. It germinated in the heart and mind of all the four strong pillars of Indian society: the four Varnas. The pillars crumbled under outer pressure and inner struggle. When the robbers found India weak and divided they saw an opportunity to rule over it. Eventually they established their empire here. The broken, down and out pillars never became united. The pillars have broken down to small stones: powerless and ineffective.

India was heading on the right path and making great progress till queens remained *Rājamātā*, but once the role reversed and family feuds came out in the form of conspiracy and killing, India lost the caring mother. People are still searching for the caring *Rājamātā* but there is none in the country. When the women of the country are not ready to be recognised as *mātā* then, from where *Rājamātā* can appear?

Once, Indian Citizens bore the responsibility of feeding the country: the people of all the four *Varnas* and *Āshramas*. The taxes that they paid in ancient times were only for the king; and were used for internal and external security. The kings did help the people but only in a crisis. They were not supposed to do business or anything else. They framed the rules and saw that the rules are according to the Scriptures and obeyed by the people. The present Citizens pay or evade the taxes and become free from the responsibilities of looking after the country and the countrymen.

The traders are no longer *Vaishyas*. The people of all the *varnas* have become traders; that does not know the tradional values, rights and duties of the traders. They are making associations and fighting for this or that but not trying to learn how to become a Vaishya. Vaishya too stands for qualities not for caste. Among the modern traders there is neither the caste nor the quality of Vaishyas.

Only the farmers are doing their work to the best of their ability and trying to cultivate as much of land as possible and grow as much as they can. But the present farmers are a broken lot. They have lost the maximum of fertile land; they have no cattle, their fuel supply has vanished with the vanishing trees, they are under loans and the loans are growing. The price of their produce is fixed by others; while the price of factory products are fixed on the basis of cost plus profit plus the discount to be given to the retailers. They were once independent; now they are dependent for everything. The situation is alarming at all the fronts.

The regional leaders are unable to think and diagnose correctly and do something concrete and effective and unfortunately there is no national leader. The leaders neither know the country as a whole nor are trying to know it. They can't grow into a strong national leader without knowing the whole country and without working for all without any prejudice.

Labourers too are now divided in two modern categories of skilled labourers and unskilled labourers. It's very unfortunate that the respectable teachers are counted among the skilled labourers. If and when they are just skilled labourers then they are no longer the respectable teachers of the yester years. Neither they will possess the wealth of knowledge nor can offer *Vidyādāna*. When they won't possess then they won't give knowledge. The teachers may be happy that they are getting enough money but they have lost the footing; the shining and strong pedestal on which they had been down the ages. As labourers they work or evade work.

Indian labourers, in some form or the other are behind each development in the world. They are found everywhere in the world. They simply work and hardly try or fight for recognition.

☛

Hindu Festivals of Vrat and Parva

Hindus lead a life of festivals and festivities; and thus of ecstatic pleasure; mental satisfaction and inner development as with the *Vratas* and *Parvas* they become ready for the coming months and season. Happily enough, all the *vratas* and *parvas* of India are festivals. They work in many directions, serve different purpose and have something for each *varna* and each age group. Above all, they are the means of getting pleasure and success in life, and achieving spirituality. The *vrats* and *parvas* encourage us to lead a pious life and also keep relaxed and give immense pleasure sharing them with the family and society as they are leisure and engagement: both holidays and happydays.

Control, discipline and abiding by rules are the first things taught by the *vratas*. Worshipping of gods is its integral part and the apparent reason. *Vratas* make and keep us conscious towards our goal in life: both to immediate goal and future goal. While observing fast or engaged in a *vrat* the Hindus keep the lustful and filthy ideas away from them so physical vices, vocal, mental and vices that come from contact remain away. The mind is deliberately taken off from them.

Vratas are observed in two ways by observing complete fast for a day or by taking food once on the fasting day. The first one is divided in three categories: *Vāchika*, Vocal; *Kāyika*, physical; and *Mānsuka*, mental. Primarily there are three kinds of *Vratas*: *Nitya*: for immortality; *Naimitika*: for a particular purpose and *Kāmya*: for the fulfillment of a definite desire. The spirituality of a *vrat* depends on the pure, simple, and virtuous deeds and behaviour that are observed consciously with dedication. There are numerous

Vrats, one for almost everyday; but everyone is not required to observe all. It's on the need and wish of a person which *vratas* he/she observes.

Parvas are held for giving instant pleasure and for keeping one busy in some generous and pious deeds and for forgetting the jealousy, lust and enmity. *Ānand*: physical, worldly and spiritual is the aim of the life of a Hindu along with keeping the *Chit*, mind, full of *Sat*, pure energy and benevolent ideas. The whole culture of India is based on this finer and fundamental principle. The *Parvas* beer the seeds of the culture and the fruit of culture blooms to create seeds for the continuity: seeds of *Parvas* turning into the tree of culture and the tree of culture bearing fruits so that new seeds are grown for fresh and new trees of culture and refinement.

Though there are provisions (*vidhāns*) at places; strict provisions to be rigorously followed by all worshippers; but in personal matters, family or village traditions (*kula* and *ghrām paramparā*); they are all free to follow what suits them, is convenient to them or what they usually do.

There are standard list of articles to be used and offered in each *poojā* but Hinduism is so lenient that one can use all, most of them, a few of them, one of them or none of them and perform his or her *poojā*. It's a matter of faith, belief, the acceptance of that belief and inner purity.

Like *Vratas Parvas* also have been divided in three categories on the same pattern and same names. But the *Parvas* are divided in the following nine kinds:

S.N.	Kinds	Cause	Example
1.	Divya Parva	Peculiar position of celestial bodies	Samkrānti, Kumbh, Vāruni, Eclipses
2.	Deva Parva	During Northern sun; Shukla paksha and on the defined days of different gods	Ganeshchaturthi, Ekādashi, Pradosh
3.	Pitri Parva	Complete Āswin Krishna Paksha; and the day of death	Pitripaksha, Vārshika Shrāddha

4.	*Kāla Parva*	The first day of creation; decade and year	New Year's Day on *Chaitra Shukla Pratipadā*
5.	*Jayanti Parva*	The birthdays of Incarnations and great souls	*Ramanavami,Dhanaterash, Janmāshtmi, Gurupurnimā,*
6.	*Prāni Parva*	Hinduism has gods for matter and living beings	*Nāgapanchami, Gopāshtmi*
7.	*Vanaspati Parva*	Hinduism has gods for divine and medicinal plants	*Vatbrikshapoojan; Baikuntha Chaturthi;*
8.	*Mānava Parva*	*Yagya, kathā, satsang, krishi,* harvesting, birthdays	*Bhagawat saptāh, vasantpanchami, Viswakarmāpoojan,* Birthdays, marriagedays, *Grihapravesh, Navānesti*
9.	*Teertha Parva*	The places of Incarnations	*Prayāga,* Gayā

It is very obvious that Hindu Vrats are related to body, existence, feeling and thinking while the *Tyohārs* (festivals) are related to pleasure and entertainment. But all of them are based either on body, food, and agriculture or religion, wisdom and happiness.

Four Āshrams

Hinduism divides or we can safely say, that the wise men of the remote past divided human life in four stages called *āshrams*. They are: *Brahmacharya āshram; Grihasta āshram; Vānaprastha āshram* and *Samyāsa āshram*. Usually people believe that they are given 25 years each. But it's not so. The first one is given the first twenty-five years of life; the 2nd is given the next thirty years of life till the age of 55; the third is given only twenty years up to 75 years of age. If *Vānaprastha* is delayed, its time will be reduced. *Samyāsa* begins from 75. The limitations are not rigid. Exceptions are accepted. In rare cases one can opt for Samyāsa at an early age but it's treated as an incomplete life; not fully lived and well utilized. Such persons are either escapist or rare sublime figures.

Brahmacharya

Brahmachārya āshram: The teachings begin at the age of five. (It's not true in modern context when parents send the kids of just over two to Preps for their physical freedom and, thus are snatching the childhood away from their children.) The *Shāstras* are clear in perception and teaching. For the first five years give as much care and love as you can; then send them to school even against their wishes and of course by force for a minimum of ten years. Treat a boy or a girl as a friend if he/she attains sixteen:

Lālyet panchvarshāni dashvarshāni tādayet,
Prāpte tu shodashe varshe putram mitrawat samācharet.

लालयेत् पंचवर्षाणि दशवर्षाणि ताड्येत् ।
प्राप्ते तु षोडशे वर्षे पुत्रं मित्रवत् समाचरेत् ॥

The shloka clearly mentions 'son' but it's in the case of a father; in the case of a mother, not the son but the daughter will be behaved like a friend. She can't be a friend to her father as the son is admonished from becoming friendly to the mother or mothers, even to sister or sisters.

Brahmacharya is the age of growth, the period of storing energy, of studying everything, and learning control, collecting self, gaining knowledge (knowledge comes dropping slow), forming character, getting refined and living on meager and of becoming cultural and refined.

During this period one is only a *Vidyārthi* (student) gathering knowledge and growing strong for taking the hard life ahead. He should eat little, live away from home with his *āchārya*, read the books, sleep least; half awakened like a dog and concentrate hard like a heron. The following are the said five characteristics of a student:

> *Alpabhogi grihatyāgi shāshtrānusheelanratāh,*
> *Swāna nidrā vako dhyānam*
> *vidyārthinah panchlakshanam.*
> अल्पभोगी गृहत्यागी शास्त्रनुशीलनरता: ।
> श्वान निद्रा वको ध्यानं विद्यार्थिन: पंचलक्षणम् ॥

During the *Brahmacharya* one must and painstakingly avoid the following things: honey; meat; fragrance; garlands of flower; women; intoxicants; violence; unguent, (cream, ointments and pastes to smear the body and face); collyrium (a watery substance applied to eyes, *anjana*); shoes and umbrella; sex, anger and lust; dance, song and music; gambling; abusive-fights; unscrupulous talk; telling lies; looking at women; hugging women; and hatred and disrespect towards others:

> *Varjayenmadhu mānsam cha gandham*
> *mālyam rasāna striah,*
> *Shuktāni yāni sarvāni praninām chaiwa hinsanam.*
> *Abhyangamanjanam*
> *chākshanorupānachchhatra dhāranam,*
> *Kāmam krodham cha lābham cha*
> *nartanam gitavādanam.*

Dyutam cha janavādam cha parivādam tathā nritam,
Strinām cha prekshanālambhamupaghātam parasya cha.

वर्जयेन्मधु मांसं च गन्धं माल्यं रसान् स्त्रिय: ।
शुक्तानि यानि सर्वाणि प्राणिनां चैव हिंसनम् ॥
अभ्यंगमंजनं चाक्ष्नोरूपानच्छत्रधारणम् ।
कामं क्रोधं च लाभं च नर्तनं गीतवादनम् ॥
द्यूतं च जनवादं च परिवादं तथा नृतम् ।
स्त्रीणां च प्रेक्षणालम्भमुपघातं परस्य च ॥

मनुस्मृति २: १७७-१७९

It is very sad that under outer influences the students and Brahmachāries are being forced to do all these things that they must avoid. The whole of society including the leaders, teachers and guardians are helping them to get deeply indulged in these acts. All good things that have positive values have deliberately been taken off from their eyes and reach; and they have easy access to all the vile things that is corrupting their mind and character. When they enter the next phase of life they carry over all these ills and thus, the whole of the society is getting corrupt. It's the conspiracy to make all others bad and immoral so, there will be no question of legal, moral or ethical or even religious. There will be no morality in the society. The western people, under that conspiracy, are trying to follow Indian ways to become refined and cultured; and throwing others, particularly to Indians, into the drain of sex, physical relations, nakedness, wine, snacks and all other character-pollutants.

During this period one has to grow and be strong and responsible enough to take the responsibilities of a householder.

Grihastāshram

Grihastāshram is the toughest period in the life of a human being. He has to do a lot during this period and has to live always under pressure and demand. Neither the pressure will be released nor the demand will be reduced. One has to cope with it. The expenses and the responsibilities will increase during every passing year.

In *grihastāshram* too Hindus are detached in attachment. They work and earn but not only for themselves but for many. In his earning; not only his family members but; the religion, society, the king, the country, thief, beggars, downtrodden, animals, birds and insects too have their share. He works hard to fulfill the needs of the family, the society and others. He earns for them too and willingly shares his earning. He has control over his 'self' and senses. So, even under duress he works hard and for all. He faces every situation boldly and endures.

There is a definite reason behind it. All the persons living in other three *āshrams* are totally dependent on the *grihastas*, the householders for almost all worldly needs. He spends least on himself and maximum on the family and society. He does not have to accumulate wealth for he has to spend his earning. He raises a family not for himself but for the society and humanity. That sense of doing for others gives him immense satisfaction. Moreover, only diligent men of character and control over self can succeed for the collective demands are very high:

> *Yathā wāyum samāshritya vartante sarvajantawah,*
> *Tathā grihasthamāshritya vartante srva āshramāh.*
> *Yasmāt trayo apyāshramino shānenānnena chānwaham,*
> *Grihastenaiwa dhāryanate tasmājjeshthāshramo grihi.*
> *Sa sandhāryah prayatnena swargamakshayamikshitā,*
> *Sukham chehechchhatā nityam yo*
> *adhāro durbalendriyaih.*

> यथा वायुं समाश्रित्य वर्तन्ते सर्वजन्तव: ।
> तथा गृहस्थमाश्रित्य वर्तन्ते सर्व आश्रमा: ॥
> यस्मात् त्रयोऽप्याश्रमिणो शानेनान्नेन चान्वहम् ।
> गृहस्थेनैव धार्यन्ते तस्माज्ज्येष्ठाश्रमो गृही ॥
> स सन्धार्य: प्रयत्नेन स्वर्गमक्षयमिच्छता ।
> सुखं चेहेच्छता नित्यं योऽधार्यो दुर्बलेन्द्रियै: ॥

(मनुस्मृति, ३/७७-७९)

(As all the living beings survive on the 'life-element' in them, in the same way all the members of the society survive on the *grihastāshramis* (householders). In other words householders are the life element of others. Only the householders earn, collect and give *vidyā* and *anna* (fulfill everyday needs) of other three *āshramas*; and hence, they are the best. He, that wishes to get heaven after death and pleasure and happiness in this life, should carefully enter the *grihastāshram*. Those, that are weak and have no control over body, mind and senses, can't enter and fulfill the responsibilities of this phase of life.)

The entry into *grihastāshram* begins with marriage. One has to get married after taking permission from the elders, parents and guardians. Either they select a cultured and suitable bride themselves or the guardians will select the bride. Usually, in marriages, the elders, that are experienced persons, think of *chāsā* (achievements and chances) *bāsā* (residence and living) *dashā* (present condition) and *dishā* (direction of growth and development) of both the bride and bridegroom; that the younger generation and inexperienced people will not think of and compare before giving final consent. As these things are not being considered nowadays, so, the failure of marriages surface; and even the brides are attacked, killed or burnt alive. It's the most heinous crime and the fall of man to the nadir.

One must make one's mind clear about the dowry that has taken the most ugly turn. It's not for taking money but for giving the most essential articles for starting a new household. There has never been any demand. Demanding money or articles is definitely degradation. It shows the lust. It's useless to marry a daughter in a family where the lust rules or a son in a family that has ego coming directly from out of wealth. One should directly refuse to marry the girl into that family if there is a demand; and also refuse to marry a son into the family that offers money. Dowry is never the sale of a son or bribe for a girl.

The situation was totally under control before independence. But it's alarming now. The elders must meet, discuss and come to a consensus and abolish it. It has taken the sap from the life of each and every family and parent. They, that take huge amount, are definitely losing their sons.

Those, that don't have a balanced view and behave miserly neither get respect nor are happy. Those that escape from such huge responsibilities are the weakest thread in the social set and the lineage of living human beings. Those that indulge into immoral acts are not human beings. They are like small insects or huge demons (*laghu krimi athwā brihad daitya*).

Vānprashtha

The beginning of the 6th Chapter of *Manusmriti* deals with the *Vānaprashthāshram* and from there on it deals with *Samyāsa*.

When a person has attained the age of 55; has fulfilled his social and family responsibilities, has grown weak and the sense organs are growing weaker; has got grandchildren, then one can accept *vānaprashtha*; give the charge of the family and its traditions and leave the house. One can leave his wife behind under the guardianship of his elder son or can take with him but he is not allowed any physical relationship with her or any woman. He can't earn during that period. He will have to depend on alms so that he gets rid of his ego and become humble. He will have to share the alms with others that visit his *āshram*. He will have to take bath thrice and remain busy in self-study of Scriptures. Manusmriti 6:8. There is another grand binding, mostly for energy and digestion; that he can't take cereals or anything produced on cultivated land. Like Rishis he will have to live on the fruits of uncultivated lands and the vegetation in water. Even if he is hungry he can't eat them. (Ibid 6:13-16.) He can keep eatables either for a day or maximum for a month. He has to lead a really very hard life, to make his body lean and weak from outside but strong from inside. For it he must go to a plain at the hilltop and face the rain in the open; and wear wet clothes during the winters. He can't indulge in anything that gives pleasure, observe celibacy, sleep on earth, should not feel attached to the temporary residence, and prefer to live under a tree. Begging is allowed only in the case that one is not getting fruits or roots of plants to eat. In that case one can take only eight morsels. All those that do it are accepted and treated as Brāhmins; because he tries to get revelation, to purify and know the inner self. If there is *Vānaprashtha*, there will be no problem of old age and no need of old age houses. Such houses are providing luxury and taking away the opportunity of further purification of mind and soul. Those that accept it become pure like 24 carat gold after spending over a decade in forests or at uninhabited places far away from the pleasures and luxury of life.

A person with weak willpower will not agree for it. The love for luxury, easy life and physical pleasure has weakened and weakening the Hindus. As a result very few persons are opting for *Vānaprashtha*; and incidentally, without being burnt in the testing fire of *Vānprashtha* one can't be a *Samyāsi*.

Samyās

Only those that spent a decade or so in *Vānaprashtha* are capable of and eligible to become a *samyāsi* (mendicant). Only after attaining the age of 75 one can accept *samyāsa*. The moment one accepts it he becomes free from *varnās*. He is no longer a Brāhmin or Kshatriya or Vaishya or Shudra. He can't bring harm to any living being. No one is afraid of him and he has no fear: *bhayam nāsti kutashchana*.

A *Samyāsi* can't move in a group and except for the four months of rainy season he can't stay at one place for more than three days. He can't carry or store anything other than *Danda* (staff); *kamandalu* (an earthen, wooden pot or one made up of skin of gourd); *kanthā* (a patch-work garment) and *kaupina* (a small piece of cloth to cover the private parts). He can't touch women or wealth including gold for detachment is his wealth. He can go to a habited area only once in a day and beg and eat once only. (Ibid 6:43-59)

Sanyāsi should not wish to die or try to live longer. By controlling the senses, by getting rid of love and hate, by not inflicting any mental or physical injury to any living being a *Samyāsi* gets the Nectar, the *Moksha*, Salvation and bliss:

> *Indriyānām nirodhena rāhadweshakshayena cha,*
> *Ahimsaā cha bhutānāmamritatwāya kalpate.*
>
> ***Manusmriti 6:60***

इन्द्रियाणां निरोधेन रागद्वेषक्षयेण च ।
अहिंस या च भूतानाममृतत्वाय कल्पते ॥

❧

Solah Samskãrs

Sixteen Samskãrs in Hinduism are bindings for keeping one under discipline so that one can be free from anxiety and acquiring inner power. It is for the refinement, for making one cultured, civilized and sublime. In the long run it helps in smooth running of the society and development and growth of an individual in right direction.

Sixteen samskãrs give solid base to individuals and families for progress and prosperity. Life begins from imperfection and moves towards perfection. Whether perfection is achieved or not that is a different matter. The most important thing is that a person or a family tried for perfection or not. One must observe and absorb the best human and divine qualities. One can't do it on his own. Hinduism aims at giving opportunity and aid to individuals through rites and rituals and these samskãrs are the best way that bring the experienced closer to an individual and provides opportunity to an individual to learn the intricacies and complexities of life.

In every ritual the pandits teach what is provided by the Scriptures, the parents and grand parents teach what is in the family traditions and what are variations in different families and *varnas*. This is the most practical way of teaching. The *jagyopavit samskãr* makes one *dwij*, gives a new life; and one feels reborn and rejuvenated while the *vivãha samskãr* prepares the bride, bridegroom, their respective families and societies for the marriage, that ensures its long life. Till it was observed strictly according to the rituals there were virtually no divorce in Hindu families. The western influence and the modernity have changed the scenario and many untoward incidents are regularly occurring.

Sixteen Samskārs are based on deep psychological thinking. The theory is not taught but the applied psychological treatment frees one from depression and other such diseases. For example: the last rites after the death of a person. The death of a family member is a shock and it shakes all the members, relatives and the near and dear ones. There is a lot of psychological pressure. For four days after putting a dead body on the pyre, a few rituals are observed only in the early morning and early evening but from the fifth day the cleaning of the abode begins. Members take bath and the dirty clothes are given to the washerman. He deliberately comes early and starts asking for the clothes. They make hurry to give the dirty clothes. Such intruptions, works and preparations for the final *shrāddha* on the 10th, 11th, and the 12th, days provide natural distraction to mind. The weeping of other members, stops and that of the widow or the children is reduced to bare minimum. Yet some weep at certain hour. But the engagement in the rituals and feast lessens the mental burden. It provides relief. Only the Hindus perform this peculiar and essential ritual.

The following are known as *Solah Samskars* (Sixteen Samskārs). One can be baptized into the following 16 different ways at different stages of life for different gains. They are:

> *garbhādhānam punsvanam seemanto jātkarma cha*
> *nāmkriyāniskramane annāsam vapankriyā.*
> *karnbedho vratādesho vedārambha kriyāvidhih*
> *keshāntah snānmudwāho vivāhagniparigrahah.*
> *Tretāgnisangrahscheti samskārāh shodash smritāh*

Vyās Smriti 1/13-15

गर्भाधानं पुंसवनं सीमन्तो जातकर्म च ।
नामक्रियानिश्क्रमणेऽन्नाशनं वपनक्रिया ॥
कर्णवेधो व्रतादेशो वेदारम्भक्रियाविधि: ।
केशान्त: स्नानमुद्वाहो विवाहाग्निपरिग्रह: ॥
त्रेताग्निसंग्रहश्चेति संस्कारा: षोडश स्मृता: ।

1. Conception (*garvādhānan*); for better children

2. Fertilization (*punswan*), three months, after conception for 'life-being' and safety

3. upgradation of limitations (*seemantoannayan*), a month before delivery for safe and secure birth

4. The ceremony performed at the birth of a child (*jātkarma*), performed just after the birth to be sure that all necessary precautions have been taken

5. Naming (*nāmkaran*), eleven days after to give an individual identity

6. ceremoniously going out (*niskraman*), after four months the child is taken out into the open to face the wind and sunshine

7. Ceremoniously giving a child its first cereal food (*annaprāshana*) after six months

8. Sowing seeds (*vapankriyā*)

9. Investiture with the sacred thread (*upnayan*)

10. piercing of ears (*karnabedha*)

11. Offering of hair (*keshant / shamshru*)

12. Initiation into study (*vedārambh*) to start study

13. Convocation or Baptism into Vedas (*vedasnān*),

14. Marriage (*vivāh*)

15. Encircling the marriage-fire (*vivāhgniparigrah*)

16. Baptism into the conservation of fire (*tretāgnisangrah*); to start a domestic life.

❧

Varnāshrama Dharma

Manu is blamed, for 'dividing' the human beings in four different categories; by ignorant people that have either not read Manusmriti or have not understood it adequate enough to realise their fallacy. He classified the human beings on the basis of the works that they were doing. This classification has nothing to do with the birth. Manu has clearly stated that **everyone is born as Shudra**: *janmanā shudro jāyet*. The difference lies in the conscious effort of a person and the **inner growth achieved**, *samskārāta dwija uchyate*. The better one grows the higher or different status one gets. It seems very easy to be born as Brāhmin and enjoy the privileges of a Brāhmin. It's not easy, it's exceedingly difficult to be a Brāhmin and remain a Brāhmin.

Mostly because the persons born in different Varnas grew up to, opted for the related work and became eligible to be called a person of that *Varna*. So, in the course of time, '*Varnavyawasthā*' was either willingly accepted or forcibly accepted 'by birth'. Birth has nothing to do with the *Varnavyawasthā*. It's the work and growth that determines the *Varna* of a person. If a person born in a Brāhmin family joins military service he is not a Brāhmin but a Kshatriya; if he starts a business and becomes a trader then he becomes a Vaishya or if he works as a labourer he is a Shudra. A guard at the gate of a big factory or a small shop cannot be a Brāhmin. He is a Shudra and he should be treated like that. A person teaching somewhere successfully cannot be a Shudra, he should be treated as a Brāhmin. There should not be confusion about it. *Varnavyawasthā* should never be accepted on the ground of birth. It cropped up and was enflamed during the Middle Ages to divide the Hindus. It was successfully done. Hindus were and are divided. People should be bold enough to claim their Varna on the basis of the work that they are doing. In the Gitā Krishna has openly and clearly stated,

"I have created the men of four Varna on the basis of *guna* (qualities) *karma* (profession) and *vibhāga* (division or gradation)":

chāturvarnyam mayā srishtam gunakarmavibhāgashah. (The Gitā 4:13)

"Brāhmin, Kshatriya, Vaishya and Shudra have been divided according to their *karma* (profession), *swabhāva* and *guna* (quality)":

Brāhmankshatryavinshām shudrānām cha paramtapa,
Karmāni prabibhaktāni swabhāwaprabhwairgunaih.

ब्राह्मणक्षत्रियविशां शूद्राणां च परंतप ।
कर्माणि प्रविभक्तानि स्वभावप्रभवैर्गुणै: ॥

गीता १८:४१

In the body of the society, country or religion Brāhmins are the mouth, Kshatriya are the chest, Vaishya are the thigh and the Shudra are the legs. They have their respective importance, are the integral parts of the whole and keep the whole active. At some places it's symbolically presented but the fact remains that the *Varnadharma* was created on the basis of the division of labour. Maharshi Vālmiki has imagined them in that way. In the *Aranyakānda* of his *Rāmāyana* *Jatāyu* says to the God's incarnation Rāma, "Brahmins appeared from the mouth, the Kshatriyas from the breast, the Vaishyas from the thigh and the Shudras from the feet."

Mukhto Brāhman jātā urasah kshatriyāstathā,
Urubhyām jagire Vaishyāh padābhām
Shudrā iti shrutih.

मुखतो ब्राह्मणा जाता उरस: क्षत्रियास्तथा ।
ऊरूभ्यां जगिरे वैश्या: पद्भ्यां शूद्रा इति श्रुति: ॥

(वाल्मीकि रामायण, अरण्यकांड १४:३०)

It can be made debatable but the fact remains that all of them combined together make the greatest and the most ancient, original and Eternal Religion. Those that try to divide them, have only one thing in mind to weaken the country and the religion. A united India is always a power to reckon with. It was divided after Harshavardhan and the country faced resultant slavery for about 1200 years. Some people wrongly argue that if a person changes his profession once or twice then in which Varna he would be placed? His Varna is the Varna according to his present profession. If he changes the profession his Varna will automatically change. This question has come to light when the census is done on the basis of caste, sub-caste and creed that are other ways to divide the society and maintain the distance. A united society will automatically become strong.

The skill and success of a person depends mostly on the family background and the environment. Personal devotion, confidence and concentration also help him. In India a weaver, a carpenter, a mason, a fisherman or a washer man, etc. usually earn enough to feed and foster their family members. They are very skilled and very laborious. Earlier on they used to serve the society in many ways but the western materialism has affected their life too. They are now working overtime for money. In that process they have lost the pleasure and are unhappy. After independence their financial position has improved but the social and spiritual aspects of life are no longer visible. They are losing fast their grip over the soil, climate, nature and natural living.

So far the profession is concerned the Varna has helped the Hindus. One becomes easily skilled in one's paternal profession. It's easier for the son of a carpenter to know his trade as he sees, handles and uses the tools from childhood. The same thing happens to the son of a businessman. He learns it easily and automatically. The son of a Brāhmin reads and recites shlokas from very early stage. Moreover, there is neither jealousy among the persons of different trade and professions, nor one wishes to take over the profession of others. Among the four Varnas there is no other difference. Their souls are the same, they can grow well, work and worship and get salvation. If and when one does his duties well and plays his role to the best of his ability, he gets transformed. The reward is always there.

Brāhmin: According to Shri Krishna (Gita 18:42) they are Brāhmin that are self-restraint, have won over their senses, readily suffer for religion and can forgive others. They have a simple and humble heart and tolerant body, are theists, possess knowledge of the Scriptures and have experienced the absolute truth. These are a part of the nature and life of a Brāhmin:

Shamo damastapah shaucham kshāntirārjavamewa cha,
Gyānam vigyānamāstikyam brahmakarma swabhāvajam.

शमो दमस्तप: शौचं क्षान्तिरार्जवमेव च ।
ज्ञानं विज्ञानमास्तिक्यं ब्रह्मकर्म स्वभावजम् ।

(गीता-१८/४२)

In the *Vanparva* of Mahābhārata (180:21) it has been clearly stated, "O the Serpent King! He is said to be a Brāhmin that has truth, charity, forgiveness, morality, humbleness, penance and sympathy and kindness":

Satyam dānam kshamā
sheelamānrishansayam tapo ghrinā,
Drishyante yatra Nāgendra sa brāhman iti smritah.

सत्यं दानं क्षमा शीलमानृशंस्यं तपो घृणा ।
दृष्यन्ते यत्र नागेन्द्र स ब्राह्मण इति स्मृत: ।।

(महाभारत, आदि पर्व-१८०/२१)

Kshatriya: According to Shri Krishna (Gitā 18:43) the warriors are the Kshatriya. They have valour, brightness, patience, wisdom and presence of mind and they never run away from the battlefield. They are charitable and have a sense of owning others. So, they rule according to the Scriptures and save the interest of all. They work for everyone's welfare. They treat the people as their sons and foster and protect them. These are in the nature of Kshatriya:

Shauryam tejo dhritirdākshyam
yuddhe chāpyapalāyanam,
Dānamiswarbhāwashcha kshātram karma swabhavajam.

शौर्यं तेजो धृतिर्दाक्ष्यं युद्ध चाप्यपलायनम् ।
दानमीश्वरभावश्च क्षात्रं कर्म स्वभावजम् ।।

(गीता-१८/४३)

Vaishya and Shudra: According to Shri Krishna (Gitā 18:44) agriculture, animal husbandry, purchase and sell and truthfulness are in the nature of the Vaishyas; and to serve all is the natural duty of the Shudras:

Krishigaurakshya vānijyam
Vaishyakarma swabhāwajam,
Paricharyātmakam karma Shudrasyāpi swabhāwajam.
कृषिगौरक्ष्य त्राणिज्यं वैश्यकर्म स्वभावजम् ।
परिचर्यात्मक कर्म शूद्रस्यापि स्वभावजम् ॥

(गीता-१८/४४)

According to Shri Krishna (Gitā 18:45) one becomes skilled and expert in own profession and trade and just by doing the best in his natural *karma* (work) one gets *siddhi* (prosperity, success, fulfillment and salvation):

swe swe karmanyabhiratah sansiddhim labhate narah.
स्वे स्वे कर्मण्यभिरत: संसिद्धिं लभते नर:।

Like many other things *Varnāshrama Dharma* too is not truly followed in its pure form. Once they were pillars, nowadays are breaking away. Naturally, the whole structure is falling apart. Indian society is not getting the strength from the roots, pillars, walls and stems. All the four Varnas are divided in many ways and on many counts. They have different categories and subcatagories; and numerous unresolved differences. The disintegration is obvious resulting in weakening all the four Varnas; and hence, in weakening the whole country. The process of weakening is still on; along with the conspiracies. The conspirators are wise, resourceful and active. We have forgotten that united we stand and divided we fall. We have to learn a few lessons and take strict measures to defeat the divisive forces to regain our ground and status.

Chãr Purushãrtha: Four Pursuits

Hinduism believes in and declares that a man has only four objects for pursuit in life called, *Chãr Purushãrtha*: *Dharma, Artha, Kãma* and *Moksha*. All human activities are directed towards these four directions and man has no other pursuit in life. All other pursuits that we can think of are a part of one of these general pursuits.

Manu is accepted as omniscient, *sarbgyãnamaya*. According to Manusmriti 1:102 *Swãyambhuva Manu,* the wise man created this Scripture for Human beings: *Swãyambhuva Manurdhimãnidam shãstramakalpayat.* He showed man what was to be done and what was not to be done: *prãmãnyam dharmashãstrasya kãryãkãryavyawasthitau.* In the course of deciding the duties of mankind he gave four objects of pursuit to man known as *Chãr Purushãrtha*: They are **Dharma, Artha, Kãma** and **Moksha.** Directives have also been given, how these can be achieved in life. Control and balance are two key directives. Uncontrolled and imbalance will ruin not only a person and his family, but the society and eventually humanism. It will bring pain, anxiety, wars, terror, destruction and extinction. While by following the directives man can ensure a long healthy and happy life, growth, development and prosperity to all: human and non-human. Most of the non-humans have come to the brink of extinction only because of human excesses. One has to be wise and far-sighted and follow the four pursuits rigorously to make and keep the earth as the most suitable place for life as it is the only planet that creates, fosters and enjoys life.

Dharma: In a broader sense *Dharma* is the total work worth doing. In accepted terms *Dharma* is to perform and complete the duties dictated, doctrines laid down, moral character and social responsibility spelled out by the Scriptures. One can do well for oneself by doing well to others. Whatever the position may be don't inflict injury or give pain to others; on the other hand, help all: *paropakārāya punyāya pāpāya parpidam*: It's the essence of all Scriptures according to the greatest mind of all time and editor: *Veda Vyāsa*. It's a very straightforward theory. Be selfless and get all; be selfish and lose all. It appears odd but is very simple.

Take an example of a teacher. Where lies his selfishness: in the dedicated and engrossed teaching. If he studies hard and teaches well, he will get respect from every corner; will be enriched with knowledge and teaching experience. He will grow and get promotion. It will be so, because he works for others. On the other hand he can save his time by becoming a shirker, by evading classes, by taking all sorts of leaves, by keeping engaged in different economically profitable engagements or can enter the classrooms late and leave the class early or will talk on other current topics and evade the syllabus. What will eventually happen? He won't get the respect of students or guardian or colleagues. He will be sent so cause notices, be given warning or suspended, if not, then he will come to see his institution and return back without teaching anyone. He will lose the honour and respect, though, he may get his fixed salary.

The synthesized and precise conclusion has been given by Krishna in the Gita; such a condensed statement is nowhere else to be found. It's the most concise and vividly expressed Dharma: *sarbbhutahite ratāh*, **indulged in working for the welfare of all**. Its importance can be marked and felt with the fact that in the Gitā it has been given at two places: 2:25 and 12:4.

Dharma is not one and static, in broader sense it relates to and is representative of and assimilates all the deeds of all the human beings. Our Dharma includes *Vyaktidharma* (personal religion), *Poojādharma* (worshipping), *Āshramdharma* (four stages of life), *Varnadharma* (four strata in society), *Gunadharma* (related to quality), *Nimitadharma* (specific purpose), *Sāmānya dharma* (general), *Āpatadharma* during emergency; *Yugadharma* according to the era; *Pitridharma* (duties towards father); *Mātridharma* (duties towards mother), *Putradhrma* (duties of or towards a son); *Mitradharma* (duties of and towards a friend, *Rājadharma* (duties of or to a king), *Kshatriyadharma* (duties of a warrior or guard), *Vaisyadharma* (duties of a businessman), *Samayadharma* (duties at some particular hour) and so on. It includes virtues, merit, function, attribute, nature, quality, onus, justice, righteousness, duty, law, doctrine, instructions, property, business, daily observation of religious rites, faith, sect, honesty, theology, religious rules, etc. Morally binding deeds must be performed, and performed well:

Āchārah paramo dharamah
shrutyauktah smārta yewa cha,
Tasmādasmin sadā yukto nityam syādātmawān dwijah.

आचार: परमो धर्म: श्रुत्युक्त: स्मार्त एव च ।
तस्मादस्मिन् सदा युक्तो नित्यं स्यादात्मवान् द्विज: ।।

(मनुस्मृति १:१०८)

Dharma in Hinduism is to follow the Vedas and the Smritis and to behave in the way the elders behave; *mahājano yena gatah sa panthāh* (That is the way on which the great souls move.) One should adopt the behaviour that one likes. The behaviour of other persons towards someone that is appreciated, liked and loved should be followed. If one likes respect then he must show respect to others; if he likes to be loved then must show love to others. If one does not like jealousy, hate, show of pride then he/ she should not show these towards others. One should never behave in the way that he dislikes. Mahābhārata makes it clear:

Shruyatām dharmasarvaswam
shrutwā chaiwāwadhyāyanam,
Ātamanah pratikulāni pareshām na samācharet.

श्रूयतां धर्मसर्वस्वं श्रुत्वा चैवावध्यायनम् ।
आत्मन: प्रतिकूलानि परेशां न समाचरेत् ।।

The following ten are the characteristics of *dharma* (religion) adopted and followed by a religious person: *dhritih* (firmness of mind, satisfaction), *kshamā* (forgiveness), *dama* (self restraint, endurance of pain), *asteyam* (not stealing the property of others), *shaucha* (purity, freedom from defilement, virtue), *indriya nigrah* (control over sense organs), *dhi* (knowledge, wisdom, intellect), *satya* (truth, truthfulness), and *akrodha* (lack of anger, forgiving):

Dhritih chhamā damoasteam shauchamindriyanigrahah,
Dhirvidyā satyamakrodho dashakam Dharmalakshanam.

धृति: क्षमा दमोऽस्तेयं शौचमिन्द्रियनिग्रह: ।
धीर्विद्या सत्यमक्रोधो दशकं धर्मलक्षणम् ।।

मनुस्मृति ६:९२

These original ten teachings and traits were intensively extended. In Shrimadbhāgawad Mahāpurāna they have become thirty. All of them are followed. They are *satya* (truth); *dayā* (pity); *tapa* (penance); *shaucha* (purity); *uchita-anuchita* (sensible-insensible, relevant-irrelevant); *mana-sanyam* (control over mind); *indria-sanyam* (control over senses); *ahimsā* (non-violence); *brahmacharya* (celibacy); *tyāga* (sacrifice); *swādhyāya* (self-study); *niskapatatā* (innocence); *santosh* (contentment); *samdrishti* (equality); *sevā* (service); *nibriti* (detachment); *anabhimāna* (ego-less); *ātmachintan* (meditation); *bhojan-vitaran* (giving food to living beings); *ekātmabodha* (oneness); *santvāni-shravana* (listening to saints); *guna-shravan* (listening to the qualities of the God); *bhakti-kirtan* (singing in praise of the Lord); *iswar-smaran* (remembering the God); *iswar-sevā* (to serve the Lord); *bhagawad-poojan* (worshipping the Lord); *namaskār* (greetings and salutations); *dasya-sakhya-samarpan* (to behave as the slave and friend to God and total surrender to Him). By following these thirty ways he leads a happy, healthy and complete life. His wishes are fulfilled:

Satyam dayā tapah shaucham titiksheshā shamo damah,
Ahimsā brahmacharya cha tyāgah swādhyāya ārjawam.
Santoshah samadrik sevā grāmyehoparamah shanaih,
Nrinām viparyayeheksā maunamātmavimarshanam.
Annādyādeh sambibhago bhutebhyashcha yathārhatah,
Teshwātmadevatābuddhih sutarām nrishu pāndava.
Shravanam kirtanam chāsya smaranam mahatām gateh,
Sevejyāwanatirdāsyam sakhamātmasamarpanam.
Nrināmayam paro dharmah sarveshām samudāhritah,
Trinshallakshanawān rājan sarvātmā yena tushyati.

Shrimadbhāgawad Mahāpurāna 7:11: 8-12

सत्यं दया तप: शौचं तितिक्षेक्षा शमो दम: ।
अहिंसा ब्रह्मचर्य च त्याग: स्वाध्याय आर्जवम् ॥
संतोष: समदृक् सेवा ग्राम्येहोपरम: शनै: ।
नृगां विपर्ययेहेक्षा मौनमात्मविमर्शनम् ॥
अन्नाद्यदे: संविभागो भूतेभ्यश्च यथार्हत: ।
तेष्वात्मदेवताबुद्धि: सुतरां नृषु पाण्डव ॥
श्रवणं कीर्तनं चास्य स्मरणं महतां गते: ।
सेवेज्यावनतिर्दास्यं सख्यमात्मसमर्पणम् ॥
नृणामयं परो धर्म: सर्वेषां समुदाहृत: ।
त्रिंशल्लक्षणवान् राजन् सर्वात्मा येन तुष्यति ॥

Artha: When a person enters the life of household, he needs many things for fostering his family. Till then he had been free from the burden. He has to fulfill the needs, the personal, family and social requirements. For earning these things he has to work. They work better that have prepared themselves during the period of learning. They earn well and feed their family well, that have inner ability and skill. Hinduism prohibits all from earning and collecting wealth and articles for luxury. It admonishes all to acquire wealth from wrong means. To accumulate a lot of wealth even through rightful means is also prohibited.

Shrimadbhāgwad Mahāpurāna as well as the Smritis lay stress on earning and keeping a bit more wealth than actually needed.

A dialogue between Yudhistir and Nārad is narrated in Shrimad Bhāgawadmahāpurāna. Yudhistir asked Nārad what is the Dharma of a householder? How much should he earn? In response Nārad said, "One has the right to earn and accumulate only that much which feeds him and his family or which is enough to satiate the needs of the body. If one accumulates more than that then he is a thief":

Yāwad mriyeta jatharam tāwat swatwam hi dehinām,
adhikam yoabhimanyeta sa steno dandamarhati.

यावद् म्रियेत जठरं तावत् स्वत्वं हि देहिनाम् ।
अधिकं योऽभिमन्येत स स्तेनो दण्डमर्हति ॥

Shrimad Bhāgawadmahāpurāna 7:14:8

Contentment should be at the root of artha-sanchaya (accumulation of wealth). Manusmriti (4:12) asks that those who wish to be happy must show control because contentment is permanent. Contentment is needed for happiness and discontentment is the root cause of evils and suffering:

Santosham parmāsthāya sukhārthi sanyato bhawet,
Santoshmulam hi sukham dukhmulam viparyayah.

संतोषं परमास्थाय सुखार्थी संयतो भवेत् ।
संतोषमूलं हि सुखं दु:खमूलं विपर्यय: ॥

(मनुस्मृति-४/१२)

Grihasthās has been asked to give ten percent of their earning through ethical ways to others in charity for pleasing the gods:

Nyāyopārjitah vitasya dashamāshena dhimah;
Kartayo viniyogonshcha Ishwarprityarthameva cha.

न्यायोपार्जिं वित्तस्य दशमांशेन धीमत: ।
कर्तव्यो विनियोगश्च ईश्वरप्रीत्यर्थमेव च ॥

But those that are rich enough, kind and generous, should divide their earning or wealth in five parts only: *dharma* (religion); *yasha* (fame); *artha* (business); *kāma* (everyday use) and *swajana* (relatives).

Dharmāya yashase arthāya kāmāyaswajanāya cha;
Panchdhā vibhajana vittimihāmutra cha modate.

धर्माय यशसेऽर्थाय कामाय स्वजनाय च ।
पंचधा विभजन् वित्तमिहामुत्र च मोदते ।

There are special instructions for the Brahmins. They cannot accumulate wealth. The conditions, laid down for the Brahmins and the latitude given to them, must open the eyes of all, 'How much wealth one should acquire and store?'

He was the best Brahmin that stored wealth or food for a day. He was called *Aswastanika*. The next best was he that stored for three days only, and was called *trāihika*; the next best was the Brahmin that accumulated for a year only and was called, *kumbhidhānyaka* and the last one was that accumulated wealth or money for three years. He was called *kusuladhānyaka*. It was the maximum limit. But modern man remains discontented even after earning for many generations to come. Kabir was balanced when he said that one should earn or get enough (or a bit more than) to feed self, the family and the *atithi* (guests).

It was true before our independence but most of the Brahmins started accumulating wealth. Obviously, it's falling from a height. It's deterioration. Not only they but other people too must stop for sometime and think over the 'complete present scenario' to decide the course of their life. Will they go the western way for total annihilation or change the ways for making and keeping the earth as the mother to ensure the continuity of life on the mother earth. The option is in their hand. They can go for a life of luxury at the cost of the natural wealth, natural phenomenon and the living beings of the earth or they can use restrain and save the atmosphere and the five gross elements for life to sustain. It's not for the first time that such situations have come. The fights of gods against the demons had always the smooth running of life as the real cause. The demons were destroying all life giving and life-keeping elements etc. So, they had to be defeated and killed for the survival of all. At present, human beings are being killed in thousands of ways and the family is being given compensation in money. One has to be clear in mind, is money adequate or inadequate compensation for a son or husband or a father?

Kāma: Brahman is in the form of subtle power, eternal energy, He gives energy and creates system of systems. He is the living element and the life-element. He endows others powers to create and procreate. *Kāma* (sex) is a system of creation, rather it's a system of systems and has many known and unknown forms and systems. Although, we say that the same system of procreation works in a group of living beings but it's not true. The systems differ. Despite great human effort and great human knowledge all the systems are not known. We simply make a guess with the help of hundred of things that we closely observe. In mammals it's different, it's different in marsupials. Fish have their different ways of procreation and birds have many different ways.

At least, in human beings, *Kāma* and *kāma-bhāva* is very prominent. *Kāma* is there for only procreation but modern man has declared and insists that it's for pleasure. When it's for pleasure then, there is no limitation; and if there is no control and limitation then it's a cause of great physical pain. In the beginning, it may seem to be all right, but when the body weakens, the organs get tired, then numerous filthy diseases attack. They hardly kill a person but that is the tragedy. One is cursed to live with those diseases, pain and physical and mental suffering.

As precaution and for safety, the Scriptures frame rules for it. Manusmriti (4:1) tells to finish the education in the first quarter of life and then, one should marry according to the rules and tradition and start a life of a householder: *dwitiyamāyusho bhāgam kritadāro grihe vaseta*. He directed all to marry one woman and lead life with her:

> *Ritukālābhigāmi syāt swadāraniratah sadā,*
> *Parvarja vrajechchhaināw tadvrato ratikāmyayā.*

ऋतुकालाभिगामी स्यात् स्वदारनिरतः सदा ।
पर्ववर्जं व्रजेच्चैनां तद्व्रतो रतिकाम्यया ॥

मनुस्मृति ३:४५

In the Shāshtras eight types of sexual relations or satisfactions have been described. They are: remembering the partner (memory of previous experiences); talking about physical relations; playing with the opposite sex; looking longingly; secret talk; planning, effort and determination for meetings; and copulation:

Smaranam kirtanam kelih prekshanam guhyabhāshanam,
Samkalpo adhawasāyashcha kiryānishpatirewa.

स्मरणं कीर्तनं केलिः प्रेक्षणं गुह्यभाषणम् ।
संकल्पोऽध्यवसायश्च क्रियानिष्पत्तिरेव ॥

Maharshi Vātsyāyana gave a lot of mind and energy to it for the benefit and satisfaction of the householders so that they can get pleasure and remain healthy. With their least knowledge and tremendous attractions and provocations the modern man has lost control over sex. As a result, the secretion of hormones is affected; blood becomes impure, diseases are rampant, infertility and weaknesses are growing fast, and thus, both pleasure and health are lost. It must be made a satisfying act, not a defeat.

Moksha: Hinduism declares *Moksha* (salvation, final liberation, beatitude or redemption) as the ultimate end of human life. Hinduism holds the clear view that we are born to grow from inside and to become better and better in every subsequent life with faith, devotion, humility, service to others and other good and virtuous deeds. From the very beginning one should lead a pure life, free of lust. One should not inflict injury to others. If some persons bring harm to a person he should forgive them. This way one can help one's soul to attain near perfection. With the help of self study, meditation, devotion and worshipping one can realise the Truth, see and know the self and get united with the self which is the replica of the Brahman. Manu is vociferous and direct about it. He says: "Man with his greater deeds becomes sublime and equal to gods, and with his deeds alone he transcends the five gross elements and attains salvation":

Pravritam karma sansevya devānāmeti sāmyatām,
Nibritam samwamānastu bhutānyatyeti panch wai.

प्रवृत्तं कर्म संसेव्य देवानामेति साम्यताम् ।
निवृत्तं संवमानस्तु भूतान्यत्येति पंच वै ॥

मनुस्मृति १२:९०

There are two ways: *pravriti* (inclination of mind, tendency, pursuit or activity) and *nivriti* (repose, retirement, detachment and salvation). Hinduism accepts both the ways. By following both or any of the two, man can get salvation. If one treats all the living beings like his own self, and with his inner eye sees his own image or the self in others, he transcends all and attains heaven:

Sarvabhuteshu chātmānam sarvabhutāni yātmani,
Samam pashyannātmayājayi swarājyamadhigachchhti.

सर्वभूतेषु चात्मानं सर्वभूतानि यात्मनि ।
समं पश्यन्नात्मयाजयी स्वाराज्यमधिगच्छति ॥

मनुस्मृति १२: ९१

This is the highest goal and objective that should be kept in mind and all our actions should be such to pave the way for that. That is the reason that Hinduism lays stress on pious soul and virtuous deeds, treats all else as alter ego and tries hard to lead as pure a life as possible. If there is some mistake then it suggests expiation and atonement. It can be achieved only by truly following religion and religious Scriptures.

☙

Panch Mahãyagya

As householders the Hindus have to perform five great worshipping acts called *Panch Mahãyagyas*. These *yagyas* must be performed for becoming cultured and civilized; and to be metamorphosed into better human being and for inner growth and all round development.

Adhyãpanam brahmayagyah pitriyagyasu tarpanam,
Homo daivo balirbhito nriyagyoatithipujanam.

अध्यायनं ब्रह्मयज्ञः पितृयज्ञेषु तर्पणम् ।
होमो दैवो बलिर्भितो नृयज्ञोऽतिथिपूजनम् ॥

To teach Vedas is called *Brahmayagya*, the duties performed for the Creator. It includes self study. Tarpan or offering water to the dead is *Pitriyagya*, the duties performed towards the parents and ancestors. The worshipping of Gods and offering fruits, flowers and incense is *Devayagya*, the duties performed towards the Gods. Sacrifices, charity and others are *Bhutayaga*, the duties performed towards the society and other beings. To be hospitable and treat the guests as gods and to worship them is called *Manushyayagya*, the duties performed towards other human beings. One, that performs the *panchmahãyagyas*, gets freedom from debts to 'all' others

Brahmayagya: Brahmayagya is related only to Vedas but it includes both the study and teaching of Vedas. The recitation of *Gãyatri Mantra* is also a part of this *yagya*. As a pupil or student or *Brahmachãri* one has learnt as a householder he has to share that knowledge with others. He has to teach those things to the members of his family, community and society, and to others, if and when possible. He should keep on studying a part of it everyday or whenever possible to keep them fresh in mind. It sharpens the mind, keeps one ready and gives insight into the things and happenings all around. The persons that perform this *yagya* get a graceful personality, brightened face, healthy body and long life; and they prosper well. Brahmayagya is dealt in detail in *Shatpatha Brāhmin* in the 11th Chapter (11:5:6:3-8).

Pitriyagya: *Pitriyagya* has two broader divisions as *tarpana* and *shrāddha*. *Shrāddha* is performed after the death of an adult person, at least whose *jagyopavita samskāra* has already been performed, a year after the death too, and every year or it can be submerged with the *pindadāna* at *Gayā*, a sacred place for *Pindadāna*. After that, it's no longer needed. But only they are allowed not to perform again whose both father and mother are dead. Others can go to *Gayā* umpteen times but will have to perform it every year. It can be done with the help of a *pandit*. But in *tarpan* (ritualistic offering of water, flower, linseed, and fruits) a *pandit* is not needed. A person can perform it on his own, daily or after every bath, or once in a month or once in a year. According to **Yāgavalkya Smriti**: father, grandfather and great grandfather are like Vasu, Rudra and Āditya. Predecessors and forefathers maintain unbroken tradition of a family tree. They are pleased when they are remembered, worshipped and offered sweets, fruits and fragrance by their children and grandchildren. They bless them with long life, children, riches, knowledge, pleasure, empire, happiness, heaven and even salvation:

Vasurudrātisutāh pitarah shrāddhadevatāh,
Preenayanti manusyānām pitrin shrāddhena tarpitāh.
Āyuh prajām dhanam vidyāh swargam
moksham sukhāni cha,
Prayachchhanti tathā rājyam preetā nrinām pitāmahāh.

वसुरुद्रातिसुता: पितर: श्राद्धदेवता: ।
प्रीणयन्ति मनुष्याणां पितृन् श्राद्धेन तर्पिता: ।।
आयु: प्रजां धनं विद्या स्वर्गं मोक्षं सुखानि च ।
प्रयच्छन्ति तथा राज्यं प्रीता नृणां पितामहा: ।।

याज्ञवल्क्य स्मृति १:२६९-२७०

Offering water and *pinda* (ritualistic mounds prepared under instruction specially for the purpose that can't be used in other rituals) are deemed necessary for the pleasure and satisfaction of the forefathers and for one's own prosperity and peace. It's said in the **Manusmriti** 3:82 that a householder should perform *shrāddha* everyday (in practice, as far as practicable but definitely once in a year):

> *Kuryādahrahah shrāddhamannādyenodakena wā,*
> *Payomulaphalairwāpi pitribhyah pritimāwahan.*
>
> कुर्यादहरह: श्राद्धमन्नाद्येनोदकेन वा ।
> पयोमूलफलैर्वापि पितृभ्य: प्रीतिमावहन् ॥

(मनुस्मृति-३/९२)

Devayagya: Through *Devayagya* gods, deities, demigods are worshipped. Oblations are offered to deities in Fire with the citation of 'swāhāh'. Deities are not in physical form. They are in subtle body. That is the reason that we try to please them with fragrance. Moreover, burning the chosen articles of oblation cleans the atmosphere. *Devayagya* is very common in Hinduism.

Bhutayagya: *Bhutayagya* is to give food to men and women suffering with deadly diseases; and to non-human beings like dogs, cats, pets, crows and other birds, ants and other insects. In Hinduism feeding a cow is treated very sacred simply because Indian cows know and eat many herbal medicines and hence her milk and other things prepared with it has curative effect:

> *Shunām cha patitānām chabhwapachām pāparoginām,*
> *Wāyasānām kriminām cha shankairnirwaped bhuwi.*
>
> शुनां च पतितानां चभ्भपचां पापरोगिणाम् ।
> वायसानां कृमीणां च शनकैर्निर्वपेद् भुवि ॥

मनुस्मृति ३:९२

Manushyayagya: In performing the *manusyayagya*, a man has to help other human beings and to ensure the continuity of life by keeping the atmosphere clean and by maintaining ecological balance and by avoiding inflicting injury and pain to other human beings. It has now been centralized at entertaining guests and even the meaning of guest has changed. All visitors, including relatives, one coming after fixing prior appointment, and one coming for some specific purpose; are treated as guests while in Hinduism all these are not accepted as guests. Guests are only those persons who come without fixing a date. The word *atithi* (guest) means without a date, a person that suddenly comes without a purpose. One should welcome, entertain and feed one's dependents, servants, adopted children, *brahmachāri, yati, sadhu, yogi* and such persons:

Atithiryasya bhagnāsho grihāt pratiniwartate,
Sa datwā dushkritam tasamai punyamādāya gachchhati.

अतिथिर्यस्य भग्नाशो गृहात् प्रतिनिवर्तते ।
स दत्वा दुष्टकृतं तस्मै पुण्यमादाय गच्छति ॥

Insight into Hinduism

Symbols

Just by knowing the symbols used by the Hindus and the meaning of the symbols one can see, feel and know real Hinduism. The Hindus use numerous symbols of different kinds and variety for different purposes and at different places. Everything is expressed through symbols. The gist can be seen in a long statement from the Scriptures. It will definitely give an insight into Hinduism and make the preferences of the Hindus crystal clear:

"A forehead without a Tilaka, a woman without a husband, a Mantra whose meaning is not known, the head that does not bow before elders and holy personages, a heart without mercy, a house without a well, a village without a temple, a country without a river, a society without a leader, wealth that is not given away in charity, a preceptor without a disciple, the governance without justice, a king without an able minister, a woman not obedient to her husband, a well without water, a flower without scent, a soul devoid of purity and holiness, a field without rains, an intellect without clear concept, a disciple without a godly preceptor, a body devoid of good health, a custom without purity, austerity without the feeling of oneness, speech that lacks truth, a kingdom without good people, work without wages, Samyāsa without renunciation, legs that does not visit pilgrimages, determination without discrimination, a knife without sharp edge, a cow that does not give milk, and a spear without a point are all condemnable. They exist in name only."

AUM : AUM is the self created celestial *Nāda* (sound), Word, Brahman and Life. One must practise to make this sound of AUM from the navel and not from the throat.

Swastika : Swastika is the symbol of well being and good omen. It ensures peace and prosperity in all the four directions and throughout the four stages of life.

Deepa : Deepa (earthen lamp) is Light, and Life in mundane form and represents struggle for existence and victory over darkness and ignorance.

Dhupa : Dhupa symbolises fragrance and cleanliness; and keeps both the mind and environment clean and fresh.

Chandan : Chandan is fragrance on the one side, medicine and health on the other.

Tilaka : Tilaka symbolises religiosity and spirituality. It's placed on the forehead as a mark of auspiciousness. It can be sandal paste, sacred ashes or *Kumkuma* (a red turmeric powder). The devotees of Lord Shiva apply *Bhasma* (sacred ashes) on the forehead, arms, and chest and even on body, the devotees of Vishnu apply sandal paste and the worshippers of Mā Shakti apply *Kumkuma*.

Bell : By mistake people think that Hindus use the bell to call the deities. Bell is a declaration that someone is performing poojā, or a poojā is being performed somewhere and it's a call to the listeners to come to that place to take part in it.

Incense : Hindus use fragrance.

Flowers : Flowers stand for purity, fragrance, and tenderness and show devotion. Flowers can't be plucked during night. One can't pluck flowers after taking a bath. Some flowers like that of *Ketaki* won't be offered to gods and deities. Usually, fallen flowers are not offered in pooja but *Pārijāt* (harsringār) *Champā* and *Molsri*, etc. have the right to be placed on the gods even when they have fallen to the ground. *Pārijāt* has special value as the smell of even a single flower will easily reach the navel.

Shankha; Conch : *Shankha* is very pious in Hinduism. It is blown on many occasions. It symbolises action; both the start and finish. It gives a clarion call. It was vehemently used during Mahābhārat. There are certain people that join two or three conches and play rhythmically. Though, it has its peculiar sound yet experts blow it in different ways.

Fish : Fish symbolises *Jeejiwishā*, the will to live. It shows the struggle for existence.

Fruits : Fruits represent purity and piety; and are vehemently used in *Poojā* and *Prasāda*.

Sweets : Sweets to Indians compensate for the short calories. They are an integral part of Indian festivals and feasts; rites and rituals. They are one of the three things that Indians are proud of: Sweetness, Light and Fragrance.

Shahad, Madhu : Honey symbolises sweetness and purity. Though mostly used as a part of medicine, as āyurvedic medicines are usually taken with honey, but honey is used in rituals and rites with equal frequency and greater respect.

Milk : Cow milk is complete food and hence very sacred. Indian cows graze in the field and eat herbs. Hence, the milk and other products have great medicinal values.

Cowdung : Cowdung is one of the five things of cows used in sacred ceremonies. The other four are *godugdha; gomutra; dahi* and *Ghee*.

Durvā : *Duba* or *Durba* is a type of green grass. It has its medicinal value and its juice is poured in drops in ears when a scorpion stings. Cats use it to clean their stomach and strengthen their digestive system.

Kusha : *Kusha* is a kind of grass with needle like leaves. It symbolises roughness and toughness. It's taken off along with the roots. It's used in various ways in *Yagyopavita* (Sacred Thread Ceremony) and other rituals but it's mostly used to make mats. *Kusha* mats are used for sitting during *poojā* and meditation. Although dry, yet it's taken as good conductor of electromagnetic waves. Kusha-rings are worn in fingers in certain yagyas and poojas. A kush ring is known as *pavitri*. In certain region *yagyopavit* of *kusha* are also placed on shoulder with others.

Thorn : Many thorns as symbols are directly related to rituals. The thorn of cotton silk is used as medicine. Ladies pinch their tongue with the thorn of a grass (*rengani*) after cursing their brothers in 'Curse Ceremony.'

Gold : Gold represents purity and has a special place in Hindu rituals. It's essential to wear a gold ring in many customary rituals and *poojās*. Ladies use it while wishing long life, long married life and bright sons.

Silver : Silver is cool and stands for purity. It's not only for ornament but also for gift and charity.

Copper : Copper is a great purifier and killer of germs. Hindus keep water in copper vessels and drink in the morning for a strong digestive system.

Iron : Iron obviously signifies toughness, and it gives relief against tough opponents, planets and zodiac. The much used and rough iron of horse-shoe is worn as ring by the Hindus to give toughness to nature and for victory against tough customers and situations. It's astrologically related to Saturn.

Ashtadhātu : *Ashtadhātu* is an alloy metal and accepted as pacifier of Planets and worn for *Grah-shānti*.

Kartāla : *Kartāla*, a living symbol of *Bhakti*, is a musical instrument. It is used as an accompaniment to *Kirtan* and *Bhajan*. It is known as a favourite to both Nārada and Hanumāna.

Veenā : *Veenā* stands for higher attainment, dedicated practice and used in classical music. It's the musical instrument of Saraswati, the Goddess of learning.

Music is a part of Hinduism as well as Indian social and cultural life. Indian musical instruments are endless. Not even the musicians can claim to have seen all of them. Only such instruments have been selected here that work as a symbol.

Dhola, Tablā, Drum : Different types of percussion musical instruments are used by the Indians but *Dhola* is the most popular as it is played also by women and used both in religious rituals and festivals.

Nagārā : *Nagārā* produces a very highpitched sound and it's the symbol of call and awakening.

Damru : *Damru* symbolises ecstasy on one hand and Time on the other. As it's the favourite *tāla vādya* of Shiva so it's used in all sorts of worshipping of Shiva.

Bānsuri : *Bānsuri* has the sweetest and the most loving sound. It's the most mellifluous musical instrument and is rightly associated with Lord Krishna. It's the most popular musical instrument among the villagers.

Peacock Feathers : Peacock Feather is the symbol of prosperity and ease. It's believed that the person that keeps it is never restless. It's favourite of Lord Krishna.

Vaijyanti Flower : The *Vaijayanti* flower is for Krishna and a garland made up of it is usually offered to him.

Sadābahāra : *Sadābahāra* means evergreen and ever in bloom. It's a unique flower. If the plant is there then flowers are bound to be there irrespective of the season or climate. It's the right medicine for sugar patients. Earlier on it was found at each well. Now it's becoming rare yet it is valued and taken care of.

Mango Leaves : Mango leaves are sacred and symbolise greenery, growth and prosperity. By using it one wishes and guarantees prosperity, health and happiness.

Pālo and Parihat : Yoke and harrow are used in ploughing and represent the farmers and farming. Its use is declaration that Indian soil is to be used for growing crops and plantation. This alone can feed all.

Cow : Cow, the symbol of non-violence, is the most sacred creature for Hindus. Along with some Goddesses and the earth, cow is also like a mother to them. It's because of the quality of milk and other products that we get from her as well as because of the calves that become oxen and are the backbone of Indian agriculture.

Peacock : A peacock is liked for its colourful feathers and because the feathers are related to Lord Krishna.

Pigeon : Pigeon, the symbol of peace, is the most common pet and at places they are protected in thousands. Although, psychologically, they don't suit the Indian mind but they have carried messages in the form of letters for quite a long time so they are a part of Indian living.

Trishula : *Trishula*, the trident is the most sacred weapon. It symbolises Time and destruction. Because it's the weapon of Shiva so it's worshipped. In certain families, as a part of family tradition, it's washed and kept at the place at the time of the *poojā* of *Kula Devatā*.

Alpanā : *Alpanā* represents arts, artistic values and aesthetic sense. Ladies, preferably girls decorate the floor at the doors with rice paste in numerous patterns. It shows the refined taste and artistic bend of mind.

Rosary : For Hindus any round small hard and dry fruit-stone or seed can make a rosary. Yet they prefer the rosary of *Rudrāksha,* lotus seeds and Basil Beads painstakingly prepared from basil stem.

Tulasi : Green leaves of Basil (*Tulasi*) are the greatest preventive medicine known so far. Hindus use it regularly in almost all the rituals and rites; in *prasāda*; in food; in hot drink or eat with *Gola Mircha* and *Namaka*.

Important Concepts

Six *Teerthas:* (Holy Places): Hinduism takes its strength from very pragmatic approach. One has not to go visiting places, running from pillar to post for anything: *Brahman*, God, *Devatas*, Planets, Constellation, Temples or Places of Pilgrim. They are within him. The heart is the biggest and greatest temple. His life, character, body, pious living, possesses all. They are all within him and around him:

if one accepts each stone is the idol of God;

māno to deva nahin to patthar;

the most sacred river is in a shallow wooden tub;

man changā tab kathauti mein gangā.

Hindu Scriptures help them in such realisations. They give them the widest latitude. Take for example the sacred places of pilgrims. In India alone there are thousand of such sacred places for the pilgrims to visit. Modern men will hardly tell about a few dozens among them. The people from villages can count in hundreds but no one will give the complete list. In certain specialized books more than one thousand such places are given.

But both *Shrimad Bhāgawat Mahāpurāna* and *Padmapurana* say that one does not need to go to visit such places. They say that a devotee, a *guru*, the mother, the father, the husband and the wife are six great places of pilgrim.

Bhakta Teertha: The heart of a true devotee is a great temple. It's the place known where god resides. They make the places worth living. Their places are like sacred pilgrim places where one finds God:

Bhavadwidhā bhāgawatāsteertham bhutā swayam bibho,
Teerthi kurwanti teerthāni swāntah sthena gadābhutā.

भवद्विधा भागवतास्तीर्थं भूता स्वयं विभो ।
तीर्थी कुर्वन्ति तीर्थानि स्वान्त:स्थेन गदाभूता ॥

Srimadbhāgwad Mahāpurāna 13:10

Guru Teertha : The sun gives light during the day, moon gives light during the night, lamps give light at homes, but a teacher always keeps the heart and mind of his disciples lighted. He replaces the darkness of ignorance with the light of knowledge, so, a guru is a sublime place of worship:

tasmd guruh param teertham shishynmawanipate.
तस्मद् गुरुह परम तीर्थम् शिष्यनमवनिपते

Mātā Teertha; Pitā Teerth : For welfare, prosperity and salvation the father and the mother are the greatest *teerthas* for the sons. If one has not worshipped his parents then, what can he get from reading the Vedas? For a son worshipping the parents is the religion, the sacred place of pilgrim, the *moksha* and the best deed in this life: For a son there is no *teertha* better than the mother and father:

nāsti mātrisamam teertham putrānām cha pituh samam.
नस्ति नात्रीसमम् तीर्थम् पुत्रानाम् च पितुह समम्।

Pati Teertha : The lady that treats her husbands right leg as *Prayāga* and the left leg as *Pushkar* and takes bath with left over water and lives under him gets the virtues of taking bath at those pilgrim places. The husband is like all *teerthas* and all *punyas*:

sarvateerthamayo bhartā sarvapunyamayam patih.
सर्वतीर्थमयो भारता सर्वपुण्यमयं पतिह।

Patni Teertha : If in a household there is a wife that follows the rules of morality, has good moral character, and is engaged in religious deeds and tries to learn new things; then, the gods, the sacred rivers, the *yagyas*, the *rishis* and the sacred places reside in that house. For welfare, pleasure, happiness and salvation, there is no *teertha* better than the wise, no pleasure that can compete with her and no virtue that can equal her:

Nāsti bhāryā samam teertham nāsti
bhāryā samam sukham,
Nāsti bhāryā samam punyam tārnāya hitāya cha.

नस्ति भार्या समं तीर्थं नास्ति भार्या समं सुखम् ।
नस्ति भार्या समं पुण्यं तारणाय हिताय च ॥

Padma Purāna, Bhumikhand 59: 24

Panch Devatā :

1. *Shri Ganesh*
2. *Bhagawāna Shiva*
3. *Mā Shakti*
4. *Surya*
5. *Vishnu*

It's believed that they are all one but because of their appearance at five different places, they take five names. *Surya* is present before us and obviously give us heat, light and energy. Lord *Shiva* is the god of prosperity and also of destruction. He is easily pleased and is very lenient in blessing others and fulfilling desire. *Vishnu* is omnipotent God. Mā *Shakti* is the mother of all living beings. She is the perennial energy. *Shri Ganesh* is the god of prosperity and of everything good. He paves the way by taking away the hurdles and obstacles.

Panch Māta : Mother, mother-in-law, queen, teacher's wife and friend's mother.

Panch Pitā : Father, father-law, king, teacher and God

Panch Kanyā : Ahalyā; Draupadi; Kunti; Tara; and Mandodari.

Pancha Kawal : It's also known as *panch grās*: Five morsels of cooked food kept apart by the Hindus for a dog; sinner; leper; sick and for a crow.

Panchgabya : The five articles yielded by a cow: milk, curd, ghee, dung and urine; and its mixture is distributed after performing some poojas.

Panchāmrit : A pious mixture of milk; curd; honey; ghee; and sugar to be offered to a deity and distributed among the people.

Panchapallava : The leaves from five trees: mango; rose; apple; citron; and *bilva* (stone apple); used in *yagyas* by Hindus. They are used for their medical values and the quality to clean the atmosphere. The leaves of lemon/ citron are the best purifier of ghee. Old and a bit contaminated ghee is heated with a few lemon leaves and it's again clarified and becomes pure.

Panchmakāra : Five essential things for a *Vāmamārgi*, each beginning with M sound: *mānsa* (meat); *madirā* (wine); *machhali* (fish); *moodrā* (gesticulation); and *maithuna* (copulation). Those that practise it are called *'Aughar'*; they look unpleasant; behave awkwardly and are mostly indiscreet. They have never been in the main stream. They claim to be the worshippers of Shiva and Shakti/ Shiva or Shakti. They lack piety and are least beneficial for the society.

Panchmahāpātaka : According to Manusmriti, there are five great sins that includes: murder of a Brāhmin; drinking wine; theft; cohabitation with preceptor's wife; and association with the persons that commit such crimes.

Panchratna : Five precious gems: gold; diamond; ruby; pearl and amethyst.

Panchasunā : The five things of a householder that unknowingly destroy other living beings: fireplace; curr-stone; broom; mortar and pestle and waterpot.

Panch Kosha: (Five Shells) : The five Kashas are repository, shell, treasury, strong room, treasure house, or pericardium. There are five independent impure elements or matters that make these five shells impure and weak. The ways and means to be free from these impurities are given in *Karmamimānshā shāstra*. They can get impure by visiting some places or touching something or eating something. Nowadays, a few restrictions are rigidly followed, rest are seldom obeyed and only by selected families.

(i) **Annamaya Kosha: (Physical Body):** The impurity of the Physical body is *mala* i.e. excrement or muck faeces.

(ii) **Prānamaya Kosha:** The impurity of (Organic body/self) is called *vikār* i.e. alteration, deterioration, perversion. This *vikār* increase after touching dead body or in the burning ghāt while assisting or performing the last rites. So, there is strict instruction (and it is strictly followed by one and all) *awagāhan*, to take bath, to touch iron, gold, fire, oil, etc. after performing the last rites and returning home.

(iii) **Manomaya Kosha** : The impurity of Mental body is called *vikshepa* i.e. deflection, dissipation, perplexity, celestial latitude, scattering, dispersion as it can happen because of any one of them; the method and occasions are not fixed. It can happen even during solar or lunar eclipses.

(iv) **Vigyānamaya Kosha** : The impurity of (Spiritual) body is called *āwarana* i.e. screen, shield, obstruction.

(v) **Ānandamaya Kosha** : The impurity of Blissful body is called *asmitā,* i.e. vanity, pride, ego.

Panch Pratishthā (Five Respectable Possessions): The following five things are accepted as the causes of honour and respect. He is the most respectable that possesses all; he too is respectable that possesses more than one.

(i)   To have wealth.

(ii)   To have uncles and friends.

(iii) To be very elderly in age (In Hinduism an 80 years Shudra too is respectable).

(iv) To have the knowledge of Shrutis and Smritis.

(v)   To follow the dictates of Shrutis and Smritis.

Dash Tyājya (Ten Abuses) : One must get rid of the following ten sins or abuses for a satisfactory, peaceful and happy life.

vi.   To think to grab else's property.

vii.   To wish to commit a crime.

viii. To treat physical pleasure to be all.

ix.   Harsh words.

x.   Telling lies.

xi.   Making slanderous remarks.

xii.   Idle talk.

xiii. To take something without being given.

xiv. To give pain.

xv.   Immoral relation with other man or woman.

Wealth : Hindus accumulate virtues. They don't prefer to accumulate wealth for the posterity. They have a very plain theory:

putra kuputra tab kā dhana sanchay;
putra suputra tab kā dhan sanchay

If the son is corrupt, impious and without character then there is no use of wealth because it will be soon wasted; and if the son has virtues, wisdom, piety and character then there is no need to accumulate wealth. Such a son will earn a lot.

Japa : *Jāpa* is very common among the Hindus. *Jāpa* takes the mind off from the materialistic concerns and helps in concentrating on spiritual realities. The mundane world is left behind and the soul enjoys the pure pleasure. The mad rat race is totally stopped during that period. The body and mind gets ready to transcend. It's also a form of meditation. Those that are not adapted to the inner silence and the silence of Nature helps them in moving towards their cherished goal in their own way and at their own pace. The constraints and restraints of concentration are not there. The soul is left free on its own to absorb whatever it can and to accept whatever it likes. It's the most natural path to sublimity and the easiest one.

There are different types of *jāpa* and in every *jāpa* a name of the favourite god or goddess is repeatedly chanted. The most common is the *jāpa* done according to the rules and one follows all the regulations. Even they count it on rosary. Then, there is a *jāpa* that is hardly audible; another one is silent *jāpa* and yet another that is done in mind. The last one is the best one. In ascending order each one is ten, hundred or thousand times better than the first one:

Vidhiyagyājjapayagyo vishishto dashabhirgunaih,
Upānshuh syāchchhatagunah sāhastro mānasah smritah.

विधियज्ञाज्जपयज्ञो विशिष्टो दशभिर्गुणै:।
उपयांशु: स्याच्छतगुण: साहस्त्रे मानस: स्मृत: ॥

Salutations and Greetings among the Hindus

Only the cultured and refined can give honour and respect to religion, tradition, values and relations. Only they can pursue the four pursuits and mix and mingle among the people with the head held high for they have done nothing wrong. But the people that indulge in immoral deeds prefer to remain closed in their comfortable dens and announce that the other people are living below their standard so they won't mix with them. To go to the open field or to be a part of the larger society is not mixing with them, it is facing them; it's facing the blows of air, the showers of rain, the burning heat of the sun and the enquiring eyes of the people, moving or standing around. If one is pure and has done nothing wrong then he can face the society, if otherwise, he needs security. When one is out in the society he/ she needs greetings and salutations.

Hindus have a great tradition of salutation: from folded hands to prostration; from touching the feet to putting hands on the back and patting. Both honour and assurance is silently communicated. It makes the ties stronger. They are not treated well that turn their face and pass on in a hurry to avoid a person: elder or younger. It's a great sight, in some parts of India, particularly Bengāl; when a grandmother or great grandmother bows down and touches the feet of a 5 or 15 years old girl. It's a way of teaching and showing respect to the growing girls that will someday give birth to other human beings. It's the salutation to the future mother, grandmother and great grandmother. Hindus treat it to be the success of life when they give a daughter in marriage to a groom. It's known as *Kanyādāna*; the greatest *dāna* according to Hindu Scriptures. The girls are Laxmi. It's a shame that science has paved the way of knowing the sex of a child when it's in the womb and getting abortion if she is a girl child. It's a shame on the human beings and human values. The parents must realise that they too were born only when there was a girl that became her/ his mother. Modernity or demonic spirit is the worst curse, and somehow all are suffering.

They don't get respect because they don't show respect; they are not saluted because they fail to salute. The ignorant men and women have forgotten that if they will not show respect to their elders and younger brothers, sisters, relatives or others; then neither the younger nor the elders will show respect to them. It's a mutual process of give and take and it's definitely reciprocal.

There are five things that give respect: knowledge; wealth; uncles and brothers; old age; and deeds according to Scriptures:

Vittam bandhurvayah karma vidyā bhawati panchami,
Yetāni mānyasthānāni gariyo yadyaduttaram.

वित्तं बन्धुर्वय: कर्म विद्या भवति पंचमी ।
एतानि मान्यस्थानि गरियो यद्यदुत्तरम् ॥

Manusmriti 2: 136

If one wishes to get respect from the elders and younger alike he must observe the rules of salutation and greetings. He must mention his name and add *bho* while saluting the old men as they might not see him clearly or may not recognise him as: *abhivādaye prasoon nāmāham bhoh*: (Main Prasoon Pranām kartā hun) I'm Prasoon saluting you. The elders must reciprocate it with: *āyushmān bhava soumya* (*Soumya! Tum āyushmān howo*); Live long! O, gentle boy!

While greeting a person either ask welfare; or enquire about health. If one is not related (with blood) to a lady while addressing her: one should use the words like *bhawati*! or *Bhagini*! or *Subhage*! If she is a girl then use '*āyusmati*'. One must salute everyday the related and elder ladies by touching their feet. Elder sister, *Mausi*, *Buā* should be treated as mothers though mother should be given preference.

Sparsh (touch) is very valuable. It heals wounds and brings us closer so while blessing a younger person that is related with blood; either touch his/ her head or pat on the back.

Those that follow the rules; and salute or greet others or serve the old men; get longer life, wisdom, fame and strength:

> *Abhivādansheelasya nityam vriddhopasewinah;*
> *Chatwāri tasya vardhante āyurvidyā yasho balam.*
> अधिवादनशीलस्य नित्यं वृद्धोपसेविन: ।
> चत्वारि तस्य वर्धन्ते आयुर्विद्या यशो बलम् ।

Manusmriti 2:117

The service rendered to mother, father and Guru is said to be the greatest penance: *teshām trayānām shushrushā paramam tapo uchyate*.

Pathādhikāra (Right of way): Who should go ahead? The horns ask for a right of way. One can see written in bold letters in the back of vehicles; horn please; stop; pass signal when there is space. The infinite space is showing no space. It's not filled up with living beings. Living beings have been drastically reduced. It has been filled up with vehicles. There is no money with the governments to put a shed over the head of the poor but there is a lot of money in the coffin to construct multi layer car-parkings. It's the safety of vehicles that are more important than the safety of living beings because no money is needed to have a child; they are born in thousands everyday but one pays lakhs of rupees to purchase a car. A car is more valuable than a child. When a child is hit by a car and dies, he is paid a meager amount as compensation; but when a car is hit and damaged, a lot of money is paid as compensation because many people will get share from the money sanctioned or passed for payment to the car-owner.

The ways (roads) are constructed. Money is taken as loan from World Bank. For it fertile and habited land is acquired. The road is ready in order to clear the jam but when the road is finally opened, the jam is there from the very first day of official inauguration.

It's not the Indian and natural way of living. There were clear instructions who would be given the right to pass first. There was no wordy dual then, and people never drew swords or a revolver to kill the erring driver. Today, a minute's delay will hear hundreds of blowing horns asking for the right to go ahead. They are fined from breaking the rules but everyday the traffic rules are broken. The growing challans are proofs in themselves.

According to Manusmriti the following should be given way first:

(i) Persons in vehicles
(ii) Very old men
(iii) Patients
(iv) Load bearers
(v) Women
(vi) *Snātaka* (Graduate whose convocation is over; now a learned man)
(vii) Kings
(viii) Groom

Learned men and kings should be given preference. A king should clear way for a learned man.

Hindu Scriptures

The most ancient *Rishis* had *Sanātana Dharma* (Eternal Religion) in mind when they thought about the human beings and their Dharma that was another or similar word to *Karma*. To give substance and meaning to its original name and concept and in keeping with and establishing a rich and lively tradition for human beings the *Rishis* created myriads of immortal Scriptures. It is a grand, vast, immaculate and indomitable world of knowledge. It's known as Vedic *Wāngamaya* (the World of Vedas). They include *Shrutis*, the books of knowledge and *Smritis*, the books of religion, rites and rituals. They cover each aspect of life and knowledge. They are great books of Science, Arts, Literature, Sculptors, Medicine, Weaponry, Warfare, Math, Astrology, Astronomy, Humanities, Religion and Spirituality, etc. They were thousands in number. About 80% of them were destroyed, looted, burnt or carried away from the 7th Century to 20th Century.

They are written in *Samskrit*, the most ancient language known as *Deva Vāni*, the language of Gods, it was invented in Deva Nagar so the script got the name: *Deva Nāgari Lipi* It's so sublime and perfect that all the languages of the world that came at a later stage; and are still being improved, have never matched it.

Veda: *Shrutis* and *Smritis* (Books of Knowledge and Religion) are sub-divided in many groups that are given below.

(1) *Mantra Samhitās*

Branches of Vedas

   (a) *Rig Veda*
   (b) *Sāma Veda*

(c) *Yajur Veda*
(d) *Atharva Veda*

(2) *Brāhmin Granthas*
(3) *Āranyakas*
(4) *Upanishads*
(5) *Sutra Granthas* in *Vedas*
(6) *Prātishākhya*
(7) *Shikshā*
(8) *Kalp*
(9) *Vyākaran.*
(10) *Nirukta*
(11) *Chhand*
(12) *Jyotish*
(13) *Up-Vedas*
(14) History: Epics: *Purānas*
(15) Philosophy: *Darshan*
(16) *Niti Shāshtras*
(17) *Smriti Granthas*
    (a) *Manusmriti*
    (b) *Yāgyavalkya Smriti*
    (c) *Vyās Smriti*
    (d) *Vishnu Smriti*
    (e) *Parāsher Smriti*
    (f)*Āitreya Smriti*
    (g) *Vashishtha Smriti*
    (h) *Markandeya Smriti*
    (i) *Āpastamba Smriti*
    (j) *Shankha Smriti*

The *Rishis* are usually found in penance, i.e. deep meditation and research. In whatever direction they moved to and whatever subject they took for meditation or research, they completed it, reached up to the end of it, grasped and expressed the whole truth. It was very easy to understand during their respective periods because the people knew that language and were versed in it. Concept and understanding was easier and clearer. But since, at present we don't possess that height or depth in knowledge and language, hence, we are not able to understand the obvious as well as the hidden meanings. The reason is that we are not growing from inside and unable to grasp a single part fully. Our knowledge is imperfect and partial. We are following such superfluous ways that everyday it's becoming exceedingly difficult for us to establish a rapport with existing knowledge and wisdom; and see the whole. The other reason is that; the Rishis saw and have described the 'whole' in short and in profane and mystic language that is very ambiguous for us.

The not so-enlightened modern men (because of changed preferences, luxurious life-style and food habits) fail to give adequate time to the grand classical treatises of knowledge and religion, could not read the texts well, get the actual meaning and subtle suggestions, perceive the inner reality, and know the whole. The whole (even the completeness) eludes them.

It's our shortcoming. We have to overcome it. There is nothing wrong with the treatises. Of course, most of the treatises are missing. They would have filled up the gap and provided the missing links. But what is lost is lost. In place of crying for split milk we must foster well the milch-animals to get more milk.

The modern man will have to work harder and ascertain deep involvement and concentration to be able to read, analyze and explain the apparent and hidden meaning; only then he/ she can be able to grasp a lot and provide some missing links.

This can be done and achieved by only pious means, life and living. With blackened eyes, disfigured heart and prejudiced mind one can't dive deeper into that wide and fathomless ocean of knowledge or fly higher into the cosmic truth to bring out star-like self-illuminating facts.

The Rāmāyana, The Mahābhārata (including the Gitā) and Srimadbhāgawad Mahāpurāna are called *Granth-trai* and are believed to be the Scriptures of Hinduism by general Hindus. Whenever someone will ask, "What are your *Dharma Shāshtras*?" The answer will invariably come in the form of these four books. As most of the Hindus have seen a separate book called *Srimadbhāgwadgitā*, so they treat it as the fourth Scripture. These books are in the form of stories and are recited and chanted everywhere in India; mostly for a week or fortnight or a month at one place. The recitation goes on throughout the year. The *pandit* or *mahātmā* reciting these Scriptures also explain and elucidate the *Shlokas* in a very lucid style. The common people listen to them, try to understand it, they discuss among themselves and follow the dicatates. They take the help of pandits for performing rites and rituals. This way they easily get acquainted with what is there in the Scriptures for the Grantha-trai is physical illustrations of the subtle qualities and characteristics described in other books.

They are taught that good behaviour and pure deeds give long life; desired child; permanent property and the signs of bad days are eroded. So they perform moral and religious deeds:

Āchārālalbhate hyayurāchārādipsitāh prajāh,
Āchārād dhanam akshayam āchāro hantyalakshanam.

आचाराल्लभते ह्यायुराचारादीप्सिता: प्रजा: ।
आचाराद्धनमक्षय्यमाचारो हन्त्यलक्षणम् ॥

Such confident teachings in millions and billions have moulded the life and mind of the Hindus. They have a peculiar way of teaching. Whether one reads or not, likes or not but everything important will be made known to all at some stage in the very first part of life. Hinduism takes its strength from there and grows incessantly in every direction.

Development to Completeness and Fullness

The Ways of Worshipping

The Hindus have adopted all the ways of worshipping. Whatever the way of worshiping a man can think of has been already there in Hinduism. They can worship the God in only a loincloth (almost naked); half clothed, or completely dressed. They can worship the God before sunrise, after sunrise, during the day, before evening, after evening or during the night. Prostration and touching the head to the feet of God are the most common ways but they can only bow their heads and that will be all. The ladies too can worship immediately after taking bath with untied plait or after being ready in all respects.

The Hindus can worship the God while standing, sitting, prostrating or relaxing in a cosy bed. They can worship God with folded hands, empty hand, with flowers, with clothes, fruits, gold or jewel or anything that they can get or is available; for they believe that everything is the gift of God, we only return his gift or worship Him with the things that He has given:

twadiya vastu govindam tubhyam yewa samarpayet.
त्वदिय वस्तु गोविन्दं तुभ्यं एव समर्पयेत्।

Hindus believe that only by worshipping the God or a god they can get bliss and salvation. It is so because for them Brahman, Krishna, Rāma, Shiva, and others are one and the same. The name is not a hindrance in their prayer, worship, devotion and final salvation. They need devotion and they must surrender to that God. They must help others with their heart, mind and act. That is the only thing needed. They don't need *yoga, yajna, japa, tapa* or *upawāsa*, austerity and penance. Purity of heart and benevolence in deeds are all. Such simple souls will get satisfaction and contentment and the power to endure and thus happiness and bliss.

Nawadhā Bhakti

Nine types of devotions have been preached in *Srimadbhāgwat Mahāpurāna* that widens the scope and allows a lot of free thinking and movements. It's known as *'nawadhā bhakti'*:

> Shravanam kirtanam vishnoh smaranam pādsevanam
> Archanam vandanam dāsyam sakhyamātmanivedanam.
>
> **7:5:23**

(i) *Shravan* (listening to the Name) (ii) *Kirtan* (to recite the Name) (iii) *Smaranam* (to remember the Lord) (iv) *Pād sevanam* (serving the Lord) (v) *Archanā* (to worship the Lord) (vi) *Vandanam* (to salute the Lord) (vii) *Dāsya* (as a servant) (viii) *Sakhya* (as a friend) (ix) *Ātma Nivedanam* (to request the Lord). Two other forms are also added to it: **prem lakshanā** and **parā bhakti**: to make it 11. "Even one out of these ways will give solace and satisfaction, closeness and intimacy, fullness and richness; which will keep one charged with energy and emotion." Its advice to all is clear and open that all of us should seek the 'closeness of the Lord.' The Hindus sing loudly the devotional songs but strangely enogh, accepts **silent and inner worshipping as the best.** For them, the faith, devotion, surrender and purity of mind and deeds are the most important aspects of life and religion.

Daily Prayers

Regarding the daily prayers for the Hindus neither the time nor the place, neither the occasion nor the times of repetition is fixed. One can pray anywhere, anytime, in any posture or dress, any god or goddess, alone or in company and any number of times. It depends on the mood, wish, time, etc. of the person concerned. There is no binding for anyone. It's the individual freedom as also the daily worship. Neither an idol nor a temple is needed. Neither there has to be a mat of *kusha* (a kind of grass thought to be good conductor of electromagnetic waves and used for sitting and other purposes for the religious and spiritual observances); nor a rosary. The availability of such things will make things easier but lack of any such thing is not an obstacle in worshipping and prayers. If one uses a rosary then there is no binding about the type of beads used; beads of basil stems (*tulasi*) are as good as that of *rudrāksha* (the seeds of a tree known as Eleocarpus ganitrus used in rosaries). It's the latitude and freedom that has kept the interest of common man alive till date.

Just on the other hand, Hindus can take all pains to visit a temple or a place of pilgrimage or a particular god or goddess or to fulfill a vow or a promise. One can go to an extent to collect one particular article needed in performing a particular ritual. They are so committed and so particular about the rituals.

The Hindus, customarily pray before leaving the bed. Those that know recite the following shloka:

Samudra vasane devi parvat stan mandite; Vishnu patri namastubhyam pād sparsham kshamaswa mey.

समुद्र वसने देवि पर्वत स्तन मण्डिते ।

विष्णु पत्नि नमस्तुभ्यं पादस्पर्षं क्षमस्व मे ।

There are many that don't know the *shloka,* only salute the earth and remember their personal deity and leave the bed. In most of the homes morning prayers and worshipping are done both separately and collectively before eating anything. Most of them take bath before that but nowadays the others perform the ritual without taking a bath. Bath cleans the body and lightens the mind.

Almost all the shopkeepers touch the land closer to the door or shutter before inserting the key to open the shop. Incidentally, Hindus don't say that they are closing the shop in the evening they say 'enlarge the shop' (*dukāna barāhwo*). Customarily, they salute the shop before closing it.

All the shopkeepers, including the hawkers, salute Goddess *Lakshmi* everyday when they get the payment to the first sale. They salute the weighing machine (balance) and the cashbox.

Every trader or professional, without making a fuss or show, salutes the instruments or the most important thing that helps most in earning. All the traders and businessmen will worship his/her deity (mostly Laxmi and Ganesh) without fail and definitely before starting the day's proceedings. They paint *Swastika* and *Shubh-Lābh* at different places including the cashbook and ledger and the portable wooden temple. Most of them hang lemon and chilly outside to keep the side effects of Saturn away. It's natural to the Hindus. It's not superstition. It's a way to accept the power and contribution of the unknown entity and show the gratefulness.

In no country and no religion, except among Hindus and in India, the Sun is worshipped so much and so well. At some other places only the rising Sun is worshipped. In India both the rising and setting Sun are worshipped as *prātah poojā* (morning prayer) and *sāndhya vandanā* (evening worship).

As a part of that ritual, the kids are anointed on the forehead. In many cases and at many places, usually at the time of greater rituals, the heads are shaved clean (called tonsure in English) except the choti, a lock of hair left after tonsure at the crown, above *Sahasrār Chakra*).

Worshipping in Every Season

For the Hindus every day, every season, every *tithi* is fit for worshipping. If they have none to worship, they worship seasons. They prefer closeness to Nature, a life that is environment friendly. It's because of the prayers in Vedas. *Sāma Veda* says:

"Rejoice all the moods of Nature; experience the unseen divine glory manifested in various forms. Spring is the season of flowers and scented breeze that gladden the hearts; Summer follows with its peculiar beauty and music; then comes the rain with its dark clouds and dazzling flashes and drizzling water that bathes the entire earth to show her splendid splendour while Autumn and Winter manifest themselves with their individual and magical beauty and charm."

The Atharva Veda too sings in similar tone and tempo: "Maintain us in well-being during Summer, Winter, Dewtime, Spring, Autumn, and Rainy Season. Grant us happiness in cattle and children. May we enjoy Your unassailed protection."

What a grand and unique day. Time, way or mode of showing reverence and devotion to the Omnipotent!

Pancha: Dash: Shodasha: Upachār Poojan Vidhi

Hindus are fond of *Poojā* that they perform at every opportune moment and both for valid and important reasons or trivial causes. While doing so they have to perform sixteen functions known as

Shodash Upachāra. But the latitude in and elasticity of Hinduism is apparent here too. If the needed articles or time is not available then they can perform only ten functions called *Dashopachāra* or only five, known as *Panchopachāra.* As there are some deviations so more than sixteen Upachāras are given. The details are given in only *Shodash Upachāra; Panch* or *Dasha* can be taken from there.

At present these are in vogue. There is a chance that the earlier forms were different. Only the *Mantras* for each act and the commentaries that were written during the recent past are available. We have definitely lost the original and genuine form. One basic difference is obvious. Everything is kept ready and the worshipper simply touches the cloth or ornament and it is accepted as offered. We hardly spend adequate time on the poojā.

Panchopachāra

Gandha
Pushpa
Dhupa
Deepa
Naivedya

Dashopachāra

Pādya
Arghya
Āchamana
Snāna
Vastra
Gandha
Pushpa
Dhupa
Deepa
Naivedya

Shodash Upachāra

Āwāhana : We keep the symbolic figure of the wished God and Goddess and pray them to come to the place so that they can be worshipped.

Āsana : With the expectation of the arrival of the wished God and Goddess we offer a suitable seat to them. In absence of permanent place we offer *Kusha* or *Durvā* or *Pushpa*.

Pādya : With a view to wash the feet we offer water. Sandal (or fragrance) mixed water is kept in a vessel and offered with the help of *Durvā* or a mango leaf.

Arghya : We take *chandan, Akshat, Supāri* and *pushpa* and offer with the related *Mantra*.

Āchamana : Water from Ganges or Yamunā or from other sacred or clean places are kept in a pot and offered with wooden *āchamani* or a mango leaf.

Snāna : The idol or idols, placed at the place of *poojā*, is/are given bath with pure water.

Vastra : After bathing new clothes are offered.

Abhisheka : The idols are decorated with chandana, etc.

Ābhushana : As needed ornaments are offered.

Gandha : Fragrance of one or different variety or fragrant flowers are offered.

Pushpa : Only those flowers, that are allowed, are offered.

Dhupa : We burn *dhoopa* preferably in an earthen pot and offer its smell.

Deepa : Earthen lamp/ lamps are lighted either in mustard oil or in pure ghee.

Naivedya : Sweets and fruits are offered as the food. Similar *prasāda* is distributed among the persons present at the place.

Tāmbula : After food as mouth freshner beetle leaves and beetle nut are offered.

Stavapātha : Prayers and eulogies are chanted to praise the deity.

Tarpana : Water is offered to deities and forefathers.

Pradakshinā : At least seven rounds around the deity is taken to show respect.

Namaskāra : Either through prostration or with folded hands the deities are saluted.

Pushpānjali : While praying flowers are kept in the folded hands and offered at the end of the prayer.

Ārati : Usually an earthen lamp is placed on rice in a pot or only wick or camphor is burnt in a dish and shown to the deity and *ārti* is sung or chanted.

Fasting

Fasting is an integral part of the life, worshipping and rituals of the Hindus. But it's done mostly to give rest to the digestive system, to increase the resistance and sustenance, and to show regard to the prevalent system. Women are far ahead of men in fasting. Though *Pratipadā, Chautha, Ekādashi, Terasa* and *Poornimā* are favourite days but fasting is observed on any day (specially, Tuesdays, Thursdays and Sundays; at certain places Monday too) and on the days of *Vrata* and festivals barring Holi and Deepāwali. The climax is that they observe fast even when they are not healthy. These are done as part of the ritual and definitely in the name of religion and because of deep faith. People may not observe fast if it's not associated with religious rituals. They have a latitude: if the body demands then it can be satisfied with water, fruit-juice, milk, fruit or sweets. But some men and women don't take even water and call it *"Nirjalā Ekādashi"* etc. On the other hand some take food (as light as possible) once on the days of fasting and that is all.

They believe that the functioning of organs and diet control is done with mind control. So, fasting is prescribed and observed as a part of self-discipline. In that way they can govern their sense organs in place of being governed by them. That way the requirement of the body can be reduced and there will not be any danger of obesity. In the recent times the women in the cities have ignored it and hence they are paying heavily for the disregard to fasting. They don't believe that it's the time tested and proven method.

Balancing the *Pancha Tattwa*

The Hindus govern their body and sense organs by ensuring positive alignment to and of *Panch Tattwas*. That way they revitalize their organs and resources for better functioning and use in future. That way they expand their physical, mental and spiritual energy. It's a part of both their worshipping and selfdiscipline. That way they try their level best to maintain a balance among *Vāta*, *Pitta* and *Kaffa*. Fasting and balancing give them time and opportunity for reflection and introspection. It gives them understanding of different perspectives and also gives greater power of tolerance. The act of balancing is the secret of their system that helps both in inner and outer growth but mostly inner growth as the Hindus take physical growth to be inner growth as it is affected from inside. The growth is seen through naked eyes but everything in our body grows from inside.

Ritual Bathing and Walking on Foot

Though, the means of transport have grown and are available yet the Hindus prefer to go on foot for ritual bathing or offering water. For it they usually select a distance of eight *Kosha* (about forty kilometers). Some cover this distance in five or six days and some in just 24 hours. The miracle is that the person completes it and it makes no difference whether he/she is a child, young or old. This adds to the confidence and physical fitness.

In certain cases and on particticular days and at designated places (*Kumbha Melā* for example) people from distant places throng to take ritualistic bath. They sustain the rigours. It's the cause behind the living nature of the Hindus. They never feel defeated because they live in harmony with the self, environment, community, society and above all God, Religion and Rituals. It easily gives them balance between the inner self and outer realities both on material plane and subtle plane. All these, including the tradition and culture, are a part of our being and make them strive hard towards achieving the right balance.

Only Hindus Perform Poojā

All the religions of the world show respect in different ways to the Absolute God but only Hindus perform *Poojā*. In that they have adopted and follow all the ways of showing respect to the God and worshipping Him.

Though there are provisions (*vidhāns*); at places strict provisions to be rigorously followed by all worshippers; but in personal matters, family or village traditions (*kula* and *grām paramparā*); they are all free to follow what suits them or is convenient to them or what they usually do. They maintain a strange balance between the strict discipline and total freedom.

There are standard list of articles to be used and offered in each *poojā* but Hinduism is so lenient that one can use all, most of them, a few of them, one of them or none of them and perform his or her poojā. It's a matter of faith, belief, the acceptance of that belief and inner purity.

It's needless to state that most of the Indians spend most of their energy in subduing desires, and most of them get reasonable success. Their tolerance, satisfaction, contentment, endurance, peace and pleasure come out of that control (*sanyam* and *indriyanigrah*).

Shāntipātha

After every *Yajna*, Ceremony or Ritual the Hindus pray for peace. The very wording is enough in itself to prove that they had the whole earth (world) in mind and prayed for peace in the world, the world of herbs and plants, the water and that of the God of the world. The prayer for peace for the Brahman, Peace and ALL is its climax:

> *AUM dhau shāntih antariksha shāntih prithvi shāntih*
> *āpah shāntih aushadhayah shāntih vanaspatayah*
> *shāntih vishwedevāh shāntih Brahma shāntih sarva*
> *shāntih shāntih ewa shāntih sāmā shantiredhi.*
> ॐ द्यौ शान्ति: अन्तरिक्ष शान्ति: पृथिवी शान्ति: आप: शान्ति:
> औषधय: शान्ति: वनस्पतय: शान्ति: विश्वेदेवा: शान्ति ब्रह्म
> शान्ति सर्व शान्ति: शान्तिरेव शान्ति: सामा शान्तिरेधि ॥

Hinduism: Complete and Eternal Human Religion

Hinduism is the 'whole', nearly the perfect, and the first and original 'Religion'. It's the complete religion. It's the natural religion. It's the most human religion. It depicts, deals in, determines and preaches 'religious, human, moral and ethical behaviour of mankind towards all living beings: human and non-human.

Hinduism possesses, depicts, shows and gives all ideas, philosophy, schools of thought, ways of good, healthy, happy and blissful living and dying; and in the process developing towards the spirituality to achieve that pious state that makes the union of the 'Soul" with the Almighty, and its ultimate freedom and salvation possible.

Hinduism is the complete religion, even if it's not perfect religion. So, the world suffers from inferiority complex and out of that complex tries to belittle everything Indian and particularly, Hindus and Hindu Religion. The word Hindu too was created with the same intention. The most tragic part of this adverse situation is that unknowingly and out of ignorance most of the Indians are bringing harm to Indian life, culture, civilisation, religion and Scriptures.

The others are amazed at its possessions, perfection, performance and permanence. They may be jealous, Hinduism knows no jealousy; and never at the growth and prosperity of others: it's satisfied with its own *sattu* and *sāga* and will not look with lust and expectations on someone else's *puā*.

Hinduism is the Complete and Eternal Human Religion. It has already been simplified. We don't see the whole and select the best way for ourselves keeping in mind our mental status and physical surrounding as well as the inner strength that can empower us to sustain during and win over the anxieties. Each one must read at least the *Grantha trai*, one *Smriti* and a few *Niti Granthas*. Then we can see the path clearly and move on confidently. Clarity in mind and concept is the most important thing.

The saints and seers with their commentaries, analysis and speeches have tried to simplify this great religion and make readily available to each individual. The mothers take trouble and pain to give us life; we don't take trouble and pain equal to their one tenth, to make the surrounding a better place to live happily and with contentment. We are all the time adding something to already existing immense dangers. We have consumed most of the things essential for life and are consuming fast the remaining things. Without changing our approach, philosophy and behaviour can we save the birds and animals that are at the brink of extinction? Can we save the trees and forests and plants that are our life? We know that we can't exist without them, yet we are cutting them down for various uses and numerous infrastructures. We have to be sure that we can't survive on the constructed house or printed money or minted coins. We can survive only on grass, cereal and other plants, small and big trees, herbs and medicinal plants, and by keeping the environment clean and healthy.

We have forgotten the most common incident. Once, a king was riding a horse. On the outskirts of a village he saw a very old man planting a mango sapling. He wondered, 'What is the use of planting the sapling when the old man can survive only for a couple of years?' His curiosity grew. He went to the man and repeated the question that was giving him trouble. The old man came with a simple answer: "I ate the fruits of the trees that my grand father planted; I'm planting this sapling so that my grand children can eat the fruit."

Are we conscious of our grand and great-grand children? Are we planting enough trees for their comfort and survival; for shade, firewood, fruits and medicines? No, we are accumulating printed notes and getting tall buildings constructed. Although, we know that in remote past, every township with brick-built houses was abandoned: from Indus-Valley Civilisation to Aztec, including Olympia and Gaza. Our forefathers built great palaces and temples but preferred to live in huts and *āshrams*. They built *Pushpak Vimāns* and preferred to travel on horsebacks, tongas and bullock-carts. They had invented *Brahmāshtras* and other deadly weapons but allowed only tridents, lances, swords, knives and staff for the people to keep and use. They had sat together and coolly decided the best and most healthy way of living.

The others wonder at its long life, immortality and continuity. We will have to sit together, see the whole truth of the religion and society, think deeply and widely on the prevalent problems and crisis, and take a decision to ensure the survival and continuity. One man, one caste, one community, one region, one place or one meeting can't be enough to solve this great problem of survival or extinction; religious deeds and irreligious acts; and of consuming or saving the life giving and sustaining matters and elements.

Tolerance and Ego-less-ness

Hinduism has no ego and boasts of nothing. So, if one says 'his religion is older'; another says, his religion is greater, yet another claims that Hindus have borrowed it from our religion, or yet another says his religion has fostered Hindu religion or another one claims that his religious people saved Hindu Scriptures. Hinduism keeps mum, often accepts, bows in reverence, shows gratitude and raises no objection; for Hindus know, the Scriptures are the proofs, what has happened during the last about one thousand and five hundred years? The humble self of Hinduism absorbs all, tolerates all and endures against all odds. The destructive elements strengthen it; the weathering forces test it and turn aside when it proves its mettle and worth.

Health and Mental Preparations

Believe it or not but in Hindu Religious Rituals and Social Customs religious factors play least role, and Āyurveda and Psychology play major roles. They shape, mould, modulate and even mend them. It would have been safe to say 'in most of the religious rituals and social customs' but it's correct to say, that 'all' the religious rituals and social customs are based on these two factors: Health and Mental Preparations.' Those that discussed and gave them final shape were highly health conscious. They considered and gave top priority to both physical and mental health on the basis of the needs of the body, local geographic conditions, available Nature' gifts and the changing seasons.

It's not an exaggeration to say that they considered even the financial health of a person and his family. That is the reason that after every cause of major expenditure, like construction of a house and *griha pravesh*; marriage or death in a family they realistically admonished from holding another function of similar magnitude for the next fifteen months.

Hinduism Needs No Clarification

Hinduism needs no clarification. Two opposite phenomenon can't be mixed and claimed to be complicated. If one sees 'the whole' of Hinduism and is not centred round to a single part or is not mixing the opposites then Hinduism needs no clarification. There are too many things but all are well arranged, and have their separate identity and existence. The existence of opposites is the eternal truth: Opposites do exist; and even simultaneously together. The darkness and light co-exist; the nights and days are always there. The end of one is not the beginning of other. It's our illusion; the *Māyā*; that we can see only one of them at a time; either day or night. Physical is as real as the spiritual; the body is as real as the soul; the concrete is as real as the abstract; *Brahman* is as real as Rāma; the *Nirguna* is as real as the *Saguna*; Cosmic energy is as real as Durgā. We have to resolve the opposites. This is *gyāna*, revelation. There is no contradiction and there should be no controversy. It's not only the analysis that gives knowledge; assimilation and synthesis requires greater wisdom. That Union, Oneness, Amalgamation, Complete Surrender, Total Identification with the Absolute is not possible without knowing and following the Hindu philosophy.

Hinduism needs no clarification because the Hindus will not accept one and deny the other. They accept all. They know the physical self and the spiritual body; they accept the existence of man, gods and demons; of spirits, *gandharvas* and *gans*. They are all faith and least or no doubt. The Hindus have been treading on this well illuminated and well-crowded path for myriads of years and can continue on that path fearlessly. They have two distinct paths:

Swãntah Sukhãya: for the satisfaction of the self. This path comes out from the infinity and narrows down steadily to the micro being, the atom, the Brahman or the self, to *Aham Brahmãsmi*. The other path is just opposite to it: *Bahujan Hitãya*. The journey begins from the micro self and steadily and incessantly gets larger and larger and, eventually, identifies with all and becomes Cosmic and gets dissolved into the infinity: *Ãtmawat Sarvabhuteshu*. The world is a gyre. Hindus look at it as it is; and they also turn it upside down. The bigger mouth goes down but the gyre remains the same. The Hindus realise that both are important: What you see? How you see?

Different Government Organisations or NGOs should take the burden of preparing a correct or complete list of any one of the following; and many such organisations can participate in doing all by taking one each. It's a challenge for them to complete any one of the following in a decade. List of

◆ The Gods and Goddesses of Hindus

◆ Temples and *Mã Shakti Sthãns* in India

◆ Castes, Sub-castes and *Gotras* and Sub-Gotras in India

◆ The Famous Fairy and Moral Tales from India

◆ Variations in Rituals and Rites in India

◆ The books taken away by others

◆ The Variety of Food Eaten in India

◆ The Names of Highly Respected persons of India

Under such circumstances when 'Diversity' is the greatest cause of 'Unity' in India, it's clear that Hinduism needs no clarification. It's crystal clear and most dynamic and living in its ever-changing and ever-lasting form. It's our personal approach, deeds and behaviour that make us live happily and fully here on the earth, help us rise above the mundane self, attain spirituality, get attainment and final bliss and beatitude.

Hinduism is altogether too Simple

Because of the fact that Hinduism covers all and has something for all, so it's too vast to be kept in mind, counted on fingers or phalanages, noted down as within a dozen tenets, followed by an individual or the inhabitats of one place. This simple fact has to be made clear. One must keep it in mind that one Hindu or one Human being can't humanely see or cover or follow all that Hinduism possesses or gives. It gives something to all. All is not devised for all to follow. Nine types of devotions are there. It's an open secret that neither one can follow all those nine types of devotions nor it is expected from any individual. There are about 33,000 Gods and Goddesses in Human (Hindu) Religion; none can remember their names, none can know the details even about a hundred or so. Hindus are wise enough. They don't try to know them all. They don't need so many Gods. These Gods are there to fulfill the personal needs and aspirations of different persons, community and customs because of the geographical and climatic variations; and also variations in agricultural produce and food and living habits.

Moreover, an individual does not have to possess the religion, to carry the weight of religion, to polish and brighten the religion. An Individual is possessed by religion, carried by it and polished, brightened and emancipated by religion. Purity, devotion and worshipping are important. Hinduism clearly draws distinct lines to distinguish false show, genuine presentation and real inner change. An incident will illustrate it:

Nārad considered himself to be the greatest devotee of the Absolute God, Nārāyan. He would repeat His name: Nārāyan, Nārāyan; thousands of times every day. To satiate his ego he wanted the cofirmation from the Lord. He asked and got no reply. Doubt entered his mind. He started asking the same question everyday: 'Who is your greatest devotee?' One day the Lord said that in such and such village a farmer named so and so is the greatest devotee. It was a jolt to Nārad. He could not resist his temptation and went to meet that farmer. The farmer was ploughing his field. Nārad met him, introduced himself and waited there to learn the way the farmer performed his poojā and chanted the name of the Lord. He remained with him like a shadow. The farmer did nothing. Once while he started taking his meal, he remembered his God. 'Nārāyan, Nārāyan' – said the farmer; again when he was going to bed he repeated the name. Nārad could not sleep. He thought that the farmer might be doing the worshipping under the silence of night. The farmer slept well and when he awoke in the morning, he remembered his lord and repeated the name. Nārad remained

there for a few days but there was no change in the worshipping of the
farmer. He was angry and showed his anger to Lord: 'The farmer repeats
your name only thrice a day, how can he be your greatest devotee?' The
Lord's answer was simple and straightforward: 'The farmer does his
duty well and honestly and yet finds time to remember me thrice. You do
nothing else but repeat my name. The farmer is far greater than you.' Is
it not the most simple and the best way to show one's devotion by being
honest and dutiful and not to forget the Lord?

Hindu religion is so simple that it appears to be most complex.
It appears so because the *shat-vikārs* are in us. We are not trying to
know the reality; we are not the real devotees. We are not religious.
We are unable to know rather we don't know. It's our ignorance.
There is no complexity in the religion. The ego, desires and
complexity are within us. We are not purifying ourselves rather we
are accumulating impurities. We are not selecting and following
that which we need the most. We have changed our preferences,
we have shifted our positions, we have lost the real and smooth
track; and we are not true to ourselves for we are not performing
our duty. We are not spiritualists. We are materialists. We are not
religious. We have become atheists. We are not humans. We have
awakened demons within us.

Our *Karma* is not in accordance with the Scriptures. It's our
fault. We have to mend ourselves, change our ways, adopt correct
means and lead a pure and simple life with high and divine
thoughts to illuminate the inner self. We don't need to change
the religion. We don't have to make a show of the religious spirit.
We have to imbibe the spirit; the spirit of religion and the spirit
of virtues, so that we can be blessed; and get the desired boon. If
we can make the necessary adjustments then we can sustain and
survive; then we can lead a healthy life, get bliss and beatitude;
and attain salvation: be free from the endless cycle of numerous
births and deaths.

There are hundreds of *Upanishadas* and the message is clear:
read or know one and follow it. That is all. You will get wisdom.
There are hundreds of *Smritis* and the message is clear: read or
know one and follow it. That is all. You will be able to perform all
the rituals and rites. There are hundreds of schools of philosophy
and the message is clear: read or know one and follow it. That

is all. You will acquire the knowledge. There are hundreds of medicines for one disease and the message is clear: know one and take it. That is all. You will be cured. There are thousands of Gods and the message is clear: Worship and pray to One. That is all. You will be emancipated.

Hinduism is crystal clear and most simple in its ever-changing and ever-lasting form.

"Any conclusion, enlarged with details or synthesized with precise statements, about Hindus will remain inconclusive for Hinduism includes and inculcates 'All'. The life force and the living element in Hinduism are so forceful that the continuity of life is regarded as the supreme duty: unsaid, undeclared but meticulously followed. Hinduism is natural, unprofaned and simple, and convincing so much that it keeps on inspiring each sane man of each religion and of each generation. It makes no difference whether they agree with it or not.

Hinduism has not and will not come to a saturation point for it keeps on flowing: neither it turns into solid nor changes into gaseous and light. Hence, it was neither broken nor blown out. It will remain inconclusive for it will keep on growing and flowing like cosmic energy in every direction to cover greater space.

The most important and noteworthy aspect of Indian life, culture, knowledge and philosophy is the too deep attachment with all: body, mind, soul, self, ego, lust, children, family, wealth, relations, society, country, humanity, religion, spirituality and god; and totally non-committed detachment from them all.

The people, the teachers, the saints, the philosophers and the numerous gods here are all deeply engrossed and plainly aloof, simultaneously together. It's in itself a rare phenomenon. Both the deep attachment and complete detachment are natural and an integral part of being and thinking here. One day the father is ready to sacrifice everything for his son, to sacrifice all including character and morality and it may happen that the next day or from the very next day he will neither talk to him nor about him, neither think of him nor do anything for him. This rare phenomenon is common in the Indian people of each strata and every sect.

This paradoxical mix-up is the unseen, unknown, unfelt and undeclared but immortal gift, effect and master stroke of the

268 ■ Hinduism Clarified and Simplified

most simple rendering and teachings of the Vedas, the Rishis, the Gita, the Epics, the poetry, the music, the teachers, the sages and the saints who honestly, impartially and deliberately devoted themselves to bring out the essence, the fundamental truth, the basic and universal reality and the most simple and lively ways to enable the mass to attain spirituality and to get immense worldly pleasure without indulging too much in luxury; just by living a complete and balanced life without attachment and a lot of dedication like the honey bees moving from garden to garden, from flower to flower, collecting pollen without inflicting injury; and changing it into Nectar like sweet and useful honey. Thus the bees and the Indians give three best gifts of sublime divinity and highest culture: Sweetness; Light; and Fragrance.

These three superior qualities of the most cultured: Sweetness. Light and fragrance: are embedded well in the very fibre of the being of the Indians. They are there as natural possessions by birth, as cosmic gifts by gods, predecessors and the tolerant and energetic parents.

People of the world must remember and realise that in the whole of the world India is the **only country** that truly possesses and amply gives: **Sweetness; Fragrance; Light** and **Delight.'** *These four are the qualities of the most **cultured** and most **civilized**; most **refined** and most **religious**; and most **spiritual** and most **human**.* That is the real reason that Indians are always proud of their country, their culture, religion, knowledge and civilisation.

Now, it's crystal clear that Hinduism is as old as human existence and knowledge; as simple as breathing because it's the purest air that man should breath in; as deep as human experience; as high as man's inspirations; as essential as life; and as pious as the existence of God in living beings.

☜

www.ingramcontent.com/pod-product-compliance
Lightning Source LLC
Chambersburg PA
CBHW030410100426
42812CB00028B/2899/J